Your Child's Career

A Guide to
Home-based Career Education

Garth L. Mangum
G. Donald Gale
Mary L. Olsen
Elwood Peterson
Arden R. Thorum

Olympus Publishing Company
Salt Lake City, Utah

Library of Congress Cataloging in Publication Data
Main entry under title:
Your child's career.

Includes index.

1. Personnel service in education. 2. Vocational guidance. I. Mangum, Garth L.
LB1027.5.Y68   370.11'3   77-22791
ISBN   0-913420-75-1

Contents

Illustrations

CHAPTER ONE

Your Child and Career Education

This is a book about children and their parents. It is a book about your child, whatever that child's age or sex or physical condition may be. It is a book about a most important part of your child's life. You may call it "work," or a "job," or an "occupation," or a "career.". . . Whatever you call that part of life, you must admit that it will occupy a great deal of your child's energy, talent, and concern during most of his or her lifetime. You must also agree that some day your child's relationship to a career will have a great influence over his or her happiness and satisfaction.

This is also a book about you—you as a parent and you as a worker. It will remind you of your own career development and how you got where you are today. It may help you make some decisions about your continuing career development, because career development is a lifelong process. More importantly, this book will tell you how you influence your child's career development—whether you want to or not—and what you can do to make that influence a positive one. Finally, the book will introduce you to a new emphasis in education called "career education." This new approach is probably already a part of your child's school curriculum, if you have a child in school. In the following pages, we will tell you why career education is important, what it is doing for your child, and how you can work with the school to help your child.

But our concern with career education begins long before the child enters school. It begins at birth, because that is when the child's career development actually begins—during the first year of life. Sometimes it is difficult to realize that what you do with a child during the first year of life—and every year thereafter—can actually have a tremendous influence over how that child feels about work and the choices that child makes with regard to a career when he or she becomes an adult. But the fact is that most of our attitudes are developed during those early years *before we go to school,* and they are very difficult to change thereafter. In fact, the probability is slight that those attitudes will change profoundly by the time we are ten, or twenty, or fifty.

Thus, the preschool years are key years in career education, as they are in all aspects of growth and development. However, all is neither lost nor done when those years are past. Not only can attitudes and habits be changed with sufficient effort, but since career development is a lifelong process, there is always a subsequent stage during which the parental influence can be potent.

WHAT IS CAREER EDUCATION?

In Chapter 3 we discuss the concepts of career education in some detail, but two basic principles are worth noting at the outset. First, the term "career" as used here is *not* interchangeable with the traditional usages of such terms as "work," or "job," or "occupation." When we talk about a person's career, we include all of those things . . . but we also include much more. As defined in Chapter 3, a career "is the totality of work done in one's lifetime," while work is "all conscious effort aimed at producing benefits for one's self or for others." That means that "career" includes school work, homemaking, volunteer work, child rearing, and even some hobbies. A person's career may include several occupations and many jobs during a lifetime. Thus, it includes most of the non-recreational activity in which we participate. The main point to keep in mind is that "career" as used here is a broad term and is not confined to a single, specific pursuit.

Second, because "career" is used so broadly, that means that "career education" also has broad application. It applies to everything a person does in order to learn about or prepare for work. In a sense, of course, all education is career education, because all education helps us to prepare for an occupation, or to perform better within an occupation, or to do a better job with the volunteer duties of citizenship, or to develop attitudes about work. But the objectives of education are not limited to career preparation, and much of education's career contribution is incidental. In most cases within these pages we prefer to separate those components of education—both formal and informal—which have direct bearing on career success and identify those components as career education. For example, a child in school learns about the world around him or her in all its aspects, including its people and its customs and its physical makeup. The career educator would identify those portions of that learning which deal directly with the kinds of work that people do and the necessity of work to social conduct, and those components would be called "career education."

The best way to understand what we mean by career education is to think about your own career—all aspects of it—including the school work you did, the work you did at home as a child, the work you do on the job, the work you do at home now, the volunteer activities in which you participate. Think about how your attitudes concerning work developed, about how you learned the skills you need to do all that work, about why you work, about how you decided to do the work you do, and about everything you experienced which helped prepare you to work.

That's what career education is all about.

Career Education Begins Early

The more you think about your own career education, the more you will realize that it began very early in your life, probably before you can even remember. It began when someone told you to put away your toys, or when someone helped you learn to zip a zipper or put on a shoe, or when someone used the word "work" and you wondered what it meant.

Those early years are vital career education years, not because a child learns work skills during those years— although many work-related skills are certainly learned then—but because the child learns what to think about work and how to feel about it. In other words, those are the years when work attitudes and values are learned. For instance, imagine what a child will think about work if it is often used as punishment: "If you don't eat your spinach, you'll have to clean up your room!" The child is bound to have the impression that work is an undesirable thing, that it should be avoided, and that it can be avoided if one eats the spinach ... or whatever the adult equivalent to eating spinach might turn out to be. The message to the child is that when he or she is working, that is a form of punishment.

Or suppose for the first five years of life the child hears mother tell her friends on the telephone that she hates housework, that it is boring, that she will do anything possible to put off cleaning the cupboards. How can that child possibly develop a good attitude toward work? The child will have trouble finding any kind of work satisfying at any time in his or her life, because those negative attitudes which were indelibly impressed in childhood will always be present to some degree.

Or imagine a parent coming home after a hard day at work. The parent complains at the dinner table about how tough it was "at work," about how the boss was critical "at work," and about how inept a co-worker is "at work." The child, who is listening and learning, doesn't quite know where "at work" is or what father or mother does "at work," but the child knows it is a bad place where parents spend some unhappy time. Surely, "at work" is not a good place to be. That impression will stay with the child throughout his or her lifetime.

And after dinner, father thinks he has earned a rest, and so he settles in his most comfortable chair before the television set . . . and stays there, at least until the child goes to bed. The child learns that adult males are tired a lot of the time, sit in chairs a lot, and watch television a lot. The child has no way to know that father earned his rest, because the only time he or she sees father is when father is home sitting in the chair. The message is that when you get to be an adult you don't have to work any more . . . unless you're a mother, and then you have to do all that boring housework.

Another kind of message comes from the mother who works all day and then must prepare meals and do the housework when she comes home. She never has time for anything but work, and so work becomes a barrier between mother and child. To the child, work is not a useful thing but a disruptive influence.

Then there's the father who understands all this about career education, and so almost every evening he tries to have at least one job to do around the house so the child can see him working . . . and perhaps even enjoying it. He does his share of the housework, which includes doing the supper dishes three or four nights a week. One evening the child wants to help, and so he or she climbs on a chair and begins "washing" the dishes, just like father. But the soapy dishes are difficult to hold, and soon one drops on the floor, breaking. Father is tired and a little grumpy, and he says: "Don't do that any more! You're not old enough! You're clumsy!" The message to the child is that work is fine . . . for some people. But there are some things you can't do and shouldn't try to do.

Attitudes and Values about Work

These few examples can be multiplied by the thousands. They illustrate where we begin to pick up our attitudes and values concerning work. They are the beginnings of career education.

These examples also illustrate what an important role the home and the family play in the career education process. Actually, the home is the key to our work values and attitudes. Whatever we learn there stays with us throughout our lifetimes. It begins to show up in our school work, and it continues through our working years. There is little question that parents "imprint" their own attitudes toward work on their children at an early age. Those attitudes are passed from generation to generation as surely as hair color and blood type.

Fortunately, most adults like to work, and they find at least *some* positive values in the work they do. According to a Gallup poll published in 1973, 77 percent of workers are satisfied with the work they do. Another study found that only 14 percent of workers studied expressed negative attitudes toward their work. In their own study of work and workers, Sar Levitan and William Johnston note that:

> . . . virtually every study continues to find enormous majorities who are satisfied with their work, typically in the range from 60 to 90 percent. The Gallup poll has reported more than three of four satisfied in every survey since 1963. Variations in question phrasing, research design, and sample population have shifted the response but have not reversed this broadly positive finding.

Of course, a few observers disagree with those findings. For reasons of their own, they prefer to picture workers as dissatisfied and unhappy. But the fact of the matter is that most individuals would rather be working than not working—at least a good part of the time. They find value and satisfaction in the work they do. Certainly, workers complain. That is an accepted activity in a free society, and often it is encouraged. We see someone else with a job different from our own, and we think that would be a wonderful job to have. But we frequently see only the glamorous parts of the job. Almost every job has its tedium and its undesirable components. And every job has value and provides some satisfactions. A job that is challenging, exciting, and rewarding to one person may be boring and dull to another. As with most parts of life, it is the attitude one brings to the situation which often determines the value one obtains from that situation.

In any case, because most adults like to work, most children develop positive attitudes and values about work. Those of us who advocate career education have no reason to criticize what is happening in the home, because we see too many positive signs that career education in the home is generally good. Instead, we would like to call attention to the importance of career education in the home, to point out some simple steps that can be taken to add dimension to that early childhood experience, and to acquaint parents with the stages in career development and career education's response to those stages.

THE IMPORTANCE OF THE HOME

We have already discussed some of the values regarding work that children learn in the home. Those values will be discussed in more detail in Chapter 4. But career education is a lifelong process, and it is worthwhile to examine some of the other contributions to career development which often originate in the home.

Parents serve as role models for their children in ways that go beyond the patterning of attitudes and values. Parents provide support—or discouragement—for *all* of the decisions a child makes and most of a child's activities, including those that are work related. Consider the simple task of learning to zip a zipper. It may seem meaningless and ordinary, but it is actually an important form of skill development, requiring manual dexterity and coordination. Those same skills will be part of many work situations. The child will likely attempt to zip a zipper before he or she has developed the physical ability to do so, and will experience failure. The child's decision about when to try the task again will depend to some degree on the reactions of those witnessing the first attempt, usually parents. If the reaction is a supportive one, the child will try again soon, fully confident that he or she will succeed. If the reaction is a critical one, the child may be discouraged from trying again, feeling that new tasks are just too difficult. If there is no reaction at all, the child may become frustrated at being unable to perform the task, and the frustration may exhibit itself as anger at himself or herself or, more likely, at the garment containing the zipper. These patterns, reinforced over and over again in childhood, show up when the child becomes an adult and approaches skill development related to the workplace. The individual who received support as a child develops the inner confidence that allows him or her to work at acquiring new skills, knowing that they will eventually come. The individual who was overly criticized is reluctant to give the time and attention that new skill development requires, fearing failure. The person who received no support at all during the experimental stages of skill development is easily frustrated when trying to learn something new, and finds it easy to attach blame for his or her frustration to some person or object outside himself or herself.

This kind of support situation occurs again and again throughout childhood, throughout adolescence, and indeed, throughout life. It is the kind of support that marriage partners provide for one another in a good marriage. It is support based not on value judgments but on human values. It is support that comes from true love and respect for the individual and his or her attempts to grow.

But there are other kinds of support that can be provided in the home. One kind of support comes from simply sharing the work load around the house. It helps children to understand the nature of work in society and the interrelationships of work and mutual benefit. The child sees that if every member of the family does some of the work, all will benefit. Naturally, the young child is not equipped to share in some of the work—complex tasks, heavy work, and so on—but he or she can learn responsibility for small tasks and can join in the work activity of others. When children are young, the problem is not usually one of trying to get them to help, but one of trying to carefully assess the level of the child's development and his or her capability for participation. This is just as true for handicapped children as it is for all children. Often, the child wants to do things he or she simply cannot physically handle, and parents must be tactful in turning the child's interest in another direction without discouraging the child.

As the child gets older, the problem will be to get the child to participate at all, but if good habits are formed in childhood, that problem is considerably reduced.

The Problem of Job Stereotyping

One aspect of sharing work should be carefully avoided by parents, and that is the tendency toward job stereotyping. Job stereotyping means simply the process of classifying jobs as "female" jobs, "male" jobs, "adult" jobs, "child" jobs, and so on. If the child grows up with stereotyped thinking, her or his career opportunities will be considerably reduced. It serves to restrict the child's freedom of choice without giving him or her a "say" in the decision. Since most parents today are products of stereotyped thinking, they should make an extra effort to reduce the job stereotyping they portray for their own children. The father should certainly participate in the day-to-day housework, and the mother should join in the yard work and even such things as automobile upkeep. If the father is inept at certain household tasks, he should either learn how to do those things or at least give the appearance of assisting with the work. For instance, father may never learn how to operate a sewing machine, but he can certainly help pin up a hem. (Those who are tempted to snicker at this example should consider carefully the facts about the changing nature of work and work roles presented in Chapter 2.) The goal in eliminating stereotyping is to reduce internalized restrictions on career selection and occupational choice, not just in regard to the stereotyped jobs but in regard to the total panorama of choice. The concept of freedom of choice is often as much an expression of habit and attitude as it is an expression of available alternatives. If a young man decides he cannot be a fashion designer because his father told him sewing was for girls, then the young man's freedom of choice is just as limited as if society had told him he couldn't be a fashion designer because he was from the wrong social class.

The specific example is not so important as the overall concept: The child whose choices are restricted by factors other than his or her own talents and abilities may lose confidence in those talents and abilities. The child who is allowed to test talents and abilities in a variety of circumstances has a better chance of developing self-confidence and self-understanding.

Another kind of support for career education which can be provided by parents is related to the career awareness stage of the process. As discussed in Chapter 5, the age for formal career awareness training probably corresponds with elementary school age, but many informal exploratory activities take place before that time. Children are curious about what it means when mother or father are "at work." Perhaps the family can arrange to drive by the place of work on a weekend, or perhaps the parent can actually take the child for a visit to the work place on a working day so the child can form a better image of what happens during those hours when the parent is absent. Of course, young children cannot always grasp the meaning of what it is that a parent may do "at work," and so any explanations should be kept simple. This is particularly true for abstract work such as accounting or management or scheduling. The main thing is for the child to realize that "at work" is a specific place, that other parents work also, that work is an activity which is sometimes satisfying, and that work frequently involves a number of individuals working for common goals.

Work and Workers in the Neighborhood

This same kind of exploratory activity can occur on a daily basis by simply pointing out to the child the number of people around her or him who are working. The mail carrier who delivers the mail is working. The police officer on the corner is working. The checkout clerk at the grocery store is working. Someone had to work to grow the vegetables that are in the store, and to bring them to the store in a truck. The television announcer is "at work" in a television studio.

It is not necessary to explain any of the work activities to the child during the early years. It is enough simply to connect the people the child sees every day to the word "work." In that way, the word becomes as friendly and as acceptable as those whom it helps describe. As the child grows, she or he will begin to ask questions about the work activities of people in the neighborhood and people with whom the family comes in contact. That is the time to begin explaining what it is that various workers do and why they do it. Until that time, "work" is simply another part of the child's world, about which she or he is developing an awareness.

Once again, these simple childhood support activities will carry over into the teenage years when the child begins to think seriously about his or her own career development. The youngster who has grown up in a home where work is a common subject of conversation will find it easier to talk to others about their work, to explore the possibilities of a variety of occupations, and to understand the relationships among various fields of activity. In this way the youngster's horizons are expanded considerably, and opportunities may occur which would likely have gone undiscovered.

Support of the kinds discussed above requires little effort on the part of parents. Much of it comes normally and naturally to parents who are concerned about their children. It might be described as "just plain old common sense." Some of it requires the simple addition of a slightly new dimension to normal activities, the dimension which makes the subject of work a part of most learning experiences.

However, there is one kind of support that requires a little more effort on the part of parents than the kinds of support described above. That is the support that comes from being sufficiently well enough informed to be able to serve as a resource person for your child. It means learning a little about career education, a little about the various career development stages through which a child must grow, a little about the labor market and changing opportunities within it, and a little about how one prepares for a job and acquires entry to an occupation. The goal is not necessarily to be able to answer all of the child's questions but to be able to refer the child to a person or reference work where the questions can be answered. Reading this book about career education is one step in preparing to provide that kind of support. Other sources of information might include newspaper and magazine articles, television news reports, conversations with teachers and counselors at school, and day-to-day observations. Questions asked by the preschool child and the elementary school student will be fairly easy to answer; those asked by junior high and high school students may require a little more information.

You may recall from your own experience that the process of entering the adult world, of moving from the protected environment of the school into the work force, is a frightening process. It all seems so new and so permanent and so intimidating. Career education can help make that process much easier and much less anxiety producing. Support mechanisms from the family and the home—beginning in early childhood—are important components of career education.

HUMAN DEVELOPMENT AND CAREER DEVELOPMENT

Psychologists and educators who have studied the career development process find it to be a normal part of human development in that the phases of human development and the phases of career development are parallel. The different stages of career development—such as awareness, exploration, and preparation—correspond with stages of development the individual goes through in the broader aspects of life. Those stages very roughly parallel the three basic levels of education—elementary, middle school (or junior high school), and high school and beyond—and those levels of education also correspond with some interesting changes in personal development. Of course, all children mature at different rates, and so there will be considerable variation among children as to when they reach these stages of career development or levels of educational maturity, but there is some correlation between grade in school and stage in human development and in career development. With this in mind, career educators have designed the phases of career education to coincide with the stages of career development. Just as is the case with other developmental processes, considerable overlap exists from one phase to another. In fact, it is best to think of each phase as ongoing once it has begun. That is, the phases are sequential, but moving from phase one activity to phase two activity does not mean that all phase one activity ceases. This point will become clearer as the explanation continues.

We have already mentioned the development of work attitudes and values. These are only a part of the broader range of attitudes and values the child is developing at the same time. Normally, career educators do not consider value formation to be a separate phase, because it is actually the foundation of all development, whether it is career development or some other form of human growth. Also, value formation tends to occur simultaneously with career awareness, the first phase of career education. As the child becomes aware of work, he or she begins to develop values concerning it. Value formation continues throughout a lifetime, but as we have said before, the key years are the early childhood years. Modifications in values do take place as the individual matures, but those modifications tend to be with regard to the hierarchical structuring of the value system more than the basic formation of the values within the system. For example, the relative importance of work and play in our value systems tends to change as we grow more mature, with work achieving increasing value at the expense of play. We learn in childhood that both are important, but we change their ranking as we grow older.

Value formation, then, is the foundation of career education.

Career Awareness

The first phase of career education has been called the "career awareness" phase. It involves primarily what the words indicate—becoming aware of careers—and it coincides with the elementary school years. During those years children learn about the world around them. Until then their world has been largely restricted to the home and neighborhood, and they have been busy learning the survival skills of talking, eating, toilet training, dressing, and so forth. Now they begin to learn a little about the broader world—about science, about the customs of people, about history, and about getting along with others. They acquire a few basic intellectual skills such as reading and writing and mathematics. They learn some self-discipline and a little about themselves. Mostly, they learn a few new ways to look at their immediate environment, and they learn there is a world beyond what they can see and experience. In other words, the elementary school years are years of becoming aware. Children of that age are not able to think much beyond the moment. They cannot deal satisfactorily with abstract ideas. They cannot project much into the future. Their primary learning activities are concerned with themselves and their own sense impressions of what goes on around them. Thus, career education at the elementary school age is simply an effort to help children become aware that one of the activities which goes on around them is work. They experience work as a part of their school activity, but they also take field trips, see films, and read books where workers are featured. The teacher makes a point of calling attention to the workers and what they are doing. There is no detailed discussion, but the teacher may try to connect the various careers the students see to something concrete in their world. For example, a photo of a backhoe digging a ditch may lead to a discussion of workers laying water pipe so students can get a drink from the fountain.

We have already discussed some of the ways in which parents can support the career awareness phase. Learning takes place at home as well as in school. Children read books, watch television, and accompany parents on shopping trips or other travel. When it is convenient, parents can use those occasions to expand the child's awareness of the world of work. A trip to the hamburger stand provides a ready opportunity to talk about the people who prepare the food, who take orders, who manage the business, and who deliver the raw materials to the stand. Keep it simple. There is no need to go into explanations about how the work is done. The idea is simply to let the children know that someone is responsible for making the hamburger and the milk shake available to them. Of course, parents should answer any questions their children may have.

Career Exploration

The second phase of career education is the "career exploration" phase. As explained in Chapter 6, career exploration is an attempt to bring some organization into the study of work and careers. This occurs during the middle school or junior high school years, when the concern of children naturally turns from awareness to exploration. They want to know where they fit in this complex world, and in order to learn more about themselves they need to explore various career possibilities in relation to their own needs and capabilities. Junior high students are encouraged to look at the work people do in greater depth, to learn about life styles associated with various occupations, and to learn how careers are interrelated. Students do not make lasting career decisions at this age, but they begin to think about those decisions. Career educators try to help students organize the world of work so it can be explored easily, and they try to help students ask the important questions concerned with specific occupations.

Parents can support career exploration in a number of ways. They can try to explain to their children about their own careers and occupations. They may volunteer to serve as resource persons in the classroom so other students can ask about their careers. They can talk about the kind of training which was required to enter the occupation, the procedures for entering, the kind of life style they lead, and the opportunities they see for the future. They do not attempt to "sell" their own occupations but simply provide as much information as possible in as dispassionate a manner as possible. Parents can also encourage their adolescent youngsters to talk to relatives and friends about careers. They may lead the discussion to the subject of careers if children are reluctant to do so. Parents also can continue to expand the child's knowledge of career opportunities, perhaps by doing a little exploring of their own. At this stage, the youngster's interests may go far afield, but parents should not be overly concerned. The child has a great need to explore, and she or he will explore as many potential occupations as can be discovered. Career decisions made at this stage will almost certainly change, often on a regular basis.

The process of making decisions for one's self begins fairly early in childhood, but it becomes especially important during the adolescent years. These are years when the child tests his or her independence and individuality, often with resulting strain on parent-child relationships. Obviously, career decisions are among the most important decisions one must make, and while adolescent youngsters rarely make lasting career decisions, they do make many career-related decisions, such as which classes to take in school, whether or not to seek part-time work, what kind of work to pursue part time or as volunteer activity, and so on. Therefore, it is important to develop some understanding of the decision-making process. For that reason, Chapter 7 is concerned with decision making.

Career Preparation

The third phase of career education is "career preparation." As one might expect, this could be predicated on some sort of career decision. After all, how can one prepare for a career if one does not know what the career or occupation will be? In that sense, the title of the phase may be misleading. Specific decisions about jobs or occupations may not occur until late in the career preparation phase. Many preparations are common to most careers. For instance, one must learn where to seek a job, how to apply for a job, and what factors are important in holding a job. Those are all part of career preparation. Also important are such things as knowing what kinds of training are necessary for various occupations, where that training can be obtained, and what the entrance requirements are for training institutions. This phase of career education occurs during the high school years and after.

Parents may find it more difficult to provide support for career education at this phase than during the previous phases. Some of the information children require is specialized, and obtaining it may require the services of a counselor or the availability of special resource materials.

However, if parents have maintained an open communication channel with their youngsters regarding career questions, they can certainly offer suggestions about where the answers might be found, and they can share their own experiences regarding career preparation. Remember, the decisions the youngster makes at this age are the best decisions he or she can make with the available information. Respect those decisions as you would the decisions of any adult. Support the decisions to the best of your ability, and provide more information where you think it might be useful. It is also a good idea to encourage children to try new activities as a means of developing new skills which might have career applications. For example, volunteering to help in political campaigns or at hospitals are both good preparation for dealing with others in a variety of circumstances. Church participation, summer camps, part-time jobs, and other activities can all be valuable parts of career preparation.

THE CONTINUING NATURE OF CAREER EDUCATION

None of these phases is exclusively the province of any particular age or educational level. The thoughtful reader will recognize that career education continues throughout life. No matter what our age may be we continue to expand our career awareness, to explore career opportunities, and to prepare for advancement in a current occupation or change to a new occupation. For this reason, whatever parents do to support their children in career education can also be a part of the parents' career development.

The nature of careers is continually changing, as will be discussed in the following chapter. Parents can perform a vital function in helping their children prepare for that change through career education.

ADDITIONAL READING

Levitan, Sar A., and Johnston, William B. *Work Is Here to Stay, Alas.* Salt Lake City: Olympus Publishing Co., 1973.

McClure, Larry. *Career Education Survival Manual: A Guidebook for Career Educators and Their Friends.* Salt Lake City: Olympus Publishing Co., 1975.

Sheppard, Harold L., and Herrick, Neal Q. *Where Have All the Robots Gone?* New York: Free Press, 1972.

CHAPTER TWO

The Changing Nature of Work and Work Roles

Whenever the subject of career education is brought up among a group of individuals who are not educators, two comments are frequently heard.

The first is: "I thought that's what education was for . . . to prepare students for careers. That's the reason I went to school."

And the second frequently heard comment is: "Why do we need career education now? Our education system has worked for a good many years. Why change it? We'd be better off to stick to the basics—reading, writing, and arithmetic."

At first glance, these two comments seem quite different, almost contradictory. But the two are closely related. Both comments support a traditionalist view of education, and both comments argue for the position that the goal of education is to help students improve themselves and prepare themselves for participation in society.

Certainly, career education proponents would not disagree with either of these comments. Career educators know that certain skills and abilities are basic to literally all careers and that those same skills are necessary for such non-career activities as citizenship, social interaction, and personal development. In addition, knowledge acquired in almost any field tends to have potential for use in a very broad range of career applications, and so all education is inherently career related.

Why, then, this sudden interest in career education during the decade of the '70s?

As mentioned in the previous chapter, career education is not a new program. In a very real sense, it is a fundamental return to "basics." It is simply the application of certain principles and concepts to existing programs, not to drastically change those programs but to add an emphasis that is vitally important to students and society at the present time. The emphasis is a concern for the career development of each individual student, whether the career be paid employment, home making and child rearing, volunteer work, or avocational activity.

CHANGES IN WORK, IN THE HOME, AND IN SCHOOL

The importance of that emphasis has increased during the last quarter of a century because of at least three gradual developments: First, work itself has become increasingly complex; second, the influence of the home and other traditional social institutions has decreased; and third, society—particularly the economic components of society—increasingly demand more extensive ties between academic training and the practical application of that training.

The first of these evolutionary developments is obvious to anyone who has a job or who observes others at work. Fewer and fewer jobs are simple, single-task jobs. More and more jobs require multiple skills or the application of complex performance sequences. Even jobs which were once simple now require written reports or computational skills. And few jobs are available which do not require the ability to read, at least adequately enough to complete an application form. Indicative of the types of changes which have occurred are changes in the nature of the work force (Figure 1). In 1900, some 37.5 percent of the work force were farmers; by 1970 the proportion decreased to 3.1 percent.

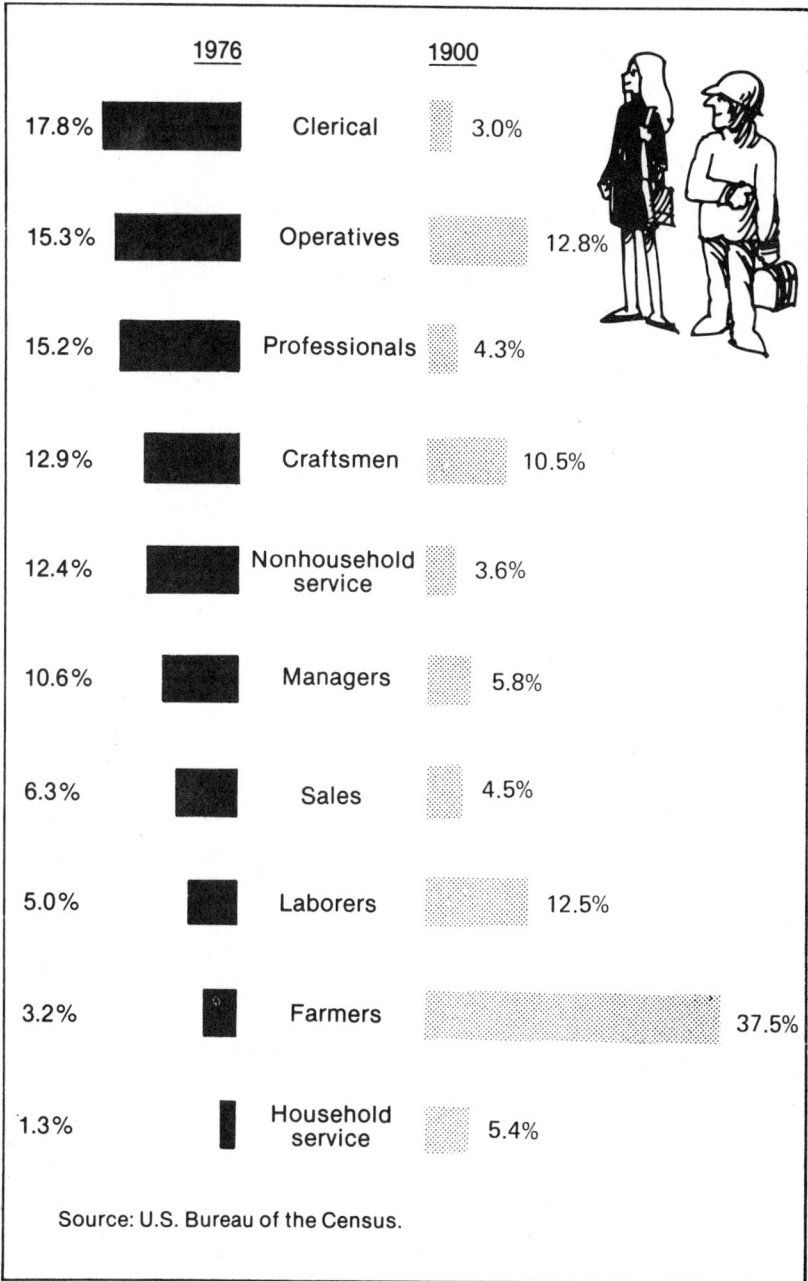

1976		1900
17.8%	Clerical	3.0%
15.3%	Operatives	12.8%
15.2%	Professionals	4.3%
12.9%	Craftsmen	10.5%
12.4%	Nonhousehold service	3.6%
10.6%	Managers	5.8%
6.3%	Sales	4.5%
5.0%	Laborers	12.5%
3.2%	Farmers	37.5%
1.3%	Household service	5.4%

Source: U.S. Bureau of the Census.

FIGURE 1. The composition of the labor force has changed drastically since the turn of the century.

In 1900, approximately 12.5 percent of the nation's workers were employed as laborers; by 1970 that figure had dropped to 4.5 percent. At the other end of the scale, in 1900 clerical workers comprised 3.0 percent of the work force; in 1970 the proportion of clerical workers had increased to 17.9 percent. In 1900, some 4.3 percent of the workers were classified as "professionals"; the proportion of professionals climbed to 14.8 percent by 1970. (Keep in mind that the total *number* of workers increased during this same period from 29 million in 1900 to 76.5 million in 1970. Thus, the actual number of clerical workers increased from 877,000 in 1900 to 13,748,000 in 1970, an increase of almost 1600 percent.)

These changes in the tasks involved with each job and in the structure of the work force itself mean that each career requires a higher level of educational preparation than it did a few years ago. The same is true of those careers surrounding the maintenance of a home and the raising of children. Homemakers today must cope with complex appliances, complex purchasing decisions, complex legal restrictions, and complex new theories of child rearing.

The Declining Influence of the Home

While the world of work has become more complex, the role of the family and the home in preparing children for participation in the world of work has decreased. This has occurred through no particular fault of parents, but primarily through unavoidable social changes. The home and family are simply not the strong influences they once were. (This is probably less true where very young children are concerned, but even at that level the influence of the home has declined, particularly with regard to career development.) A number of factors have contributed to this decline of influence. Television and urban living are prime contributors. The home and family can no longer isolate itself from the rest of the world, even on a part-time basis. In the words of Marshall McLuhan, we have all become citizens in a "global village," whose problems we share and whose influences we must absorb. The values which children develop are determined by the values they see on television and the values they confront in the neighborhood, as well as by the values they are taught at home.

Another factor is the nature of complex economic structures in which families operate today. In the past, a child could watch his or her parent at work, either in the field—if the parent was a farmer—or at the parent's place of employment, often within walking distance of the home. Such observations are no longer everyday occurrences. Parents travel long distances to their work. Frequently, employers do not welcome the presence of visiting children at the work place, since it may be disruptive or dangerous. And in many cases, children simply cannot understand the work their parents do because it is so abstract. For example, it is difficult for a child to associate the work of an accountant or a psychiatrist with the end result of that work. Therefore, it is difficult for children to come in contact with the world of work through the home in the same meaningful way as was once possible.

As a matter of fact, this situation has created somewhat of a problem with the development of work values of children. Parents work hard during the day at their jobs, and when mother or father comes home in the evening, he or she feels deserving of some quiet rest. But the child sees the parent only during the hours at home, and the child may receive the image that the primary thing a father or a mother does is rest. Under these conditions, a child has a difficult time developing meaningful work values and work attitudes. This is another reason for parents to make an extra effort to let children know what they do during the working hours, why that activity has value, and how the parents feel about it. Of course, for the young child this information must be in concrete, visible form; it cannot be presented abstractly.

A final factor in the decline of the family's influence with regard to career development is the very nature of the world of work. As will be discussed below, the world of work is so vast that few adults can fully grasp it, let alone communicate it to others. Parents can help expand their children's knowledge of the many career opportunities available today, but they can hardly cover the entire range of such opportunities. That requires the structured approach which is available through the career exploration phase of career education.

The Demand for Career-related Education

The third evolutionary development which has contributed to the increasing emphasis on career education may not be quite so apparent to the casual observer. However, the trend is frequently called to the attention of educators and those associated with the education system: Both the employing community and the students who eventually seek employment are demanding more relevant ties between academic training and practical application of knowledge in career settings. Student demands are more likely to take the form of calls for "relevance in education," while employer demands are for more adequate career preparation in the schools so that those who seek entry to the labor market have marketable skills. Students are no longer interested in simply learning to read; they want to read materials which are meaningful to their lives, and they want to develop their skills of comprehension and analysis. Employers want to concentrate their own training programs on skills intrinsic to specific jobs, not on basic reading and comprehension of written instructions.

These three evolutionary developments add importance to the career education movement, but the basic impetus behind the movement can be traced to the changing nature of work and work roles. Some of the changes have been mentioned above, but parents who want to fully understand the value of career education to their children can benefit from a closer examination of four basic changes in the nature of work and work roles: (1) expanding opportunities in the world of work; (2) evolving patterns in the structure of the labor market; (3) gradual elimination of race and sex stereotyping; and (4) the emergency of lifetime career mobility.

EXPANDING OPPORTUNITIES

The number of different career opportunities available to those entering the work force continues to expand at an amazing rate. A vast majority of the occupations available today simply did not exist half a century ago, and the activities associated with all but a very few careers are constantly changing. Over 30,000 different occupations are listed in the *Dictionary of Occupational Titles,* and that number increases each year. Many factors account for the continuing increase in the types of career opportunities, but three factors are primarily responsible: new technology, specialization and subdividing of work tasks, and re-structuring of social needs.

New technologies have accounted for the largest number of new occupations in the past quarter-century. One need not look far to become aware of the changes in the nature of our physical surroundings. Plastics, chemicals, and electronics are three components of our environment that were not nearly so pervasive one generation ago as they are today. Plastics have virtually revolutionized the manu-facturing industries. Things that were once forged, carved, machined, and bolted are now poured, cast, etched, and glued. Chemicals have changed the way we eat, the way we dress, and the way we paint our buildings. With the help of a little processing and a few chemical additives, specialists now make a handful of soybeans look and taste like a slice of ham. Electronics bring entertainment and information into our homes, dial our telephones, time the ignition in our automobiles, and sense the presence of smoke in our buildings. Fewer than ten years ago, virtually none of the occupations involved in designing and manufacturing the ubiquitous hand-held calculator existed. Now, thousands of individuals are employed in those occupations, and the calculators they produce are available even at the toy counter.

When the United States decided to send a man to the moon, the tasks involved in that goal spawned literally thousands of new occupations, many of which have now found "civilian" application. Furthermore, it seems to be an ongoing cycle: Those in new occupations dream of new goals, which require new tasks, which develop new occupations, which open up new goals . . . and so on. It appears that new technologies will continue to create new occupations for years to come.

For those readers with preschool children, the most challenging concept involved in this rapid technological change is to realize that by the time today's preschool youngster graduates from high school, the structure of the job market will be very different from today's. A few existing occupations will have disappeared, but to a greater degree it will mean that the content and requirements of many of today's occupations will have changed, while numerous new opportunities will have emerged.

A second factor accounting for the increasing number of career opportunities is specialization and the subdivision of work tasks. Specialization or subdividing of tasks usually occur because they offer a more efficient way to deal with complex tasks or processes. For instance, automobile mechanics once concerned themselves with the entire automobile, but because the systems within the machine have become so complex, mechanics now often specialize in transmissions, or electrical systems, or cooling systems, or any of the other components which make up the total vehicle. Some mechanics specialize in certain types of automobiles or trucks. This is a case of equipment becoming so complex that a single individual can be expected to fully comprehend only certain portions of that equipment. The same thing has occurred in medicine—not that the human body has become more complex, but our understanding of it has developed to the point that it is more efficient to have specialists who treat only certain parts of the body or certain diseases which attack it.

The subdividing of work tasks has also occurred for other reasons. For example, teachers are trained to teach and to participate in the administrative decision-making process of the school. It is not an efficient use of a teacher's time to spend it calling the roll, monitoring exams, or performing many of the other tasks necessary to classroom conduct. The teacher's time can better be spent in preparation or in individual student conferences. Accordingly, many schools are hiring "classroom assistants" to take over some of the work tasks in order to allow the teacher to make better use of his or her special skills. This same type of job creation has occurred in many fields.

In contrast to the explosive growth of occupations associated with new technological developments, the development of new occupations which occurs as a result of specialization and subdivision of tasks tends to be evolutionary rather than revolutionary. However, the number of occupations concerned is high, and the effects on the total pattern of occupational opportunities are extensive.

Restructuring of Social Needs

A final factor in the continuing increase of career opportunities is the restructuring of social needs in our society. In recent years society has changed its emphasis from one of production-oriented work to that of service-oriented activities, at least insofar as the proportion of the labor force is concerned. As mentioned previously, the proportion of workers in farm work and non-farm labor has declined considerably, while the proportion of clerical and professional workers has increased. Substantial increases have also occurred in the ranks of sales persons, managers, non-household service workers, and craftsmen. This change in emphasis has created many new occupations, and it has also altered the nature of other occupations. For example, at one time the blacksmith provided an important service in relation to farm production and transportation. Now, the blacksmith—an occupation currently increasing in numbers—serves the recreation industry.

And speaking of the recreation industry—hundreds of new occupations have appeared in that industry in recent years, including sports information directors, recreation planners, tour directors, and others—all "service" occupations. Another indicator of the movement toward a service-oriented economy is the fact that during the middle 1970s, Americans spent one of every three food dollars on food prepared outside the home in such places as restaurants, quick-food outlets, and snack shops. That figure will likely become one of every two food dollars by 1980.

This explosion in raw numbers of different occupational callings will likely continue as far into the future as we can foresee. Even now we see the beginnings of whole new families of occupations in the environmental fields, in communication, and in mass transportation. There is no reason to suppose that human kind—and the various societies which it creates—will stop growing in terms of seeking new and better ways to satisfy its own needs.

Increasing Range of Career Options

Accompanying this explosive expansion of occupational opportunities is another kind of expansion which is more directly related to the individual. The *range* of career opportunities available to any one person in our culture has increased tremendously in recent years as a result of changing social conditions. This is not necessarily related to expanding opportunities for certain segments within society (which will be discussed below), but to expanding opportunities for *everyone*. We have talked about equality of opportunity for many years, but that is a hollow ideal unless virtually *every* individual in the society has the same opportunity to seek entry to *every* occupation or career available in the society. In the past, this kind of opportunity has been limited due to restrictions of geography, or education, or communication, or simply "social pressure."

We have not yet achieved the ideal of equal opportunity, by any means. But virtually every young person in the 1970s has a wider range of opportunity for career choice than did her or his mother or father. Several factors account for this improving opportunity picture.

First, the mobility of the population continues to increase. Children travel—either with parents or with school groups—and they are exposed to occupational situations which are simply not available in their home towns or neighborhoods. The youngster from Nebraska visits a fishery in Massachusetts, and the child from Alabama spends a week with a cousin near a Vermont ski slope. It is not uncommon for the young person from a rural area to "try his or her wings" in the big city after graduation from high school or college. And if father works for a large corporation, the whole family may find itself changing locations from time to time. While a majority of persons still spend their lives near the place where they were born, that proportion continues to decrease, and geographic location becomes a less important factor—and a less limiting factor—in the selection of an occupation.

Second, the availability of training for a wide range of careers has improved markedly. In response to pressures from government, business, and other sources, most schools have expanded their offerings in academic as well as vocational areas to include training for careers not necessarily indigenous to the specific area. This is often difficult where no practical opportunity exists for on-site educational experiences, but the availability of audiovisual materials and well-designed training equipment has made it possible for schools to improve their services to students. In addition, other types of institutional and non-institutional training are available. Some cities have career education centers, where students can spend part of their time in training for specific occupations. The number of post-secondary vocational schools has increased tremendously in recent years, and their offerings have expanded. Job Corps centers and manpower training centers offer training for segments of the population which have had difficulty finding adequate career preparation. Unions, businesses, and other organizations have moved into the training field, often aggressively. Specialized schools and correspondence courses have proliferated (sometimes with questionable results). The availability of "non-traditional" programs through some colleges and universities makes it possible to obtain college degrees—including even advanced degrees—without ever visiting a college campus. And where economic status formerly limited availability of training for many prospective students, certain government and institutional programs have reduced that limitation through scholarships, grants, and other subsidies.

Third, this very spread of social opportunities creates its own new set of occupations. Health care occupations have experienced explosive growth, in part, because as incomes rise, families can afford to spend more on their health needs. But the provision of publicly supported health care through Medicare and Medicaid and other public health programs has also been involved. Similarly, the social work profession expands along with publicly supported welfare programs, while public housing programs open another range of occupations, as do remedial education, training, and manpower planning activities. The pursuit of energy independence will generate another flock of new occupations.

Fourth, the individual has a wider range of career opportunities simply because he or she is likely to be more aware of those opportunities than ever before. The information and communication systems within society have proliferated at an incredible rate. Television and radio are the most pervasive communication sources ever known. Over 99 percent of all homes in the United States have television sets. (Indeed, more homes have television sets than have telephones or indoor plumbing.) The average child spends more than four hours per day watching television, and in that time he or she is exposed to more different occupations than many pre-television citizens contacted in a lifetime. (More viewers watched "Hamlet" on the one night it was presented on television than have seen it in person in the three hundred and fifty years since it was written.) Home television viewing is supplemented by radio, educational television in the school, illustrated books and magazines, audiovisual materials, movies, and advertising. By the time a youngster reaches high school, she or he has observed thousands of occupations—often presented haphazardly and with some confusion, but nevertheless offered to the young person as potential opportunities for career pursuit. (One of the key goals of career education is to organize this information and present it in a systematic way so that young persons have a better opportunity to study it in a more realistic context.)

Fifth, the individual is under less pressure to "conform" to some preconceived notion of parents or social groups. There is much still to be done in this area, particularly with regard to race, sex, and handicapping conditions—but for the most part young people are becoming increasingly independent in career choices. Some of this can be attributed to a reduction of certain economic pressures, but much of it results from changes in the attitudes of society. The son is no longer pressured to follow in his father's footsteps. The laborer or the craft worker need no longer fear a loss of personal status because she or he is not a professional person. We are making some strides in efforts to minimize career stratification in favor of the view that *all* jobs are vital to the functioning of society and that *all* jobs can bring satisfaction and personal reward to the individual. Some parents who formerly might have insisted that their child attend college now accept the fact that the child may find just as much personal meaning and satisfaction in going to a trade school. This reduction of "pressure" from parents and others has broadened the career horizons of a great many young people.

Disadvantages of Expanding Opportunities

Before we leave the subject of expanding career opportunities, something must be said about the disadvantages involved. One has little "freedom to choose" if the choice must be made between two or three alternatives. The degree of true freedom expands as the number of alternative choices increases. However, the higher the number of alternatives, the more difficult it is to make a choice. One is no longer faced with selecting from among a few distinctly different alternatives; one must choose from literally hundreds of alternatives, many of which are only marginally different from the others. This means that factors outside the occupation itself begin to intrude on the decision-making process; i.e., location, life style, promotion potential, security, and many other factors. This places additional complications into the problem of selecting an occupation or occupations. Thus, the penalty for increased career opportunities is an increased complexity of career decision making.

The proponents of career education maintain that a good career education program in the school system can help reduce the difficulty of career decision making. Career education is designed, in part, to help students understand the decision-making process, and to assist them in identifying and analyzing the factors which should be considered when one is attempting to make career decisions.

EVOLVING JOB STRUCTURE

In addition to expanding opportunities, another significant change which has added impetus to the career education movement is the evolving nature of the labor market and job structure. Three of the more important changes which have occurred—and are continuing—are changes in the proportions of the labor force which are in so-called "white collar" and "blue collar" jobs, the increasing demand for "service" workers as opposed to "production" workers, and the gradually rising level of education for all workers at all strata of the labor market.

The statistical evidence for the changing proportion of blue-collar and white-collar workers has been cited above: The percentage of workers in farm work has declined markedly; a similar decline has occurred with regard to laborers and semi-skilled workers; and large proportional increases have occurred with regard to clerical workers, professional workers, technicians, and other support-type jobs. More subjective evidence is apparent in our daily environment. Machines can do many jobs more efficiently, less expensively, and with more reliability than humans. For instance, a backhoe can dig a ditch much more effectively than a crew of human laborers. Of course, the machines must be designed, engineered, constructed, marketed, purchased, scheduled, and operated by people, but most of those jobs require white-collar workers or skilled workers . . . or both. Furthermore, once the machine is in operation, it must be periodically serviced and repaired, jobs which require skilled workers.

Since machines have expanded our capacity to produce work, it has become increasingly necessary for society to establish standards regarding the quantity of work which should be done, the quality of work to be done, and the conditions under which that work should be done. To avoid confusion and to guard against faulty products, society must regulate how many water lines should be laid in trenches, where they should be laid, how large they should be, what standards must be employed to ensure long-term operation of the lines, and what safety conditions ought to be imposed on the machinery in order to protect workers and passers-by from injury. This means an increase in government workers—society's representatives—many of whom are white-collar workers. It also means an increase in those technical and support jobs which help to determine the standards and to decide upon how they should be enforced.

Much of the above discussion points to another aspect of the evolving job structure—the increasing demand for "service" workers. The shift toward a service economy was described by labor economists Sar Levitan and William Johnston in these terms:

> Manual labor once equated with work is becoming increasingly rare, antiquating the notion that work requires physical strength or skill. More important than the shift from brawn to brain has been the change from producing goods to performing services. Today more than 60 percent of the work force takes no direct hand in the provision of the goods by which the society lives. We have more cosmetologists than plumbers, more social workers than tool and die makers, more musicians than coal miners. A century ago society could afford to divert only a tiny fraction of its work force from the tasks of growing, making, and distributing goods. Today the majority exists on goods it has no part in producing. This shift in work roles will undoubtedly continue as the human effort required to survive is mechanized.

Part of the impetus behind this shift to a service base can be attributed to our increasing reliance on machines. It is a reliance which begins with the largest factories and permeates down through our society to include every human being. Food preparation, transportation, shelter, communication . . . all are dependent on machines. A second part of the impetus is our increasing dependence on government and government services. This dependence does not imply weakness; it simply states the reality that our society and our economy have become so complex that each citizen must increasingly look to government to represent his or her interests and to protect him or her from unforeseen danger. In our particular system, government is rarely involved in the actual production of goods; it performs a service function.

A third part of the impetus toward a service economy is the affluence in which a majority of our citizens lives. The availability to each individual of more money means that a larger proportion of that money can be devoted to things outside the immediate human needs of food, clothing, and shelter. Thus, citizens of the United States spend large portions of their incomes on such things as recreation, education, travel, personal services, and convenience goods. Spectator sports are big business, as are such participator sports as tennis, golf, skiing, and fishing. Adult education—from correspondence courses to community colleges—is one of the fastest growing segments of education. Many communities consider the tourist business as their most important activity. We spend unbelievable sums of money for such personal services as beauty care, legal advice, home repairs, counseling, and pet care. Gimmicks, gadgets, and gimcracks are available in every supermarket, drugstore, and gift shop, while "quick food service" runs from the traditional hamburger, to fish and chips, to fried chicken, to complete steak dinners. All of these marks of affluence are more likely to require service workers than production workers.

Levitan and Johnston summed up the trend away from "production" as a two-level development:

> First, the primary production of goods is no longer the focus of most work. Rather, the distribution, maintenance, and trade of these goods employ most people, together with an enormous work force which simply keeps track of this system. Second, a sizable and growing percentage of the population is being diverted from even secondary relationships to the circulation or production of goods. Services—from education to entertainment, from hospital care to hotel hospitality—are becoming employers of millions. And though these jobs range from being

president to polishing the president's shoes, they have in common their remoteness from the production of the necessities which sustain the population.

. . . . Simply by weight of numbers, secretaries are many times more deserving of attention than auto workers. Public school teachers outnumber all the production workers in the chemical, oil, rubber, plastic, paper, and steel industries combined. Retail salesmen are twice as numerous as the total of all engineers and scientists in the country.

Another aspect of the evolving nature of job structure in our society is that the level of education of workers in all jobs at all levels is gradually increasing. This is particularly true of craftsmen, operatives, service workers, and laborers. In 1900 the average worker had 8.5 years of education; in 1957 the average was still only 11.1 years; but today's average worker has completed 12.5 years of school. The level of education has also been rising among professional workers and technicians, but at a slower rate. The net result is that—at least in terms of years of education—today's work force is more "equal" than at any time in history.

Whatever the reasons for the increasing level of education, the implications are clear. First, the worker who is better educated is less likely to be satisfied with tedious work; he or she wants more challenge, more meaningfulness, and more opportunity for growth. Second, the competition for each job tends to be greater, with those who have minimal education finding it increasingly difficult to enter the labor market at any level. Thus, a sort of push-pull effect occurs. Prospective employees push themselves to more education and higher levels of career expectation, while employers are able to pull better educated employees into jobs traditionally reserved for those with less sophisticated training. This may create frustration, or better job performance, or both, but it certainly changes the structure of the job market. The difference in education between the supervisor and the supervisee is likely to be small, and thus demands by employees for participation in the decision-making process may very well be both pronounced and valid.

ELIMINATION OF RACE AND SEX STEREOTYPING

Few would contend that all stereotyping by race and sex has ended in the labor market. But society has made progress in reducing stereotyping, and that progress shows every sign of continuing. Stereotyping has been evident in the practice of reserving certain types of jobs for representatives of specific groups within society and in discriminating against representatives of those same groups in jobs with which they were not traditionally associated. Stereotyping has been evidenced most with regard to racial groups (blacks, chicanos, native Americans, and others), women, and the handicapped. That those stereotypes are gradually breaking down can be seen from statistical and other empirical evidence.

Approximately 15 percent of the work force of the United States is made up of representatives of racial minorities. Accordingly, one would expect that about 15 percent of jobs at each level would be filled by minority representatives. Unfortunately, that is not the case. Minorities still hold a disproportionate share of blue-collar, laborer, and service-type jobs. However, the trend is clearly toward a more equitable distribution of jobs. For example, during the past ten years the percentage of black workers in professional and technical jobs has more than tripled, and it is beginning to approach parity with the percentage of white workers in those same jobs. With regard to managerial occupations, the percentage of black workers in those jobs has more than doubled, but it still does not approach the percentage of white workers in managerial positions. Also, in the blue-collar occupations, more blacks are skilled workers and fewer are laborers than was the case ten years ago, while a slightly larger percentage of white workers is now classified as laborers than was true ten years ago.

No one should be satisfied so long as *any* disparity exists or so long as *any* job stereotyping occurs because of racial background. However, insofar as career education is concerned, the operative point is that more and more career opportunities are available to more and more of the population, regardless of background. One goal of career education is to help all citizens deal more adequately with the problems of the labor market, including information, decision-making, preparation, job entry, and job holding.

The pressures to eliminate stereotyping by race have come from several sources in society, but primary credit must go to members of the minority groups themselves, who called attention to the existence of stereotyping and who demanded more equitable treatment beginning as far back as the 1940s, but with increasing visibility in the '50s and '60s. The media recognized the problem and contributed to its solution, first with documentaries and commentaries, then within news programs, and finally in entertainment and advertising. Over a period of years, federal and state governments established a variety of programs to either force or strongly encourage the elimination of stereotyping. For instance, any organization which does business with the federal government must maintain an equal opportunity program designed to reduce stereotyping and encourage employment of minorities. Details of the program must be on file for inspection by appropriate government agencies if the organization intends to continue doing business with the government. Finally, business groups have come to recognize both the need and the opportunity to provide employment at all levels for all groups, without the traditional stereotyping which has frequently denied certain jobs to highly qualified individuals simply because those individuals happened to be representatives of a minority race.

All of these developments have helped to open up a broader range of career opportunities to large segments of the population and to make career education more important to minority groups than ever before.

Women and Job Stereotyping

A majority group which has also been victimized by stereotyping is that 53 percent of the population which happens to be female. Society is just beginning to recognize the stereotyping problems that have limited career opportunities for women, but already some meaningful steps have been taken. The federal government has expanded its equal opportunity program to include women, and it has also insisted that those who do business with the government increase employment opportunities for women. The media are attempting to reduce or eliminate stereotypic references to both women and men, and many media outlets have established editorial policies which seek to equalize the use of feminine and masculine pronouns and to eliminate such traditionally masculine usages as "chairman" or "policeman." Publishers are aggressively seeking new materials—particularly children's books—which show both male and female workers in non-traditional occupations. Career educators are especially cognizant of this problem, and through their insistence the vast majority of career education materials currently being produced exhibits women and men in non-traditional roles and attempts to show women and men in approximately equal numbers at all occupational levels.

These efforts will have a profound effect on students enrolled in career education programs, but if equal opportunity is to become a reality it must begin with values and attitudes learned by children in the home, as discussed in later chapters of this book.

Aside from efforts to open opportunities to women throughout the entire range of occupational choices, additional factors are operating to increase the participation of women in the labor market. The most obvious factor is that more women enter the labor force now than ever before in history. Economists estimate that more than 90 percent of the women in the United States will be employed at some time during their lifetimes. In the twenty-five years since 1950, the number of women workers has nearly doubled, while the number of men in the work force has increased by only one-fourth. The proportion of women in the work force has also increased. In 1900 only 18 out of every 100 workers were women; today almost 40 of every 100 workers are women (Figure 2).

Not only do more women work than ever before, but they tend to work for longer periods during their lifetimes. (Interestingly enough, the number of years worked by women has been increasing steadily while the number of

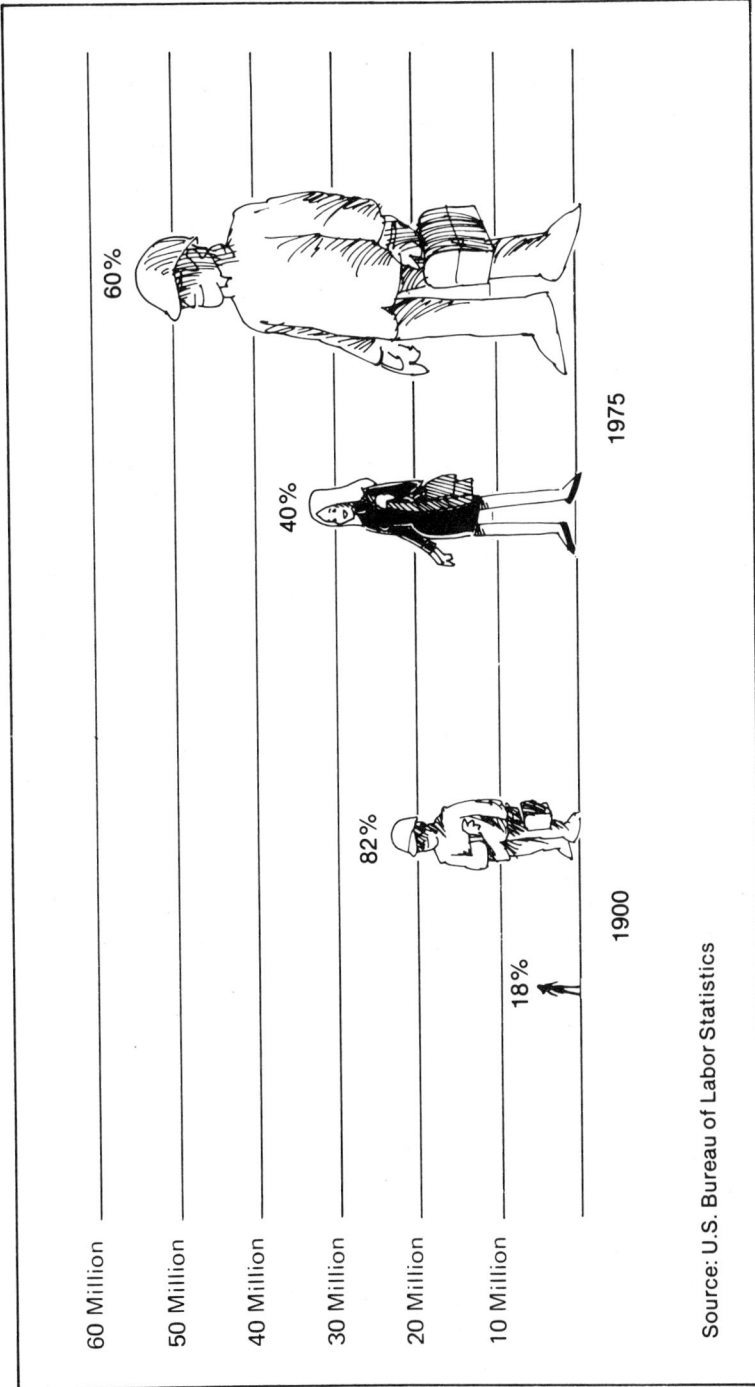

60%

40%

82%

18%

60 Million
50 Million
40 Million
30 Million
20 Million
10 Million

1975

1900

Source: U.S. Bureau of Labor Statistics

FIGURE 2. Labor force participation by women has increased dramatically in recent years.

years worked by men has been decreasing.) Many factors account for this trend. First, women live longer, which means they have more years to work beyond the child-bearing age. Second, fertility rates are low, which means women have fewer or no children, leaving them more time to work. Third, the number of women who are heads of families is increasing (by 73 percent since 1960), which means more women experience the financial necessity to work. Fourth, the demands of homemaking and child rearing have been reduced by technology and other factors. Fifth, more men are assuming partial or full duties associated with home-making and child rearing. Sixth, the difference in level of educational attainment between men and women, though still pronounced, is diminishing.

These developments account for the fact that women are entering the labor market in increasing numbers, that women are seeking a wider range of occupational oppor-tunities than those roles which have traditionally been reserved for them, and that society itself is demanding equitable treatment for that increasingly important segment of the labor force which is female.

Greater participation in the labor market brings with it greater problems in decision making. Decisions which once were not related to work and career are now integrally involved. When women simply assumed they would marry and raise children, career decisions were essentially made *for* them. Now both men and women must decide how marriage will affect their career decisions. They must decide how marriage to each potential marriage partner will affect those decisions. They must decide how children will affect the career decisions of both partners. They must decide what type of home life is most compatible with their career decisions, and vice versa. They must decide how geographic factors involved in the career decisions of one partner will affect the career decisions of the other partner. And they must decide which roles each will perform in the marriage relationship.

Of course, career education includes consideration of all these factors. It is particularly concerned with the stereo-typing, with the expansion of each individual's perception of career opportunities, and with the decision-making process as it relates to career considerations.

One more important benefit derives from the elimination of sex stereotyping in career roles. As women work to reduce that stereotyping and to expand their own opportunities, the stereotypic barriers affecting men are also reduced. Certainly, this expansion of opportunities is beneficial to the male members of society who may find just as much satisfaction in traditionally female roles as they find in any other career activity.

Discrimination and the Handicapped

Another minority group which has been discriminated against in many areas, including careers, is the handicapped. Depending on how one defines "handicapped," the number of handicapped individuals in society may go as high as one in every ten citizens. In the past, handicapped persons have frequently not been welcomed into the work force except under special circumstances, such as in a "handicapped center" or "sheltered workshop" of some sort. Most handicapped individuals are handicapped only in one specific area or field of activity; they can operate fully in all other capacities, and they should be given the same career opportunities as all other workers, outside that single limitation. The current philosophy regarding the handicapped is a philosophy which argues for allowing handicapped to enter the "mainstream" of society in every respect, limited only by whatever specific handicap or handicaps may be involved. This mainstreaming concept applies to careers, as well as to other aspects of activity, and so the federal government has recently moved to encourage employers to eliminate whatever stereotyped views they may have regarding handicapped persons. Organizations which do even a minimum amount of business with the government are required to prepare and maintain equal opportunity plans for the handicapped which include not only making jobs available to the handicappd but making certain that physical facilities are constructed in such a way as to facilitate access by handicapped persons.

As job opportunities become available to handicapped individuals, they too will benefit from career education. It will provide an invaluable means for exploring career opportunities and avenues of preparation for entry into selected occupations.

EMERGENCE OF LIFETIME CAREER MOBILITY

One of the most fascinating and exciting changes taking place in work and work roles is the increased mobility people have to move from occupation to occupation throughout their lifetimes. Often in the past, one became "locked in" to an occupation in youth and had little opportunity to change it—other than normal advances within the occupation—until it became time to retire. Many factors contributed to this immobility, including time restrictions, economic restraints, lack of training opportunities, the need for job security, and built-in restrictions on exit and re-entry. Much of that is changing.

It simply doesn't make much sense any longer to be bored with work. If one doesn't like a line of work, he or she can plan to change to another.

Perhaps this is an oversimplification, but in a very real sense it is a distinct possibility under current economic conditions. Furthermore, it is being done by more and more individuals every day. A stockbroker from New York became tired of the pressure and the pollution of the big city and opened a restaurant in a small town in Wyoming. A truck driver from Omaha moved to Atlanta to work as a gardener for a large nursery. A successful middle-aged pharmaceuticals sales representative quit his job to go back to school and became a college professor. An advertising specialist in Chicago bought a weekly newspaper in the southwestern United States, where he earned happiness and less than one-fourth of his previous income. These stories could be multiplied by the thousands. Each year in the United States more than 500,000 new businesses are opened, often by individuals who want to make career changes. That's almost 1,400 new businesses per day.

Most Americans have more free time and more disposable income than ever before, time and money which some use to prepare for career changes. And to facilitate those changes, avenues for career preparation have multiplied greatly in recent years. Many schools operate at night to accommodate those who work during the day. Community colleges have appeared in many cities to provide college-level education, and the community high school which offers adult education classes is becoming commonplace. More and more communities have excellent trade and technical schools, and labor organizations have steadily improved the quality and availability of their training programs. In response to demand, most universities are increasing their offerings during the evening hours and on weekends, and a surprisingly large segment of the college student population consists of men and women who are over 30 years of age. Many colleges and universities are experimenting with programs under which adults get academic credit for "learning by experience" rather than in the classroom. Coupled with courses taught off campus in work and community settings, such programs make it possible for adults to achieve college degrees without ever becoming students in the traditional sense. Most universities offer correspondence courses, some of which can lead to the attainment of college degrees. Other correspondence schools provide specific training in hundreds of career fields.

Another development has occurred which also has meaning for career mobility throughout a lifetime. That development is the increase in opportunities for volunteer work in the community. Volunteer work is available in hospitals, political parties, church groups, social action groups, communication media, schools, health organizations, youth groups, senior citizen centers, and hundreds of other organizations which exist in almost every community. Aside from the important contributions these groups make to society, volunteer work associated with them offers at least two valuable benefits to the individual. First, volunteer work can provide meaningful and satisfying activity for the individual who finds little satisfaction in his or her paid employment. Second, volunteer work can be an excellent training ground for the individual seeking to "test out" new work experiences, or acquire new skills, or work on a flexible, part-time basis. For many individuals, the volunteer work they do is their primary work, and whatever paid work they do simply provides the economic base which allows them the freedom to perform their volunteer work. Traditionally, volunteer service has primarily been the province of women, but that too is changing as more and more men find meaningfulness in unpaid service to the community. Also, young persons are using volunteer work as a means of career exploration, and senior citizens have found volunteer activity to be a welcome substitute for the work from which they have retired.

Finally, as the career horizons of women have expanded beyond the traditional roles of the homemaker, more and more men are assuming the part-time or full-time role of "house husband." In a sense, this is a new career opportunity for men, one which should not be minimized in any way. Men can and should help their wives prepare for and perform in careers, just as many women have supported their husbands in the past. Sharing the duties of the home and the successes or failures of the job can help to strengthen the family, and if it is done well such sharing can multiply the satisfactions of both marriage partners.

The main purpose of this discussion is to emphasize the fact that mid-life career changes are becoming more likely in modern society. Some of the changes are forced changes. Firms go out of business or change locations, forcing some employees out of work. Technology makes some jobs obsolete. The economics of the marketplace reduce the demand for certain goods and services, which means some workers are no longer needed. Poor health forces workers to change locations and jobs. But many of the mid-life career changes are voluntary. Women faced with an excess of leisure time change from being homemakers to some new career. A couple decide they would like to spend the last fifteen years of their working lives in a warmer climate. A man loses interest in his work and decides to try a new career. A woman wants to change from being a volunteer fund raiser to being a paid consultant in the field.

Many valid reasons might cause one to want to change jobs in the middle of life's career experience. When the reasons are sufficient, one should not hesitate to make the change. It is one of the luxuries afforded by our high standard of living. But one should not change careers without careful thought and preparation, since to do so might lead to frustration and disappointment. For this reason, the wise course of action is to be continually in the process of exploring and preparing for new careers. Such exploration and preparation may take the form of a hobby, volunteer work, independent study, or formalized training.

Lifetime preparation for career changes is the logical extension of career education. Since career changes are a fact of life, it is part of what is learned by those youngsters who have the opportunity to partake of career education in the school. It should be part of the work attitudes and values which young children learn in the home. And since career change is a reality for many parents, preparation for change should be considered as part of regular family activities. One of the basic principles of career education is that it should begin at birth and continue through old age. As career education establishes itself in the school and in the home, it will undoubtedly move into the community to help expand those programs designed to assist all citizens in lifetime career development.

SUMMARY

Work and work roles in society are constantly changing. In recent years, those changes have become pronounced, especially in regard to the expanding number of career opportunities, the evolving structure of jobs and the work force, the reduction of job stereotyping by race and sex, and the emergence of lifetime career mobility. Not only are more different types of careers available today, but they have fewer entry restrictions than ever before, and the likelihood of having to make more than one career choice during a lifetime is increasing.

This multiplicity of career alternatives—coupled with an unavoidable weakening of the family influence—means that workers and potential workers need assistance in approaching and entering the job market, the kind of assistance which career education can supply. First, parents need assistance in helping their children develop work attitudes and values which are compatible with existing conditions in the labor market; i.e., which allow full exploration of possible careers, which provide work habits likely to facilitate successful entry into the labor market, and which minimize any trauma associated with periodic career changes.

Second, students need some sort of structured method for exploring potential career opportunities in order that they might have an understanding of the alternatives available to them at various stages of their lives.

Third, students need assistance in the decision-making process, particularly as it pertains to career decisions. The more alternatives which are available, the more difficult are decisions likely to be. Since alternatives are expanding exponentially, the need for decision-making skills is also increasing.

Fourth, students need guidance and training with regard to career preparation, job entry, and job retention. Students need to know where to go in order to acquire skills necessary for specific careers, how to obtain entry to training institutions, where and how to enter the occupation or occupations of their choice, and what skills may be necessary to stay in an occupation and advance within its structure.

Fifth, all those currently in the labor market need opportunities to explore new career possibilities, develop new skills, and prepare for career changes.

ADDITIONAL READING

Best, F. *Future of Work*. Englewood Cliffs, N.J.: Prentice-Hall, 1973.

Extended Learning Institute, Northern Virginia Community College. *Emphasis* (I. Change 1; II. Decisions; III. Work;

IV. Preparation; V. Change 2; VI. Self). Salt Lake City: Olympus Publishing Co., 1977.

Levitan, Sar A., and Johnston, William B. *Work Is Here to Stay, Alas.* Salt Lake City: Olympus Publishing Co., 1973.

Mangum, Garth L. *Employability, Employment, and Income.* Salt Lake City: Olympus Publishing Co., 1976.

Sheppard, Harold L., and Herrick, Neal Q. *Where Have All the Robots Gone?* New York: Free Press, 1972.

Terkel, Studs. *Working.* New York: Avon Books, 1975.

U.S. Department of Health, Education, and Welfare. *Work in America: Report of a Special Task Force to the Secretary of Health, Education, and Welfare.* Cambridge, Mass.: MIT Press, 1973.

CHAPTER THREE

Career Education Concepts

The parent who would assist the career development of children in the home and interface with the schools' efforts to do the same should be familiar with current developments in career education. Career education is not a program or a course so much as it is a concept—or rather, a series of concepts. It is not an addition to the school curriculum so much as it is an emphasis within that curriculum. It is not a new direction for education so much as it is a broadening of the path of the current direction. It is not an encroachment on traditional learning activities so much as it is an enhancement of them.

Career education was developed to help schools and their students cope with the problems discussed in the preceding chapter. It has already been accepted by many school districts throughout the United States, and it has become a part of the educational offering in thousands of elementary schools, middle and junior high schools, and high schools. In most cases, it has a remarkable record of success. As one junior high school teacher put it: "Career education makes the teacher more interesting and the students more interested."

But if career education is to achieve its full potential, it must include not only the school but also the home. We have already discussed the importance of the home to career education, and we have indicated some of the support mechanisms which originate in the home (Chapter 1). Indeed, one of the basic principles of career education is that it must involve parents and the home at all levels. This involvement can begin with a general understanding of the objectives, concepts, and principles of career education, together with some indications about how those can be applied in the home during the preschool years and throughout the period of formal education.

DEFINITIONS AND GOALS OF CAREER EDUCATION

The overriding goal of career education is a satisfying and productive working career for every individual. The concept of work is an unusually broad one, however. Work is conceived of as "all conscious effort aimed at producing benefits for one's self or for others." A career is the totality of work done in one's lifetime, and it is not limited to paid employment. The effort and planning women and men put into homemaking and child rearing is work and is an important part of their careers, whether they are full-time or part-time homemakers. Work also includes the effort invested in volunteer activities in communiy or church service, in labor organizations, in political parties, or in any of the myriad of service and fraternal organizations Americans use to improve their societies outside of the commercial market place. Parenting itself can be a career or part of a career for both men and women.

Since a career includes the totality of work done in one's lifetime, and since education is the totality of experiences through which one learns, career education is the totality of experiences through which one learns about and prepares to engage in work.

Of course, work does not and should not absorb one's whole life. Yet few can find happiness and peace of mind unless they have a feeling of self-worth. That sense of self-worth generally comes as a reflection of how we feel others view us. Only our families and closest friends know our inner thoughts and yearnings, and often even they know little enough about us. Others judge us by our achievements, and it is frequently through those achievements that we also find many of our satisfactions. Not all achievement is found in work—note the satisfactions we receive from hobbies, from our own musical and artistic talents, or from competition in amateur sports, for instance—but most of our achievement probably does arise from paid and unpaid work.

For most of us, our work in paid employment or in business is not only our major source of the satisfactions of achievement, it is *the* determinant of our standard of living. It is also a major factor in determining our life styles. How we live, where we live, our residence, our friends, our amenities, our economic security . . . are all products of our employment or the employment of some other family member.

Society itself cannot survive unless most of its members are productive. Human resources have become the wealth of nations. Despite technological change and a changing nature of job structure, individual, social, and national well-being depends upon work. As a wealthier society, we can perhaps support a larger proportion of non-producers than in our past. But still, every good or service is the product of someone's work, and without that work there could be no social survival. Those who do not work may be tolerated—they may even be venerated for past work or invested in as future workers—but there is little prestige or self-satisfaction available to those who do not work and make a productive contribution to society during a major portion of their lives.

Thus, the societal objectives of career education are to help all individuals: (a) want to work, (b) acquire the skills necessary for work, and (c) engage in work that is satisfying to the individual and beneficial to society. The goals of career education on behalf of the individual are to make work possible, meaningful, and satisfying for each individual throughout his or her lifetime.

There is a general awareness that occupational skills are necessary for career success. It is less well recognized—

though obvious upon reflection—that a successful working career requires much more. The successful worker, whether in the home, in the school, in community service, or in paid employment or business will generally be found to have strong work values, a positive attitude toward work, good work habits, reasonable physical and mental health, and skills in human relations. Career education seeks to address all of these, as well as the skills necessary to carry out a particular set of occupational tasks.

For these and other reasons, the home and the family environment is a key component in career education. It is in the home where all human values begin to develop, including work values. Since the home's influence comes first and is initially all-encompassing, for most persons no other influence in life will have equal impact. No other force will ever entirely erase its influence for good or ill. The home is a work place where important production and service tasks are constantly being performed. It is also a place of refuge from work outside the home and a place profoundly impacted upon by that external work and the worker's reaction to it.

Therefore, career education's goals for the home are: (1) to ensure that the home's influence on the careers of family members is positive through the values and attitudes it inculcates and the habits it develops, and (2) to increase the productiveness of the home as a work place through improved attitudes toward the tasks performed there and increased skill at doing those tasks. The rest of this chapter illustrates how various career education concepts contribute to the accomplishment of these twin objectives.

PHILOSOPHICAL ASSUMPTIONS OF CAREER EDUCATION

The following assumptions underlie career education concepts and activities. They are extracted from the writings of career education's foremost advocate and philosopher, Kenneth Hoyt, Director of the U.S. Office of Career Education. Parents wishing to participate in the career education movement in order to enhance the career prospects of their children should understand these assumptions and their relationship to home and family contributions. Comments on each assumption may point up that relationship.

    (1)   If students can see clear relationships between what they are being asked to learn in school and the world of work, they will be motivated to learn more in school.

This is the basic assumption of the in-school component of career education. Too many students fail to take schooling seriously, because they do not see that it relates clearly to important aspects of their lives. That is also true in the home. Children, especially adolescents, resent being told to do something "because I say so," but they are self-interested enough to do whatever they perceive as being of positive influence toward accomplishments they value and yearn for.

    (2)   There exists no single learning strategy that can be said to be best for all students. Some students will learn best by reading out of books, for example, and others will learn best by combining reading with other kinds of learning activities. A comprehensive educational program should provide a series of alternative learning strategies and learning environments for students.

This is also true of the far larger body of information and skills young people learn in the home and community during the years before they begin school or outside the classroom during the school years. Parents have the best possible opportunity to observe and experiment to find how their children learn best and build on those approaches.

    (3)   Basic academic skills, a personally meaningful set of work values, and good work habits represent adaptability tools needed by all persons who choose to work in today's rapidly changing occupational society.

The statement is self-evident. Most parents are concerned with helping their children achieve academically, but perhaps inadequate attention has been paid to the work values and work habits which this book emphasizes.

(4) Increasingly, entry into today's occupational society demands the possession of a specific set of vocational skills on the part of those who seek employment. Unskilled labor is less and less in demand.

This, too, is well recognized, but information on just which occupations have promise will always be inadequate since the future remains opaque. It is important to gain a knowledge of the available sources and be willing and able to interpret and use them. It is even more important to stress adaptability so directions can change as the outlook changes. Fortunately, the basic requirements for success are the same for all occupations. Specific occupational skills should be acquired just before one enters the labor market to put them to use. With a firm base of values, attitudes, and general knowledge and skills, career redirection, including retraining, can be accomplished if necessary.

(5) Career development, as part of human development, begins in the preschool years and continues into the retirement years. Its maturational patterns differ from individual to individual.

The wise parent recognizes this from personal experience as well as from observation of children. Gaining basic skills, developing values, becoming aware of a broader world and of self in relation to that widening world, exploration of self and society, the making and implementing of personal choices are all a continuing process throughout a lifetime. This human development process has its parallel in career development. One becomes aware of the role of work in life, finds joy in achievement, develops work values, becomes aware of the world of work outside the home, fantasizes about "what I want to be when I grow up," begins to explore alternatives and become more realistic, alternately chooses (whether by deliberation or default), prepares for and tries out many work roles, and becomes more settled in a work role . . . but never sets aside at least the possibility of change.

(6) Work values, a part of one's personal value system, are developed, to a significant degree, during the elementary school years and are modifiable during those years.

This is said concerning the elementary school only because that is where formal education starts. Actually most basic values are already formed from experiences in the home and neighborhood before one enters school. The parent will always be the key influence for good or ill. The schools can only hope to either reinforce or modestly redirect what parents and the home have already done. The most significant influence of all is whether the child has found joy in achievement and visualizes work as a desirable and positive force in life.

(7) Specific occupational chores represent only one of a number of kinds of choices involved in career development. They can be expected to increase in realism as one moves from childhood into adulthood and, to some degree, to be modifiable during most of one's adult years.

The comments on assumption 5 are relevant to this one as well. However, every choice predetermines other choices. Children reach adulthood with many options blocked by values and attitudes which may be dysfunctional or by lack of prerequisite knowledge and skills. The parent with foresight will encourage keeping options open.

(8) Occupational decision making is a process accomplished through the dynamic interaction of limiting and enhancing factors both within the individual and in his or her present and proposed environment. It is not, in any sense, something that can be viewed as a simple matching of individuals with jobs.

All decisions are complex, but none are more complex than choice of a mate or choice of an occupation. Decision making itself is a learned skill, as stressed in Chapter 7.

(9) Occupational stereotyping currently acts to hinder full freedom of occupational choice both for

females and for minority persons. These restrictions can be reduced, to some extent, through
programmatic intervention strategies begun in
the early childhood years.

No other influence is more powerful than the home in
establishing role stereotypes. How often are children guided
in their choice of toys and games, in their expressions of
emotion and in their peer relations by such comments as
"boys (or girls) don't do things like that"? Handicapped
children or children from racial or ethnic minorities may
have their career potentials thwarted if in the home they are
led to think, "Oh, you could never get a job in that field."
Parental example and attitude will be the most important
determinants of the girl's pursuit of non-traditional jobs, the
young husband's willingness to share household duties with
his working wife, or the joy and fulfillment (or lack of it)
both gain from roles as parents and homemakers.

(10)   Parent socioeconomic status acts as a limitation
       on occupational choices considered by children.
       This limitation can be reduced, to a degree, by
       program intervention strategies begun in the
       early years.

This is as true with children of high income parents as
those from low income homes. Occupational boundaries are
limited by personal exposure and role models. The child of a
college professor who cannot visualize an apprenticeship in a
skilled craft is as limited as the craftsman's child who
cannot imagine pursuing a college education.

(11)   A positive relationship exists between education
       and occupational competence, but the optimum
       amount and kind of education required as
       preparation for work varies greatly from occupa-
       tion to occupation.

It remains true that on the average the higher the
education, the higher the lifetime earnings of the recipient.
However, as more and more graduate from college, that
margin is tending to decline. Many occupations learned on
the job or in vocational and technical schools now pay as

well and have as much security as many of the jobs normally thought to require college educations. It has become increasingly important to have clear objectives in mind in pursuing any particular educational pattern. Occupational success is not the only purpose for gaining an education, but it is usually one of the purposes. A diploma by itself is no longer as near to being a guarantee of success as it once was. The parent should therefore help the youth clarify his or her educational objectives.

> (12) The same general strategies utilized in reducing worker alienation in industry can be used to reduce worker alienation among pupils and teachers in the classroom.

One of the important insights of career education is that school work and home chores are as much work as is work in paid employment. The same techniques that employers use to stimulate and motivate their employees can be used by the teacher in the classroom and the parent in the home. Not only will they possibly get a better job done in school or home but they may help build a more wholesome attitude toward achievement through work, an attitude which may last a lifetime.

> (13) While some persons will find themselves able to meet their human needs for accomplishment through work in their place of paid employment, others will find it necessary to meet this need through work in which they engage during their leisure time.

This is certainly a pertinent thought for the home where so much vital work must be done without pay, and where the reward, if it comes, must come as a recognition for service and pride in accomplishment.

> (14) Career decision-making skills, job-hunting skills, and job-getting skills can be taught to and learned by almost all persons. Such skills, once learned, can be effectively used by most individuals in enhancing their career development.

These skills are described and stressed in later chapters as among those parents can help their children develop.

(15) Excessive deprivation in any given aspect of human growth and development can lead to retardation of career development. Such deprivation will require special variations in career development programs for persons suffering such deprivation.

This will be of special concern for parents in those families where the misfortunes of economics, health, or family structure may have limited the resources available. The parent in that circumstance must make extra effort to compensate, must seek help from society—and society must respond to those special needs. Much more is at stake than temporary discomfort. Lifetimes and generations are being risked.

(16) An effective means of helping individuals discover both who they are (in a self-concept sense) and why they are (in a personal awareness sense) is through helping them discover their accomplishments that can come from the work that they do.

Of course, as human beings, we are much more than the work that we do. Nevertheless, when work is defined as "conscious effort to produce goods and services on behalf of one's self and others," much of our very clearest realizations of who and what we are or can become does come about through various forms of work. Ours is an achievement-oriented society, and it is when we achieve in some way that we tend to think best of ourselves. Again, a self-concept as a worthwhile human being is the surest assurance of human happiness, and its lack is the surest sentence to despair. All of that is as true in the home as in adult employment. For the young, the parent is the key figure in arranging success experiences, making available opportunities for achievement, and ensuring that every achievement is rewarded.

(17) Parental attitudes toward work and toward education act as powerful influences on the career development of their children. Such parental attitudes are modifiable through programmatic intervention strategies.

This is the philosophical basis of this book. Much of subsequent career education may be an effort to reverse wrong starts in the preschool period. Those who come out of the home with confidence in their ability to succeed in the school do, and those who leave school with that same confidence rarely fail in the world of paid employment or in their homemaking careers.

(18) The processes of occupational decision making and occupational preparation can be expected to be repeated more than once for most adults in today's society.

Every adult, parent or teacher, will relate to this statement from experience, and will see the need to prepare young people with basic adaptability, self-assurance, and decision-making skills that will facilitate those repetitive processes.

(19) One's style of living is significantly influenced by occupations he or she engages in at various times in life.

Perhaps here is the real key to career decision making: Decide on the life style one prefers, and select and choose from among those occupations most compatible with that life style. If occupation is to be a part rather than the whole of life's priorities, it ought to be kept within such bounds. Thus, a young person must grow up recognizing the need to examine self and life style preferences as a preliminary to career decisions. Occupational choice will have a profound determining influence on location of residence, standard of living, choice of friends, nature of recreation, and almost every aspect of life.

(20) Relationships between education and work can be made more meaningful to students through infusion into subject matter than if taught as a separate body of knowledge.

Life is not lived in separate little boxes; it is a seamless and continuous fabric. It is difficult—especially for the inexperienced—to synthesize different bodies of knowledge and recognize their interrelationships. Career education

advocates making as obvious as possible the interrelationships among various school subjects, as well as the
relationship between school and practical applications in
daily and future life. Parents also can profit from this
insight as they seek to illustrate for children the implications of all of those parentally imposed requirements that
are "only for your own good!"

> (21) Education and work can increasingly be expected
> to be interwoven at various times in the lives of
> most individuals, rather than occurring in a
> single sequential pattern.

This seems to be a growing pattern. Youth have always
gained work experiences in summer and other part-time jobs
before confronting the labor market on a full-time and
permanent basis. For many years, Selective Service laws
forced on young men an interruption of schooling, with
many positive as well as negative impacts. There is an
increasing tendency for youth to interrupt their post high
school education for periods of work, service experience such
as Peace Corps or VISTA, recreation, or meditation. On the
other hand, more and more adults return to school
periodically on a part-time or full-time basis for refurbish-
ing, upgrading, career change, or to pursue a vocational
interest. The parents should recognize that interruption of
schooling can be a positive experience for their youth if
pursued as an exploratory period, and it may be precursor of
a standard life style for the future.

> (22) Decisions individuals make about the work that
> they do are considerably broader and more
> encompassing in nature than are decisions made
> regarding the occupations in which they are
> employed.

Before choosing an occupation, an individual must have
chosen some work values, whether or not to work, whether
to make work a means or an end in life, and selected criteria
related to preferred life style by which occupational choice
will be guided. Negative choices will also have been made by
the development of dysfunctional values and habits, or by
the neglect of prerequisite learning and skills. The parent,

having longer experience and generally more foresight, can help the child or youth explore the parameters of these broader decisions.

(23)   Good work habits and positive attitudes toward work can be effectively taught to most indivuals. Assimilation of such knowledge is most effective if begun in the early childhood years.

Every parent knows this statement is true, and parents of older children rue not having done better earlier.

(24)   The basis on which work can become a personally meaningful part of one's life will vary greatly from individual to individual. No single approach can be expected to meet with universal success.

For this reason, the wise parent will not dictate or even unduly bias the choices the child makes in the process of career development. Rather, the parent will encourage the child to explore his or her own talents, abilities, and preferences, to learn decision-making skills, to gather relevant data, and to make sound but individualized choices. Not *what* the child chooses but *that* he chooses—deliberately, based on evidence and judgment—should be the wise parent's concern.

(25)   While economic return can almost always be expected to be a significant factor in decisions individuals make about occupations, it may not be a significant factor in many decisions individuals make about their total pattern of work.

The United States has not arrived at a millennium in affluence, but it is the wealthiest of countries with the broadest distribution of that wealth that exists in any major nation. Many among the wealthy choose lives of public service. Some of modest means eschew the competitive "rat race" in preference for a simpler life. Many remain outside the employed labor force, depending upon financial support from other family members or from public programs. Many delay their age of full-time entrance into the work force. And all who survive retire eventually. But none of this means they have ceased working, only that they have abandoned or restricted paid employment. Others who have jobs pursue part-time volunteer work activities. It is now estimated that the equivalent of one million full-time jobs are performed on a volunteer basis in the United States. Work is meaningful in the lives of all, and career education is relevant to the future of all.

In each of these basic assumptions can be seen a role for the parent seeking to assist the child in establishing the basis for lifelong career success. Similarly, the teacher or counselor who would aid the parent can identify a personal role. Subsequent chapters tell how each can participate in furthering the career prospects of all of the children of all of the homes of America.

CAREER EDUCATION ROLES

Career education is perceived as a partnership, a joint venture, among students, educational personnel, employers, labor organizations and parents. It recognizes that the classroom is only one of many learning environments and not necessarily the most stimulating one. It is perceived that the home is the first classroom, and no subsequent experience will ever totally blot out the values, attitudes, and learnings from the home and family. The neighborhood, the community, and the work place are rich learning environments. The classroom tends to be a sterile learning environment. It is an efficient place to isolate the student from extraneous experiences while abstract concepts are taught. But it requires enrichment to relate those abstractions to the broader world. Therefore, it is expected that in a full-scale career education approach:

(1) All classroom teachers will:

    (a) Devise or locate methods and materials designed to help pupils understand and appreciate the career implications of the subject matter being taught

    (b) Utilize career-oriented methods and materials in the instructional program, where appropriate, as one means of educational motivation

(c)   Help pupils acquire and utilize good work habits

(d)   Help pupils develop, clarify, and assimilate personally meaningful sets of work values

(e)   Integrate, to the fullest extent possible, the programmatic assumptions of career education into their instructional activities and teacher-pupil relationships

(2) In addition to the above, some teachers will be charged with:

(a)   Providing students with specific vocational competencies at a level that will enable students to gain entry into the occupational society

(b)   Helping students acquire job-seeking and job-getting skills

(c)   Participating in the job placement process

(d)   Helping students acquire decision-making skills

(3) The business-labor-industry community will:

(a)   Provide observational, work experience, and work-study opportunities for students *and* for those who educate students (teachers, counselors, and school administrators)

(b)   Serve as career development resource personnel for teachers, counselors, and students

(c)   Participate in part-time and full-time job placement programs

(d)   Participate actively and positively in programs designed to lead to reduction in worker alienation

(e)   Participate in career education policy formulation

(4) Counseling and guidance personnel will:

(a) Help classroom teachers implement career education in the classroom

(b) Serve, usually with other educational personnel, as liaison contacts between the school and the business-industry-labor community

(c) Serve, usually with other educational personnel, in implementing career education concepts within the home and family structure

(d) Help students in the total career development process, including the making and implementation of career decisions

(e) Participate in part-time and full-time job placement programs and in follow-up studies of former students

(5) Educational administrators and school boards will:

(a) Emphasize career education as a priority goal

(b) Provide leadership and direction to the career education program

(c) Involve the widest possible community participation in career education policy decision making

(d) Provide the time, materials, and finances required for implementing the career education program

(e) Initiate curriculum revision designed to integrate academic, general, and vocational education into an expanded set of educational opportunities available to all students

(6) The home and family members where pupils reside will:

(a) Help pupils acquire and practice good work habits

(b) Emphasize development of positive work values and attitudes toward work

(c) Maximize, to the fullest extent possible, career development options and opportunities for themselves and for their children

To reiterate, the parent role is the vital one. The other actors merely reinforce what the parents have done, if it has been good, or try desperately to counteract it, if negative. That influence for good or ill is never overcome.

LEARNER OUTCOMES FOR CAREER EDUCATION

All of career education has a lifelong focus. The schools perceive it to be their responsibility to produce school leavers (at any age or level) who are:

(1) Competent in the basic academic skills required for adaptability in our rapidly changing society

(2) Equipped with good work habits

(3) Capable of choosing and who have chosen a personally meaningful set of work values that lead them to possess a desire to work

(4) Equipped with career decision-making skills, job-hunting skills, and job-getting skills

(5) Equipped with vocational personal skills at a level that will allow them to gain entry into and attain a degree of success in the occupational society

(6) Equipped with career decisions they have made based on the widest possible set of data concerning themselves and their educational-vocational opportunities

(7) Aware of means available to them for continuing and recurrent education once they have left the formal system of schooling

(8) Successful in being placed in paid occupations, in further education, or in vocations that are consistent with their current career education

(9) Successful in incorporating work values into their total personal value structures in such a way that they are able to choose what, for them, are desirable life styles

To accomplish these learner outcomes, career educators seek the following basic changes in education policy in the schools of the nation:

(1) Substantial increases in the quantity, quality, and variety of vocational education offerings at the secondary school level and of occupational education offerings at the post-secondary school level

(2) Increases in the number and variety of educational course options available to students, with a de-emphasis on the presence of clearly differentiated college preparatory, general education, and vocational education curricula at the secondary school level

(3) The installation of performance evaluation as an alternative to the strict time requirements imposed by the traditional Carnegie unit and as a means of assessing and certifying educational accomplishment

(4) The installation of systems for granting educational credit for learning that takes place outside the walls of the school

(5) Increasing use of non-certificated personnel from the business-industry-labor community as educational resource persons in the education system's total instructional program

(6) The creation of an open-entry/open-exit education system that allows students to combine schooling with work in ways that fit their needs and educational motivations

(7) Substantial increases in programs of adult and recurrent education as a responsibility of the public school education system

(8) Creation of the year-round public school system that provides multiple points during any twelve-month period in which students will leave the education system

(9) Major overhaul of teacher education programs and graduate programs in education aimed at incorporating the career education concepts, skills, and methodologies

(10) Substantial increases in the career guidance, counseling, placement, and follow-up functions as parts of American education

(11) Substantial increases in program and schedule flexibility that allow classroom teachers, at all levels, greater autonomy and freedom to choose educational strategies and devise methods and materials they determine to be effective in increasing pupil achievement

(12) Increased utilization of educational technology for gathering, processing, and disseminating knowledge required in the teaching-learning process

(13) Increases in participation in the educational policy-making process on the part of students, teachers, parents, and members of the business-industry-labor community

(14) Increases in participation, on the part of formal education, in comprehensive community educational and human services efforts

Parents should be aware of these educational objectives so they can lend their influence as patrons of school systems. Nevertheless, they must recognize a deeper and more profound obligation to their children. School work is work, and it requires the same commitments and self-discipline as work in the house and work in the job market. Children, like adults, can work as drudges, reluctantly and without pay. They can also find satisfaction and joy in achievement. Not all work will be pleasurable for child, student, or adult, but there is pride in self-discipline and in performing a task well by one's own choice. There is also the reward for choosing well the tasks to do at home, at school, or in the occupational world. That child who has learned to work successfully in the home, who has strong work values, and who enjoys achievement will be successful in school. The successful student is almost always a career success. The discipline and requirements are the same. Too much has been made of the difficulties of the transition from school to work. The transition is only from one work place to another. Few fail at that point. Somewhere before—in the home, in the neighborhood, in the community, or in the school—a syndrome of failure predicts failure in the occupational world. Career education is a concerted, long-term, joint venture in avoiding such failures, with the parent as senior partner, even if the school provides the organization and the managing executives.

ADDITIONAL READING

Hoyt, Kenneth B.; Evans, Rupert N.; Mackin, Edward F.; and Mangum, Garth L. *Career Education: What It Is and How to Do It.* 2d ed. Salt Lake City: Olympus Publishing Company, 1974.

Hoyt, Kenneth B. *Career Education: Contributions to an Evolving Concept.* Salt Lake City: Olympus Publishing Company, 1975.

Marland, Sidney P., Jr. *Career Education: A Proposal for Reform.* New York: McGraw-Hill, 1975.

CHAPTER FOUR

The Development of Work Attitudes and Values

Our values are the dominant forces in our lives. They determine the choices we make, the criteria we select for making those choices, and the way we act as a result of our choices. Values are also inextricably bound up with attitudes. One is a reflection of the other. In an over-simplified sense, what we do when we confront a situation in life is to "run it by" our values in order to determine how we can react to it, given our own particular set of values.

The values a child brings to a work situation—whether it be work in the home, work in school, or work on the job—have a great deal to do with the degree of satisfaction the child takes out of that situation. As we have said in previous chapters, most of the values we carry through life are learned in the home during the preschool and early school years. Thus, it is vital that parents be concerned with the development of values in their own children, because that value development will inevitably take place during those early years. The question is not *whether* a value system will develop, but *what kind* of values will develop within that system. Parents can (and unavoidably do) influence that process. The values which children develop are likely to reflect the values of their parents. For this reason, it is also important that parents examine their own values and attitudes with regard to work. By becoming more aware of their own values and attitudes, parents are able to emphasize the positive values and de-emphasize the negative values during those important formative years when their children are developing a system of values.

It's difficult to define what a value is, but you can think of it as something prized or esteemed, a belief or a feeling that something is worthwhile, or a criterion against which to measure importance. The term "value" may be attached to ideas, to persons, to objects, to places, to life styles, to activities, or to any of the other components of human experience.

It might seem a simple enough thing to determine what a person's values are. And indeed, that is not a difficult problem. The problem is that no single value exists alone; each value is part of the individual's value system, which is made up of hundreds of values, all competing for attention and dominance. The individual must not only select values, but must rank them in order of importance. The values don't change much during a lifetime—except that new values are constantly added—but the ranking of values is in constant flux, depending on the situation, the mood, and countless other factors. This is what makes it so difficult to deal with values in an analytical way.

Imagine a group of boys choosing up sides for a basketball game. Mike has first choice. Does he choose the best ball player? Does he choose his best friend, who is not such a good ball player? Or does he choose the new boy in the neighborhood who is having a hard time being accepted? Everyone knows that Mike is competitive, that he is a loyal friend, and that he is compassionate. The question is, which of those values is strongest at the moment? If competitiveness wins out and he chooses the best ball player, he will have a second choice, and he may want to re-order his value system. This time, friendship may be stronger than competitiveness, and instead of choosing the next best ball player, Mike may select his friend, knowing that in doing so he's taking a chance on losing the ball game.

This simple example illustrates what happens constantly with values. The order of importance changes. You might say that the value of values changes. Some would contend that Mike's value system places winning above other values, because he selected the best ball player first, which is true. But there is also the question of *how much* winning is valued over friendship. How great is the gap between the two? That is also a part of the hierarchical structuring of values—not only the ordering of values, but the relative strength of each.

Obviously, it is an extremely complex matter, and anything we say about values, value systems, and value development in one short chapter is likely to be oversimplified. But values are such an important part of each individual's life that we must discuss them. We are concerned here with values relating to work, to occupational choice, and to career development. We are particularly concerned with how and where those values originate, with how they fit into value systems, and with the role of parents in shaping those values.

WHERE DO VALUES ORIGINATE?

Most values are formed in childhood. Many are formed in very early childhood. Research shows that children learn values from other persons—parents, significant adults, playmates, teachers, television stars, and myriad other fictional and real-life characters. It also appears that the child actually originates some personal values, but that process is difficult to understand. Parents often witness the phenomenon of different children displaying different values almost from birth, suggesting that we still don't know everything about how children acquire values.

At one time in history, the development of values was almost solely the responsibility of the family and the church. However, the church has ceased to play a major role in prescribing values for a great many people. Surveys indicate that youngsters are more apt to look to the movie or television screen, to the super athlete, or to the hit song star for guidance than they are to look to the pulpit.

The family is also struggling with its role regarding value formation, although parents seem to be in a position where they inevitably and naturally communicate values to children. Since parents are with children most during the early childhood years—the most crucial years in value formation—they cannot avoid introducing, teaching, reinforcing, and imposing their own values on their children. And children cannot avoid "accepting" those values. Parents often make the mistake of waiting until their children "grow up" before introducing values, but by that time it is too late. Children have already acquired their values, almost always from the parents and sometimes by default rather than by direction. What typically happens is that parents of adolescent children don't like the values their children exhibit, and they attempt to force new values on the adolescents. But it's too late. Those youngsters picked up their values from their parents years earlier, and they cannot change those values. (This does not mean that adolescent children will not struggle against the values they have derived from their parents. This struggle is a part of the self-discovery process, and it is an almost inevitable part of maturation. In the long run, the values inculcated in childhood generally win out.)

We would make a similar point about the current interest in "values clarification" exercises in the school system. These values clarification experiences offer opportunities for children to examine their most cherished beliefs, to evaluate the consequences of actions based on those beliefs, to choose alternative actions, and to establish these actions as patterns in their lives. Some results are promising. But there are two major limitations. First, most value formation takes place before the child enters school. Later personality development is in the nature of footnotes to the main work. By the time the school can begin to exert an influence, the prime impressionable age has come and gone. Second, the most effective learning—particularly with regard to values—takes place in the context of real-life experiences, not in the classroom. It is difficult for the child to transfer values learned in the structured situation of the classroom to activities outside the classroom. Values clarification exercises are just that. They assist youth in identifying and articulating the values that are already guiding their actions and in recognizing the implications of those values. They are not necessarily designed to change values.

One important point, then, is that many lifetime values develop in early childhood, largely as a result of influences in the home. A second important point is that parents *cannot* assume that children will automatically develop a life-enhancing set of values or what we might call a "good" set of values. Parents must make a conscious, systematic effort to communicate values to their offspring and to help children develop their own value systems.

Of course, some learning of values takes place outside the home, but it apparently does not have nearly the profound impact as does the learning which occurs at home. In 1973 a study was conducted in six U.S. cities of variable size and geographic location. The study included school-children in grades seven through twelve, their parents, their teachers, their counselors, their school administrators, and church leaders. Invariably, each of these groups of people in each of the cities agreed that the most important influence on a child's choice of career is the parents. While agreeing about their influence on their children's careers, the parents lamented that they were woefully ignorant about what they should do to be a positive influence.

Another study scrutinized 600,000 children in grades one through twelve in 4,000 schools selected as representative of public education in the United States. The study indicated that home background was the most important element in determining how well the child did at school, more important than any aspect of the school which the child attended. The more the home had to offer, the stronger the influence it had in the child's school achievement. (Sources for information regarding the research cited are listed under "Additional Reading" at the end of the chapter.)

These studies graphically point out that parents will unavoidably have either a positive or a negative influence upon their child's education and career. The urgent message to parents is to discover what can be done to maximize the good influence. Children do not learn work values through some mystical psychological process. Quite simply, children learn *what* they live, and parents are very much in control of the home life.

For several years the child's only real contact with the world of work and attitudes toward work comes from experiencing father's and mother's work attitudes by watching their facial expressions and listening to their verbal comments about the subject. Unfortunately, becoming acquainted with work in this way does not always let children in on some of the positive aspects.

Imagine what your feelings would be if you were a house guest in a foreign country where you knew nothing about the culture, and your only contact with the culture was through hearing your host's conversation:

> "I'd like to stay and visit with you longer, but I have to get BOJ or they'll skin me alive."

> "I'm sorry. I would like to take you out to visit the museum tonight, but my BOJ takes so much out of me I just don't feel like doing anything at night."

> "Wow, what a rotten day I had at BOJ today. I'd like to just get away from it for awhile."

> "Can't you people be quiet? I've had a bad day at BOJ and I want some peace and rest."

Substitute "job" for BOJ and you may have some idea about how children feel when they hear parents talk about their work. It's difficult to develop positive values about a subject when most of the references to it are negative.

Often, parents make such comments conversationally. They don't really mean to be as negative as they sound. But the child has no way to sort out the real meaning from the apparent meaning. Of course, if your job seems like a prison camp to you, then you may mean what you say (and you should certainly give some thought to finding a new job). But if your job is like most, it has its positive as well as its negative aspects. If you want your children to have a positive attitude toward work, you must make a conscious effort to emphasize the positive aspects. For example:

"Today at work I am helping with some important projects. If I don't get my work done, there are some people who won't be able to have furniture for their new house next week."

"Why don't you come meet me down at the store? I'll show you some of the exciting things we are doing and we'll eat in the cafeteria. Then we can go right from there to the museum."

"Boy, what a great day I had at work today. Sometimes I get so involved I hate to stop work, but I wanted to come home and help you with the garden."

"Let's all sit down together for a few minutes to talk about the day's activities. We need to catch each other up on the family news."

Naturally, we can't always be positive about work. Sometimes, negative things do happen at work. And all bosses are not angels. But balancing the negative with positive comments will provide a more accurate, well rounded picture.

UNDERSTANDING OUR OWN VALUES

It may be a useful exercise to take a few minutes to examine your own values so you will have some idea about the kinds of impressions your child is probably receiving. We are concerned here primarily with values regarding work, but those values are inextricably interwoven with other values, and so we will have to expand our area of concern just a little. You may recognize the following as a simple exercise in values clarification, but it is a valuable exercise, well worth the time it will take.

What you are searching for in this exercise are some answers to the question: What is truly important to me?

You will need two sheets of paper and a pen or pencil. On one sheet, write the following categories, spacing them evenly down the page:

My Career Values

Income

Geographic Location

Self-expression

Creativity

Prestige

Authority (Supervisory Responsibility)

Relationships with Others

Work Environment

Now take the time to write down a few comments under each category, guided by the question of what is truly important to *you* in each of these areas. You can write full sentences or just put down a few key words, whichever is most comfortable for you. Be as realistic as you can. For instance, we would all like to be millionaires, but the important consideration about income is not how much it is but what you can do with it. Obviously, there are no "right" answers. What is important to you may not be important at all to someone else. You will end up with a completely unique set of values.

When you finish the first sheet, divide the second sheet into three vertical columns. As a heading for the first column, write "Desired Accomplishments," and then list the five things you would like most to accomplish during your lifetime. (You may have twenty or thirty important things you want to accomplish, but pick five of the most important.) Now, put a heading over the second column: "What I am doing or have done to achieve this goal." Fill in that column to coincide with each of your five "desired accomplishments." (Don't forget your schooling or special training that you have undertaken.) Finally, label the third column: "My feelings about my progress on this item." Write down your honest appraisal of your progress. You should have a sheet that resembles Figure 3, with all the blanks filled in.

The list you have made is an expression of your values and what you are doing to realize your values.

Desired Accomplishments	What I am doing or have done to achieve this goal	My feelings about my progress on this item
1.		
2.		
3.		
4.		
5.		

FIGURE 3. This form provides an outline for an exercise in values clarification.

There is a story about a millionaire who was asked to complete a similar exercise. He said that to be happy and successful, a person needs three basic conditions: (1) someone to love, (2) something to do, and (3) something to look forward to. Perhaps you will want to compare your own set of values to those of the millionaire. And perhaps you will want to look at the developing values of your children in similar terms. The child needs someone to love (his or her parents), something to do (meaningful work or its cousin, meaningful play), and something to look forward to (some goal that implies work as a means of attainment).

You can use this exercise and similar types of analysis to take a look at your own work values, remembering that your child will likely model himself or herself after you more than after any other adult. Think about where your own work values originated as you think about what those values are. Some regard work as a curse; others regard it as a blessing. In its ideal sense, work provides a means for creative expression, a means for realizing many of the non-work values we may have, some of which you may have listed in the exercise.

Some individuals are fortunate enough to be doing work that they love. Even if they are not paid for what they are doing, they would still try to find a way to spend some of their time at it. Children have natural tendencies in this direction. They are good at finding activities in which they can be totally and happily immersed. They resemble the self-actualized people of Maslow's famous study.

> In the best instances, the person and his job fit together and belong together perfectly like a key and lock, or perhaps resonate together like a sung note which sets into sympathetic resonance a particular string in the piano keyboard.

But rare is the child who can sustain this kind of absorption for an eight-hour stretch. Persistence and pacing must be learned so that one can better cope with the routine as well as the interesting. These, too, are work values. Virtually every activity involves menial aspects. Even the great artist needs to clean up the paints after he's finished.

If a child can learn at the age of four to uncomplainingly pick up the crayons when finished coloring, possibly that child can later on ungrudgingly endure some of the tedium that might be a necessary part of a job, and even find in the work a great fulfillment.

Henry Giles wrote about the potential of work as a means of fulfillment:

> Man must work. That is certain as the sun. But he may work grudgingly or he may work gratefully; he may work as a man, or he may work as a machine. There is no work so rude, that he may not exalt it; no work so impassive, that he may not breathe a soul into it; no work so dull, that he may not enliven it.

The Nature of Individual Values

We can see that values permeate the whole of life and govern the broad range of our activities. Our values are literally those things to which we give value in terms of giving them our time, our effort, our money, and our commitment. There are as many different value systems as there are different people, and what is right for one person may not be right for another.

However, there are two broad principles pertaining to values that seem to be universal and sorely needed as basic teachings from parents to children. The first principle is that there are some attitudes and values about work that historically have proved to be most effective in terms of getting the job done efficiently and with the maximum amount of satisfaction for the worker. These are often called "traditional work values." They are described by such statements as "a full day's work for a full day's pay," "be dependable," and "follow orders." Another set of work ethics is as yet unproved. It includes such ideas as working only long enough to finish the day's work, whether it takes five hours or twelve hours, negotiating actively for the rate of pay one thinks one deserves, and following one's own judgment as well as the orders of others. Some work situations require the traditional values; other situations are more flexible. The point is that a child must learn to understand that values differ from person to person and from situation to situation. If the individual's values cannot adapt to the situation, then it is best for the individual to avoid such situations.

The second principle regarding work values—and all values—might be called the principle of congruence. It means that we each have a need for our outer actions to reflect our inner values. In terms of career development, this means that the person who denies what he or she really wants and goes along with the desires of others will almost certainly never come to know himself or herself and create a career compatible with his or her personal happiness. The person who denies her values and enters law or business instead of her first love—teaching, for example—very likely will reap dissatisfation in some ways. And very likely the parents who push their child into an occupation of their choice, not her choice, are in part responsible for the unhappiness they reap as they are vicariously buffeted about with her from one uncomfortable job to another.

The idea of choosing a career compatible with one's values is not a new idea, but it is not always followed. Careers are sometimes chosen on the basis of what parents want for their children. "We've always wanted Gary to be a teacher." Or the career is chosen on the basis of the job market. Many out-of-work aerospace engineers during the 1970s could testify that this reason is not always valid. On the other hand, pursuing a career congruent with one's values releases personal energy. The individual is enthusiastic about the work and strives for competence, often becoming good enough so that he or she can hold a job no matter what the job market.

This is not to say that it is not a good idea to consider the job market and the desires of others, but these considerations must be balanced against one's own values. This problem is hard enough for adults to cope with, but it can be especially burdensome to a youngster who has had limited experiences to enable him or her to discover and develop values. Parents need to be certain to provide values clarification experiences for the child. The role of the parents is to free the child to be whatever he or she may choose to be.

The Value Development Process

Louis Raths has developed a model that parents can use to help their children with this vital process of value development and value clarification. The model is applicable to children of all ages, and it is based on three basic behavior phases—choosing, prizing, and acting. The model is summarized below:

(1) Choosing:

    (a)   Parents must allow the child to choose freely without pressure from parents.

    (b)   Parents must provide the child with alternatives from which to choose or allow the child to choose from his or her own alternatives.

    (c)   Parents must help the child give thoughtful consideration to all of the alternatives.

(2) Prizing:

    (d)   Parents should be alert as to whether the child is happy with the choice and "prizes" it. If the child is not happy, the choosing process should be followed again.

    (e)   Parents should give the child an opportunity to publicly affirm the choice to the family or to others. For instance, being free to say with confidence, "I want to be a truck driver when I grow up," is a big step forward in values clarification.

(3) Acting:

    (f)   Parents should allow the child the opportunity to implement the choice, to test it out.

    (g)   Parents should help the child to make the chosen value a pattern in his or her life.

The following story illustrates how parents can help a child clarify a value by freeing the child to be what she chooses. The story was told by a successful artist, reminiscing about her mother:

I remember a turning point in my life. My mother came home one day when I had been painting pictures. Only I was painting the pictures on the wall.

My mother walked in, and her first reaction was: "What a lovely picture you've made. You really do a nice job. How nice." And then she said: "When you make pictures, let me provide you with something to do it on. You don't need to make them on the wall, and I would rather that you not do it on the wall."

I really believe that because my mother thoughtfully said that to me instead of chastising me and scolding me, and because she helped me develop my talent, I was encouraged and went on.

A major opportunity for helping children clarify values is in the area of work to be done in the home. This raises the question of monetary compensation for work. Some work is of such a nature that its performance seems to be a natural part of one's responsibility in the family. Making one's bed, cleaning one's room, or picking up after one's self seem to fit into this category. Other work, such as cleaning, mowing the lawn, or painting, may fit into the compensation category. Parents will need to determine for their own family which work fits into which category. If the child does not do the work agreed upon, compensation should be withheld.

Unfortunately, many children come to expect an allowance or other automatic rewards regardless of performance, and they learn to expect "something for nothing." On the other hand, if the child learns that rewards are given for quality services rendered, then a positive value has been achieved. If the work is of the "family responsibility," non-compensated type, some privilege might be withheld or a natural consequence might be allowed to happen.

One father carefully made work assignments to his children and then said nothing if the work was not completed as scheduled. When the children later asked for permission to go on fun activities, he quietly but firmly reminded them that their work was not done and that they would have to do their work as assigned before leaving with their friends. His children soon learned to do their work when told without being reminded. This was accomplished without anger or vindictiveness on the part of the parent. Such a system works better with young children than with adolescents.

The Value of Positive Reinforcement

We are all aware of ways to provide negative consequences when something is not done as expected, perhaps because we are so used to having other people inflict negative consequences on us if we don't come through as promised. We are not so well acquainted with providing positive reinforcement when a child does everything he or she should. If the child's room is clean and the toys are picked up, we say nothing. If the room is messy, we say something. The challenge to parents is to learn to express appreciation when things are going well, not with the aim of controlling behavior, but with the aim of providing the same kind of recognition of efforts that parents enjoy in their own work.

One example of this would be for a parent spontaneously to say: "Julie, you have done the dishes so well and so cheerfully this week that I want you to have the next couple of days off, with no work assignments." It is amazing what a positive effect this can have on a child's attitudes toward work. A further ramification of this is to periodically schedule children for vacations of a week's duration where they have no work responsibilities. If you need further encouragement with this device just remember how good it feels to you to have a real work holiday. If you haven't had one lately, take one.

Work assignments should be chosen carefully to fit the personality of the child. A job that is one child's poison is another child's nourishment. It is a wise parent who gives a child a choice of several jobs rather than ordering her or him to do as the parent chooses. Parents are especially prone to palm off the unwanted or undesirable work on their children, and then they are surprised when their children don't like to work. If you don't like to clean the bathroom, chances are your children won't like to do it either. This is an area for mutual compromise, perhaps rotating the task or having everyone pitch in to get it done quickly so it is no longer a worry. (Incidentally, such occasions are excellent opportunities to discuss the issue of some work not being very enjoyable but being necessary to the quality of life. Since someone has to do it, why not make the best of it?) However, do make a concentrated effort to assign some work which will be enjoyable. For example, a sixteen-year-old who has just received a driver's license may find it enjoyable to drive around doing time-consuming errands for the parents, taxiing family members places, or even washing the family car. The same kind of work activity can sometimes be used for children who enjoy bicycle riding or walking.

Perhaps the most fruitful area for parent-child interaction in the learning of work values lies in the opportunity to complete tasks together. First, working together has the potential of being intrinsically rewarding because parents so seldom give children their time. Second, children are able to see their parents in action, so to speak, and to thereby gain first-hand knowledge of effective ways of working and enjoying work.

For family projects, parents should choose tasks without deadlines which are of such a nature that the children can be of some help. Part of the enjoyment of work comes from being able to ask questions, being able to experiment, and being able to make a few mistakes. The mistakes may not just be the child's error either. It may be a valuable lesson for parents to allow the child to see that they too make mistakes. For the child to see parents take both their own and the child's mistakes or failures in stride is even more valuable. All of this takes extra time and patience on the part of parents. It is well to remember that you are not just trying to teach the child the mechanics of work efficiency; you are teaching satisfaction in work. Gear yourself ahead of time to "waste a little time."

An experience that comes to mind in this regard is the experience of a busy executive who was taking a few hours over the weekend to indulge in one of his hobbies, flower growing. At the suggestion of his wife, he decided to include the children in the tasks of preparing the soil, planting, and watering the seeds. After the entire contents of the second package of seeds was accidentally spilled to the ground, the woman could see her husband was about to lose his temper. With some difficulty she caught his eye and pointedly asked, "Dear, what's more important, children or flowers?"

Not all children will respond in the same way to the same parental actions. Some children will respond to praise by performing even better; others will withdraw from the limelight. Some may grow up wanting to do what their parents did; others will want to do the opposite. Parents need to be aware of individual differences.

Peers also can play an important role in your child's values development. The people the child chooses to associate with will influence him or her toward one field and away from another field. If the child's friends are interested in the out-of-doors, the child will become interested in the out-of-doors. If they are hard working, the child will be hard working. This is as true at age 6 as it is at age 17 or 30.

Parents cannot always have control over the friends their children choose. If parents try to encourage or dissuade the child from a particular direction, chances are it will have the opposite effect. Probably the best strategy is to let the child make his or her own choices and then adjust to them. Rather than seeing the peer group as an enemy, the parent can see it in a positive way as an opportunity to get better acquainted with children of the same general personality and age. Through getting better acquainted with them, the parents can, in a sense, get better acquainted with their own child. And the more you know about the child, the more you know how to help him or her.

VALUES CONFLICTS

Conflicts will always be a part of parent-child relations. We wish to address ourselves to the positive uses of conflict in the hope that capitalizing on the positive will tend to diminish the negative. As examples of the possible positive uses of conflict, consider some examples.

Suppose your daughter is working during the summer at a fast food outlet. All seems to be going well until one evening when she comes home looking distraught and exhausted. When you ask her if something is troubling her, she replies that the manager has not allowed her to do a job that she had specifically understood as part of their initial agreement. She was looking forward to helping with the buying of supplies, thinking that this would provide her valuable experience in planning ahead and running a profitable food operation. This had been the main reason she had taken the job. Today the manager refused to let her help and was not willing to give her a reason.

This is a values conflict situation that comes up time and again in the market place—the employee values a certain activity more than the boss values letting the employee do it. Obviously one of the things you could do in this situation would be to call the manager on the phone and give him a piece of your mind. Or you could simply tell your daughter that life is like that sometimes, and she will learn to live with it. Or you could use this values conflict situation positively, as an opportunity to form a "coalition" with your daughter. You might discuss with her the reasons the manager may have acted that way, together with strategies for finding out his true reasons and for convincing him to stay with the initial agreement. You might examine alternatives open to her, such as taking the matter to the boss's boss, reviewing with the manager the terms of the original agreement and her reasons for wanting the job, or looking for a new job. No matter what you decide, you will have formed an important teaching-learning relationship with the young lady.

Another positive use of conflict might arise when a child has been assigned to perform a task in the home and does not respond. Suppose you have asked your son to clean up the backyard, and when you come home the job is barely begun and he is doing other things. You can assume he is lazy and threaten reprisals unless he does his work, or you can pause for a few seconds and try to learn the reasons for his lack of performance.

You may learn surprising things. Perhaps his feeling is that he is always getting stuck with dirty work, while other members of the family get to do the interesting work. Or perhaps someone else needed his help on other things that seemed more important. Or perhaps he's tired of constantly cleaning the yard after someone else has messed it up. Any of these situations might represent a conflict between one of his current values and someone else's values. Whatever the reason, you have an opportunity to create new, more functional patterns of interaction.

Parent-Child Values Conflicts

Parent-child conflicts arise when the child disappoints the parent or when the child chooses something that is not in line with parental values. The stage is set for a confrontation, and the child anticipates resistance from parents. Unless parents change the direction of the interaction in some way, the conflict potential will erupt and the familiar vicious cycle sets in. The more parents oppose, the more set the child becomes. The more set the child becomes, the angrier parents become, the harder they push, and the more the child resists, and so on.

Whether or not you are successful in interrupting such a cycle, should it occur, depends a great deal on your own values system. Let us suppose that your child has chosen to drop out of high school, where he has been earning excellent grades. His plans are to join a commune so that he can work the land and get in closer touch with nature. This desire is an expression of his values. Suppose that your value system dictates that he finish college and make a place for himself in the business community.

You are headed for a clash unless your value system hierarchy contains an important component—that of love for your child. In such a situation, love would manifest itself as respect for him and his right to make his own decisions concerning his life. You would be more willing to let him learn from his own mistakes (if, indeed he is making a mistake) than to impose your values on him to protect him from a mistake. You would be cognizant of the adage: "A thorn of experience is worth a whole wilderness of warning."

The value of love for your child would also manifest itself as a willingness to examine your own motives for wanting him to do things your way. Do you oppose his decision because you think it will be detrimental to his growth, or do you oppose his decision because of what your friends might think? If you are genuinely concerned for his growth, is this a situation where he is in such grave danger that you must intervene as a responsible adult?

Let us assume that your hierarchy of values is such that love for your child wins out over a desire that he do what you want him to do. Assuming that you decide grave danger is not imminent, that you are willing to risk the questioning glances of your associates, and that you have decided to let him go ahead and experience for himself, what then? What is the alternative to sitting back and waiting for the adventure to fail, as you think it will?

There are several steps you can take. The first step is to determine the degree of tentativeness of his decision. Decisions announced by youth as hard and fast decisions are not always as set as they may appear. They are often presented as such so that the child can appear to be grown up and decisive. As often as not the child is putting forth the plan as a way of testing parental reactions. If you push, he will probably push in the opposite direction. On the other hand, if you ask for more information about his plan, he may share his ideas with you. He may even end up asking for your counsel, assuming you have been willing to let him determine the particular value that lies behind his action. This has been expressed as assuming that there is an "honorable goal" behind his action. Most people have good intentions and want similar things from life—respect, security, love, freedom, and so on. We differ in the methods we employ to pursue the goals. What values is your son pursuing? Freedom? Independence? Brotherhood? Announcing your willingness to listen to his plan will enable you to discover the honorable goal and perhaps help him find alternative ways of achieving it. Remember that he derived his values from you, and so you probably have a great deal in common.

Resolving Conflicts

Attempting to approach the problem in this way can be especially useful if you get involved after the fact. Suppose your child has already done something out of line with your values, and you feel obliged to call him on the carpet. Assume that he had an honorable goal. Try asking him (without a superior, moralizing tone) what he was trying to gain through his action. Suggest to him other ways you feel he might gain the same thing. Try to work out a compromise plan about which you can both feel good.

In a career context, values conflicts with your child are mostly likely to result when she or he chooses an occupation that is out of line with your expectations. Assume that you had always hoped your daughter or son would become a medical doctor. When making an expectation of this kind, you must be certain that your expectations are in line with the abilities of your child. Does he or she really have the aptitude for medicine? If the answer is no, you would do well to temper your expectation to more nearly match those actual abilities.

Assume that test scores and academic performance prove that your child does have the ability. Everything seems on course for medical school, but just after acceptance to a quality college, that son or daughter decides to withdraw and begin instead an apprenticeship as a skilled craft worker. What do you do? Are you duty bound as a parent to persuade your offspring to continue on the road to medical school, or does your value, "Love for my child," require that you leave the decision entirely to the young woman or young man now on the threshold of adulthood.

The answer probably lies somewhere between these two extremes. Whatever the course of action you take, each will have certain consequences. If your child goes to college at your insistence, you become partly responsible for what she or he does there. If performance is poor and "proves" lack of aptitude, aren't you partly to blame? Then, if the result is a frustrated doctor who ends up disliking the medical profession, won't your part in the decision be resented? Thus, your well-intentioned pressure may have long-term consequences for your relationship with your child. The maintenance of a good relationship with your son or daughter would require that you be equally proud no matter what occupation is chosen. If you enjoy a relationship of trust, she or he will be more willing to come to you for counsel a few years from now.

The Reality of Self-conflict

Another type of conflict is self-conflict. Self-conflict is the most excruciatingly painful of all areas of conflict. The fragmentation of the self is one of the most discussed subjects of our time. In the book *Future Shock*, Alvin Toffler observes that the individual will experience extreme and conflicting pressures from the various influences competing for his loyalties unless he begins his approach to the problem "with a clear grasp of relevant reality, and unless he begins with clearly defined values and priorities. . . . Caught in the turbulent flow of change, called upon to make significant, rapid fire life decisions, he feels not simply intellectual bewilderment, but disorientation at the level of personal values. As the pace of change quickens, this confusion is tinged with self-doubt, anxiety and fear."

In other words, unless the individual acquires a clear sense of what he or she wants from life, he or she will be drawn to and fro by first this fad and then that fad. And even if the individual does have a clear idea of what is wanted from life, he or she will need to continually update and redefine as experience and awareness expand. If not, the individual will become less and less sure of what he or she stands for and what he or she wants, and self-confidence will disintegrate.

Toffler's words graphically describe many young people. But how can you help your child acquire a clear sense of what he or she wants from life, and how can you help your child to continually define his or her values as expanding experience brings him or her into contact with conflicting values?

We live in a society of façades. However, there is a difference between the façade of the movie set, where an entire village may be nothing more than a few pieces of canvas stretched over boards, and the human façade; for behind the human façade is a richness usually far exceeding our expectations. We teach facade life behavior to our children when we do not show our true feelings to them, when we try to shape them into predetermined molds, or when we punish them for showing their true feelings. Witness our uncomfortableness at the candor of children. Older people display the same strength, but we do not attempt to control it the way we attempt to control it in children. Older people have usually at long last learned to trust their inner values and resist imposed values.

We often punish children into adopting values inconsistent with their own values. For example, a young child who has just discovered a noisy new toy will employ it exuberantly and fill the house with sound. Most adults will endure for only a few short moments before telling the child to stop or before taking the toy away. As another example, how often do we tell our children to slow down, to stop running? We do not consider that perhaps it is we adults who are going too slow.

Carl Rogers explains that children will usually adopt values systems imposed by parents rather than risk losing the parents' affection. They sense that love is conditional upon compliance. Unfortunately, they are usually correct in this assumption. This is a situation that leads to values conflict in the self.

Consider the example of the young man who has learned that he will receive more expressions of love when he acts in accordance with his parents' desire that he be a lawyer than with his own desire to be an auto mechanic. After a while he may even assume that he has always wanted to be a lawyer. Imagine his bewilderment when he flunks his pre-law courses in college, even though other evidence proves that he has the ability to do the work.

Through counseling and introspection he learns that he has not been listening to his personal values.

If we can teach children to be themselves, to trust their inner voices, we will have a better chance of guiding them to make career choices compatible with their innate desires. In other words, we can teach them congruent behavior. As we mentioned previously, being congruent means matching outer actions with inner values. Congruence as applied to personal work values raises several issues. One of the hardest to deal with is what to do when a child seems to display many different preferences, some of which may conflict with one another. Which preference is the congruent one, or are they all congruent? Can your daughter be an artist, homemaker, engineer, and teacher all in the same lifetime? Can your son simultaneously pursue school politics, sports, auto mechanics, and an academic program?

One method of approaching this dilemma is to try to help the child find a career that combines all of the interests. One can conceive of a woman who works as an engineer during the day, who (with the help of her husband) manages a household during the morning and evening, who paints in her odd moments, and who teaches at a local community college one night a week. Another alternative might be to use her artistic, homemaking, and engineering skills in a combined way by designing kitchen environments as a full-time career. She might also do volunteer teaching.

Your son may find fulfillment and resolve values conflicts by becoming a mechanic who sponsors his own little league team and works actively in community politics. At the same time he may be an avid reader or continue his education part time. Alternatively, he may emphasize some other career area and work on automobiles as a hobby.

The point is that some values conflicts are conflicting only on the surface. Beneath the surface is much leeway for accommodation. It is seldom a question of either-or, all or nothing. It is rather a question of emphasis, balance, compatibility, and sequence. And it requires patience on the part of parents.

The ideal of sequence is essential to another method of resolving values conflicts. Your child may do well to consider the possibility of doing all of the things that he or she values, emphasizing each one in turn in a logical sequence. Your daughter might teach for a while, emphasize home-making for a period of time, then work in engineering, then become an artist. Your son might earn a college degree— perhaps in recreational education—work for a while organizing sports programs, then work as an automobile mechanic, and eventually enter politics. The only limits are the imagination and a willingness to keep growing and changing.

The Reality of Multiple Occupations

Other factors may enter in and not allow for a changing, sequential career. Some careers are such that a person may need to stay in the same area for a decade or more in order to achieve to a point compatible with his or her goals. Family and other obligations may dictate against starting over in a new career every so often. But the multiple career is edging out the specialized career in our fast-changing society. Most young people will change occupations a number of times in their lifetimes. Parents need to help their children to think in these terms.

Full acceptance of the reality of multiple occupations within a working career is one of the many values which parents can help their children obtain, beginning during the preschool years. Other values which will have a tremendous influence on career development are such things as life style, geographic location, size of family, status, urban or rural residence, type of associates, travel, access to cultural activities, and similar expressions of value systems.

Perhaps the importance of building a good foundation of work values in children can best be illustrated by a true story concerning two plumbers who came in to bid on a plumbing job. The first plumber was a successful contractor who had built a substantial and well thought of business over the years. But he had gradually become extremely dissatisfied with his work. He was desperate for a change, and he talked about how hard it was to go to work each morning and how he couldn't stand the thought of "just screwing pipes together all my life." Unfortunately, he hadn't done anything to change the situation but continued to work—and to prosper—in misery.

The second plumber came in a few days later. When asked what his plans were with regard to his present occupation, he could hardly say enough in praising the work of a plumber. The word that came up most often was "pride." He expressed pride in being in an occupation where he could show initiative in troubleshooting problems and in expanding his business. He talked of pride in being able to provide employment for others, and pride in his quality of workmanship, which was enabling him to branch out into other areas of home building. He was proud of being able to provide a vitally needed service. He could not have been happier.

The difference in the two plumbers was not in their occupation or in their ability but in the values they brought to their work. Those values probably began in childhood.

Parents would do well to slow down their reactions to their children's career choices and try to look below the surface. In the words of John Chapman, the subject of a recent television special, "The Secret Life of John Chapman," which described a college president who was using his sabbatical to sample various laborer's jobs, parents need to realize: There are all kinds of people out there who are happy with what they're doing. The important thing is to find a job where you can feel alive. Children need to be allowed to find their own best way of feeling alive, and they need to be given the type of value system which makes "feeling alive" possible.

SUMMARY

The process of abundant living is a process of discovering one's values, discovering what is most important to one, and living in accordance with those values. This discovery process is lifelong, but it is especially crucial during the impressionable years of childhood. Parents need to make a consistent, conscious effort to foster the development of life-enhancing values if they are to have an influence during the twenty or so years the child is in the home.

In general, there are several distinct elements that will most likely be a part of any interaction wherein a parent is helping a child to discover and implement values. The elements will need to be applied in different ways, depending on the maturity of the child and the seriousness of the step he or she is about to take.

The first necessary step for parents is to understand their own values, to be aware of their goals, biases and dreams, both concerning their own lives and concerning their hopes for their children. The second step is related and consists of gaining an understanding of the processes by which values are developed so that the parent can influence the child's value development in desirable ways. But a necessary part of this step is to recognize that the child is subject to many influences and may develop some values that the parent did not intend.

The third step consists of comparing parents' values to their child's values, realizing that unless the child is a carbon copy of the parents, which is seldom the case, there will be discrepancies. The fourth step is reconciliation, dealing with the discrepancies, resolving the conflict.

Reconciliation does not mean having one party to the interaction come around to the views of the other. Conflict resolution is more often typified by movement on the part of both to a middle ground. Successful reconciliation implies successful communication. The parent, as the more mature member of the interaction, has the responsibility to set the example by listening, being understanding, trying to see things through the child's eyes, and being open to change. The final outcome will most probably be a compromise between the different points of view.

The fifth step is implementation of the decision that has been reached, to give the child the chance to "try on" the value for size by actually beginning to live it in his or her life. Often the child will need the parents' support as he or she tries out a new idea. This may place parents in the position of supporting something with which they are not in complete accord, but the long-range benefits of letting the child find his or her own best way and learning by natural consequences far outweigh the immediate comfort of forcing the child to do what he or she "should" do.

All through the process there is the need for parents to teach the child, to show the child different ways of approaching life, and to do things together with the child to help in self-discovery. There is also the opportunity to reward the child in various ways as he or she does those things that are in line with the parents' values, but this should be done judiciously and not in a manipulative way. The important thing to remember is that the parent must be responsible in influencing the child, keeping foremost in mind the need to free the child to become what the child chooses to become.

ADDITIONAL READING

Dyer, William G. *Insight to Impact: Strategies for Interpersonal Change.* Provo, Utah: Brigham Young University Press, 1976.

Kirschenbaum, Howard, and Simon, Sidney B. *Readings in Value Clarification.* Minneapolis: Winston Press, 1973.

Maslow, Abraham H. *New Knowledge in Human Values.* Chicago: Henry Regnery Company, 1970.

Peterson, Elwood; Rowe, Fred A.; and Whiting, Lorina R. "Professional-Paraprofessional Cooperation in Career Development," *Personnel and Guidance Journal*, Feb. 1974, pp. 412-417.

Raths, Louis, *et al. Values and Teaching: Working with Values in the Classroom.* Columbus, Ohio: Charles E. Merrill Publishing Company, 1966.

Toffler, Alvin. *Future Shock.* New York: Random House, 1970.

CHAPTER FIVE

Career Awareness

Career awareness is the first phase of career education, at least as it relates to the school. It coincides with the elementary school years, which are the years sometimes called the "period of self-awareness." In other words, this is the time when the child develops an awareness of himself or herself as a functioning entity within the immediate environment. It is only proper that a part of that developing awareness should include an awareness of work and careers.

The overall goal of career awareness is to develop within the young child a positive attitude toward himself or herself and a positive attitude toward the value of work as it relates to the home and community. Through the development of these attitudes, the young child will gain the necessary insight and skills at the child's level of understanding and physical development which will lay the foundation and provide the prerequisites for later career exploration, career preparation, and entry into the labor force as a contributing member of society.

In order for the young child to develop these positive attitudes toward himself or herself and the world of work, the following objectives are included within the area of career awareness:

(1) The development of an awareness of workers and what they accomplish for the benefit of others

(2) The development of an awareness of the work to be performed around the home which will benefit family members

(3) The development of an awareness of the skills required to perform work and the development of the specific skills as they relate to the tasks the young child can perform in the home

We have talked about the important role of the home in the development of work values and attitudes during the preschool years. The home is a workshop, a learning laboratory, a consuming unit, and an inculcator of values. The family's function is to provide a setting within which the individual can develop a sense of security, of belonging, and of acceptance as a person. It is a place for relaxation, for expression, and for control of emotion. It teaches children to experience success and to absorb failure. It helps children develop value systems by observing and sharing experiences with others. These early experiences can be positive or negative, but whichever they are they will influence the child for life, both in the world of work and in other endeavors.

THE HOME AND CAREER AWARENESS

The home continues to exert its influence during the elementary school years, the career awareness years. However, instead of working alone as during the preschool years, the parents now have an ally in the upbringing of their children—the school. The school provides a number of things which parents are usually not able to provide. First, the school provides a structured setting so that education can proceed in an organized fashion, making certain that vital parts of the education process are not missed. Second, the school provides trained personnel to deal with the child's needs on a day-to-day basis. Third, the school provides an opportunity for social interaction with other children. Fourth, the school provides certain facilities and tools not normally available in the home. Fifth, the school provides a means of access to special experiences such as field trips, cultural events, camps, and other traditional activities. Sixth, the school provides periodic assessments of the child's progress as compared to other children of the same age in order that parents might learn more about the child. Seventh, the school provides special facilities and training for those children who need them.

All of these benefits to be derived from the school apply to career education, just as they do to all other facets of education. The school provides a structured way to approach career education, using trained teachers, in the company of other children, making use of the school's facilities and its ability to gain access to learning experiences, and giving special attention to handicapped children.

Nevertheless, the home continues to be the single most important influence in the child's life. It makes sense, then, for the home and the school to work together in bringing the benefits of the career awareness phase of career education to the child. That process of working together begins when parents understand what the school is trying to accomplish in its structured approach to career education.

One of the things inherent in any structured or organized approach is the existence of goals. An organization must set forth the goals it is trying to accomplish in order to (1) make plans about how to reach the goals, and (2) determine whether or not it is making progress.

Accordingly, career education has identified some goals for the career awareness phase. Those goals can be stated in terms of the capabilities a child should have by the time he or she moves from career awareness to the next phase. By the time the child leaves elementary school, he or she should be able to:

(1) Discuss his or her interests as they relate to work and play behaviors

(2) Distinguish among people who work with others, who work with ideas, and who work with things

(3) Recognize worker interdependence within the home, within the school, and within the business community

(4) Make connections between school subjects and employability skills

(5) Role-play or visually depict the worker personality characteristics associated with people who produce goods or services or both

(6) Discuss the likenesses and differences between himself or herself and family members, schoolmates, and others who are significant in his or her life

(7) Consider the many reasons why people work

(8) Attach worth and value to all who work, either for themselves or for others

(9) Display an optimism about himself or herself in direct proportion to the number and quality of direct contacts each makes with people who work

Parents who want to help their children in career education should examine this list of goals carefully. Parents can help directly in achieving some of the goals and indirectly in achieving others. Understanding these goals will help parents build supportive situations into normal, day-by-day activities, and will help them design new activities on occasion which might assist their child's development.

It is fairly obvious from this list of goals that the home can continue to play a vital role in career education during the elementary school years. Indeed, there is no fundamental principle of work itself that cannot be easily demonstrated in the home. It is there that children are first introduced to such concepts as the interdependence of workers on each other for successful production, the importance of cooperation among those who work together, the nature of specialization of work roles, the need for punctuality if a task is to be completed on time, the desirability of cleanliness in the work area, the necessity for accepting personal responsibility for performance of assigned tasks, the urgency of following instructions, the need to observe safety precautions, and the value of avoiding unnecessary waste. Think about how much of the work experience is based on those fundamentals.

Other concepts can also be learned in the home, concepts which are not as positive as those above. One learns that some routine tasks are boring, even though they might be important links in a chain of assembly-line tasks. One learns about the reprimands that are typically a part of the world of work if a worker fails to perform assigned tasks correctly. But these negative impressions can always be reduced by an overriding self-awareness that the rewards which come from successful completion of an assigned task are worth the extra time and effort.

While these values *can* be learned in the home, and while most work values will inevitably be learned there, it is difficult for parents to expose their children to a representative vista of the world of work. First, children and parents no longer find many occasions to work side by side in normal work settings as they used to do when the whole family worked in the fields. Second, it is no longer likely that the family will purchase such items as furniture or shoes that were made in "the shop down the street" where children could see the craftsmen at work. Instead, the family purchases furniture—and most other items—without having any direct knowledge of how it was constructed and often with little knowledge about what types of material have gone into the construction.

This separation of consumer from manufacturer creates a real problem for those who need to learn about workers, and interdependence, and all the other aspects of career awareness. But it is a problem the school can solve much more easily than individual parents. The school can organize field trips, obtain appropriate films, and bring in resource persons to enhance the child's career awareness activities. The school can also find ways to involve those parents who wish to be involved in the career education process. Many schools ask parents to visit the classroom and talk about their own career activities, about their life styles, and about how they feel about the work they do. Other schools ask parents to help with field trips, either in arranging the trip or in helping to supervise the children while making the trip. Of course, there are many other ways in which parents can be involved, and one of the basic principles of career education is that cooperation between the home and the school—involvement—should be encouraged as much as possible.

But what can a child learn about work and careers during the career awareness phase, and how can parents augment that learning through activities in the home?

Approaches to Career Awareness

The learning experiences of activities which promote career awareness within the child can be accomplished by using a combination of three approaches: (1) vicarious, (2) simulated, and (3) actual or real life. The vicarious approach includes such things as printed materials (books, pictures, photos, magazines, newspapers), movies, television, and other audiovisual materials which provide sources of information. During vicarious learning activities, the young child's participation is limited to that of an observer. Career awareness is developed through observation and discussion of the information with parents or others. This also includes activities where the young child may be watching and learning about the television repair person or the dentist, but does not actually have "hands on" experiences within such settings.

The other two learning approaches—simulated and actual—provide for involvement of the child at two different levels. The simulated approach includes role-playing activities in which the child acts upon the materials provided as he or she actively participates in the pretend roles of television repair person or dentist. The exception to reality is that the child uses toys and other make-believe materials in place of the actual equipment. The child's imaginary world comes alive when the kitchen chair is transformed into a dentist's chair and a teaspoon becomes the small mirror to look into the patient's mouth. Such play activity simulates the real world.

Actual or real life experiences involve observation of and participation in actual work situations, such as work tasks around the home. The nature of these experiences is determined by the child's emotional and physical capabilities, and it may include assuming responsibilities for self-care (dressing, grooming, and so on), keeping the room tidy, and accomplishing other household chores. During such experiences the child may begin to develop emotional and physical skills and self-confidence which will prepare him or her for the world of work as an adult. As the child engages in real life work experiences, he or she develops such attributes as the ability to cope with the work situation, the ability to complete a task, and the satisfaction which accompanies such accomplishments.

The Continuing Development of Values

During this period, the child continues to develop his or her personal values, to "firm them up" through testing and practice, and to clarify their relationships, particularly in a hierarchical sense. As we said earlier, most of the child's values are implanted during the preschool years, but added responsibilities around the home and the school experience give the child a chance to see how well those values work—or how poorly they work if the values have been negative. The child who has acquired a set of values about work which are generally positive will likely adapt well to the school situation and will enjoy it. The child who has negative work values may find school difficult, frustrating, and generally unsatisfying.

In a very real sense, school is the child's first "job," the first experience with the realities of the work place outside the home. The child must be at school on time, must perform cetain required tasks in a prescribed fashion, and must work with others toward common goals. This is a good description of work, and the child who has developed some positive work values will recognize it as work and will accept it willingly, finding even at that early age satisfaction in achievement.

And so parents should continue to offer the same kinds of values-building support they provided during the pre-school years. Furthermore, they should expand that support as the child's own growth continues and as the child's values-testing activities extend into new areas.

For example, at some point during the elementary school years, the child begins to see a real distinction between work activities and play activities. He or she begins to realize—often begrudgingly—that time must somehow be divided between work and play, that the two are different (though not necessarily contradictory), and that sometimes the difference is more one of attitude than of effort. We all remember Mark Twain's classic story about Tom Sawyer whitewashing the fence. Tom was assigned the job of whitewashing Aunt Polly's fence, "Thirty yards of board fence nine feet high." He dreaded the job, because he would rather have been playing or swimming on such a hot day. But he had an idea. He thought that if he could make the job look like play instead of work, he might be able to get his friends to help him. Soon Tom "retired," while his friends begged for turns with the brush and whitewash. In the words of Mark Twain:

> Tom said to himself that it was not such a hollow world, after all. He had discovered a great law of human action, without knowing it—namely, that in order to make a man or a boy covet a thing, it is only necessary to make the thing difficult to attain. If he had been a great and wise philosopher, like the writer of this book, he would now have comprehended that Work consists of whatever a body is *obliged* to do, and that Play consists of whatever a body is not obliged to do. . . .

Like the "great and wise philosopher" who wrote the book, parents can discover a "great law of human action" when they help their children reduce the distinction between work and play by showing—through precept and example—that there can be as much enjoyment in work as there is in play. A number of techniques can be used to help make work an enjoyable experience. First, parents themselves can enjoy—or appear to enjoy—some of the work they

FIGURE 4. Tom Sawyer turns work into play.

do, at least as much as Tom Sawyer appeared to enjoy his work. Second, parents can use the most effective reinforcement device yet invented—praise. Young children especially like to receive the approval of their parents. But remember, praise is not a magic wand that, waved once, will turn a shirker into a worker. It is more like a fleck of stardust; it must be repeated over and over and over again before it begins to shed any light. Third, parents can mix work with play—a race to see who can clean up their room first; the family becoming involved in a water fight while washing the car; a father playfully wrestling with his son over who has to do the dinner dishes. Fourth, parents can connect work to play by indicating that it is because parents work that the family can go on vacation, or by making work a prelude or precondition to play.

With regard to this last item, there is nothing wrong with making work a precondition for play, since that connection is a very real connection in adult life. However, parents should be careful about how the connection is made. There is a difference between using play as a reward for work completed and using work as a punishment to keep a child from play. Consider the difference in the following two situations. In the first instance, the child is on his way outside to play when he is stopped by his mother and told that he cannot go out until he makes his bed. In this case, work appears to the child to be a form of punishment because it interferes with his plan. The second situation is exactly the same, except that in this case the mother has made it clear to her son earlier that morning and on many previous occasions that he could not go out to play until his bed was made. The child knew that making the bed was a precondition to going out to play. The child's frustration in the second instance may very well be the same as that of the child in the first instance, but through proper management and follow-through by parents, the child will eventually acquire the habit of completing his work as a primary part of the daily routine.

There is no secret source for advice about how to continue the support of positive work values in a child; there is no magic formula. The examples we have presented in this book can be multiplied by the thousands, because almost every situation offers some opportunity for positive support. Values continue to develop, and to be reinforced, and to be positioned in the value system. Perhaps the most critical factor affecting values development is very simply whether or not parents *care* about their children, not just care about the moment—where they are now and how happy they are *now*—but care about tomorrow—where they *will* be and how happy they *will* be. That care should take the form of constant self-reminders about the importance of value development, of continuing parental discussions about opportunities for support activities, and of discussions with others about how *they* deal with the various difficulties that arise. Often, discussing a problem or a situation—putting it into words—helps to reveal a solution or an alternative plan of action that may be more productive.

Values development continues in the child throughout the career awareness phase, and those values begin to express themselves in the development of work habits.

THE FOUNDATION OF GOOD WORK HABITS

The kinds of work habits a child acquires are intertwined with the kinds of work values the child has adopted. It's difficult to say which comes first, the habits or the values, but it doesn't make much difference because they are both so closely related. And because school is the child's first formal "work" experience, the development of work habits is an integral part of the elementary school years, the career awareness years.

One might find some arguments about what are good work habits and bad work habits. For instance, some people agree with Oscar Wilde that "punctuality is the thief of time," just as some people agree with Charlie Brown's dog, Snoopy, that "work is the crabgrass in the lawn of life." Little can be gained by debating those questions here. We unashamedly admit our commitment to many of the so-called "traditional" work values, often referred to as the "work ethic." The work habits we discuss will be based largely on that position.

Readers should proceed with that in mind, accepting or rejecting what they will, based not only on their own perceptions of which work habits make a good worker but which work habits they would like their own children to exhibit.

There are many, many kinds of work habits, but we should like to concentrate here on three which have special relevance to the home. Those three are planning and scheduling, follow-through, and personal growth.

Planning and Scheduling

Entire books have been written about planning and scheduling. Indeed, it is a key consideration for all organizations. But a good argument can be made that planning and scheduling are also important to each individual. There is some evidence to indicate that those who are "successful" tend to be planners, and conversely that those who plan tend to be happier. It doesn't take much to observe these same phenomena in your own experience. You may notice that people around you who set goals and set out to meet them are often happier than those who simply accept whatever each day has to bring. And perhaps you can remember times in your own life when working toward a specific goal motivated you, gave you extra energy, and made life more satisfying, even though you may have been working very hard.

Planning involves setting goals, determining objectives along the road to those goals, and measuring progress toward the goals. To oversimplify, one can think of it as a football game. The goal is to make a touchdown. The objectives along the way to the goal are first downs, which come every ten yards. Progress is measured by the number of first downs or the number of yards the team has been able to move the ball toward the goal. Every work situation involves planning, either by the individual or the employer, because every work situation has a goal, a reason for being. The worker who understands the nature of goals and has experience with them has a much better chance for satisfaction than does the worker who habitually approaches life on a day-by-day basis.

Parents can do a great deal in the home to help children acquire the habit of scheduling and planning. Some parents can remember the "good old days" when Monday was wash day, Tuesday was ironing day, Wednesday was shopping day, and so on. It sounds like a dull routine, but it was much more than routine; it was scheduling and planning. It helped the whole family to know what was expected of them, and it helped the children acquire the habit of planning and scheduling. (Of course, there was another reason for it in those days—because washing *required* the whole day—but the effects were still salutary.)

The place to begin with this kind of habit formation is in early childhood. Children should learn that there are jobs which must be done every day, jobs which must be done every week, and jobs which must be done every month. They all require scheduling, and planning for other activities must take into account these routine duties. These tasks should be simple tasks for young children—putting away toys or gathering dirty clothes on wash day for example. The tasks can become increasingly complex as the child grows, but remember that the important thing is not the task itself but the habit it is developing. Play is an important activity of childhood, and the child's duties should not be so extensive as to substantially restrict play time. Some parents find it helpful to make lists showing the duties of each family member. The lists are hung on a bulletin board, and as each task is completed, the family member checks the appropriate date to indicate completion. Even children who cannot read can learn to use such a system. It's a good idea to have duties for *all* family members on the chart, not just those for children.

Another useful technique is to sit down periodically as a family and discuss the duties of each member. The family should decide which jobs need to be done, why they need to be done, and who should do them. This exercise also helps parents to see whether or not children are beginning to realize the interconnectedness of single tasks and mutual benefits. It also allows parents to openly discuss another important concept involved with planning, that of establishing priorities. Of all the tasks to be done around the house, some are more important than others; they have priority. The planning process includes consideration of priorities, and the most important task—or tasks which support it—should be planned first. For example, the preparation of food is a vital task for any family. The person who does that task each day probably should be relieved of some other duties in order to make time for food preparation. Thus, other family members who are not preparing food should take over some of the second-priority tasks. Priority also applies to talent and desire. If one family member has a talent for making beds and enjoys that task, then he or she might want to trade duties with another family member who enjoys some other type of work but doesn't like making beds.

A primary task for parents at this stage is to follow through and make certain that once a child accepts responsibility for a job—whether voluntarily or by assignment—the job must be done on schedule. Often, the work of making certain tasks are completed is more difficult than just doing the task. But parents who make a habit of doing the child's job instead of following through to see that the *child* does the job are helping themselves, not the child. To repeat, the important thing is not the job itself but the *doing* of it. Efforts spent at teaching the habit of planning and scheduling during the early years will pay tremendous dividends to the parent when the child reaches adolescence . . . and of course to the child when he or she enters the world of work.

In this regard, school work should be treated just the same as any other necessary task. Beginning in the early grades, a child should understand that a certain part of the day is set aside—scheduled—for school work. Perhaps it will be only ten or fifteen minutes a day, at first, but it should become as habitual as making the bed. Often, parents will have to provide their own "school work" for the child—a book to read, an art project, a game to play—and perhaps even work with the child. But the time should be set aside for study, with no interruptions, no friends, and no television. Let the child help schedule the time—some may prefer early morning, and others may opt for late evenings— but follow through to make certain it is observed. As the child progresses in school, the amount of time scheduled for school work can be extended, but it probably will not exceed one-half hour per day. Some days, the child may have more to do than can be done in one-half hour, but if he or she has developed the planning habit, the added work will be taken in stride.

But what about the exceptions? What about the days when grandma visits, or when illness disrupts the schedule, or when conflicting events occur? Of course there will be exceptions. Parents should not be upset by the days when the scheduled task does not get done—for good reason—any more than should children. It is not necessary (and, indeed, it may be a mistake) to fix the schedule so firmly that exceptions are regarded with hostility. They are normal and natural, and they must be accepted as such. The goal is not to create a "perfect record," but to build a foundation for good work habits. It's a good idea to justify the exceptions on the basis of priority or other reasonable cause; it's not a good idea to make children feel guilty when the exceptional circumstances occur. Often, it can be dealt with quite simply: "I knew you had to be at school early, Billy, and so I made your bed this morning. Maybe you can help me make mine this weekend."

The Importance of Follow Through

The second general category of work habits which have application around the house can be classified as "follow through."

We have discussed follow through on the part of parents with regard to making sure children do what they have agreed to do or what they have been assigned to do. Not only does that help create good habits, but it sets a good example, because children have clear evidence that their parents do not shirk their own responsibilities. However, "follow through" is also a habit that children might well acquire. It means that when someone accepts responsibility for a task, he or she will complete the task. It is the sense of "contract" that comes with accepting an obligation and then making certain that the obligation is fulfilled.

Three basic components are part of the follow-through habit with regard to work. First, the individual must know what the task is and must understand what the standards for completion involve. Second, the individual must be involved somehow in the decision-making process which leads to the "contract." Third, there must be a completion signal to indicate the responsibility has been satisfied.

With regard to setting standards for performance—which the reader will recognize as part of planning—parents frequently make the mistake of not setting any standards at all, or the equally serious mistake of setting standards that are too difficult for the child to attain. Let's go back to the example of making the bed. Parents know what "making the bed" means. It means turning under the sheets at the foot of the bed, stretching the covers, fluffing the pillow, and so on. But sometimes children think of "making the bed" as simply pulling the bedspread up over everything else to hide it. Such children are not being sly or lazy; that's their interpretation of "making the bed." But when they do it that way, parents become angry . . . and the children become frustrated. Parents must demonstrate to children exactly what it means to "make the bed," what the standard of performance is. But the child will *not* be able to make the bed as perfectly as the parent. The child's coordination, strength, and reach will not allow it. Thus, a compromise must be reached. The point is not how well the bed is made but that the task is completed to an accepted level of quality.

This same process of setting standards applies to all tasks. Does "cleaning the room" mean putting everything in the closet, out of sight, or does it mean putting things where they belong? Does "hanging up the clothes" mean hanging them on a hook by one sleeve, or does it mean placing them neatly on a hanger? Does "studying" mean staring at words on a page for ten minutes, or does it mean being able to talk about what the words say?

Of course, parents must be careful not to select tasks or performance standards that are too difficult for the child to achieve. If the child is frustrated by a task, the process will be counterproductive, leading not to good work habits but to poor ones.

Parents can do themselves and their children a great favor by getting them involved in the decision-making process at an early age. Decision making is discussed in Chapter 7, but it is worth making the point here that children are no different from adults in this respect: They tend to have greater commitment to tasks if they are involved in making decisions about performing the tasks. The sooner the child becomes involved in decision making, the more responsible the child will be. This becomes especially important during the troubled years of adolescence when children refuse to accept parental decisions and begin making their own. If they have developed an understanding of the obligations which go with decision making, they are more inclined to make sensible decisions.

The question is how to get children involved in the decision-making process. It begins simply. Ask the child to select a favorite fruit or vegetable at the grocery store, or to rearrange the seating at the dinner table, or to decide on one friend to ask over for lunch. Share some of your own decision-making deliberations with the child, letting her or him know that alternatives exist and that each alternative has certain consequences. For instance, deciding on the family menu involves alternatives of taste, cost, nutrition, and preparation time. And as the child matures, gradually turn over decision-making responsibility. For example, when your ten-year-old daughter asks if she can go out to play, don't respond with: "No. You haven't done your work."

Instead, consider this response: "Well, that's a decision you'll have to make today. Have you thought about it? Have you done all your work? Is there something else you might want to do that's more important? Do you remember that we were planning a trip to the zoo this afternoon?"

In all likelihood, the child will still decide to go out to play. But the decision is the child's. She understands that she is responsible for making that decision and for all its consequences. It isn't a strong understanding, but only a glimmer of understanding. Its effects may not show up for years. But parents must continually remind themselves that in such circumstances what one writer called "the invisible effects of habit formation" are taking place. Those "invisible effects" might just as well be related to good habits as to bad ones.

Finally, reserve the right to disagree with your child's decision. But make certain the child knows it is the *decision* with which you disagree, not the child. For example: "It's your decision. But if it were my decision, I would do it this way, because. . . ."

Once you have involved the child in decisions regarding tasks and the performance standards for those tasks, then you must make certain that the child receives adequate reinforcement when tasks are completed. Often this can be just a simple "Thank you" or congratulations for a job well done. However, once in a while consider the possibility of helping transfer your own satisfaction at the completion of the task to the child. For example, a parent might comment: "That's a good job. It must please you to be able to do such good work." That simple statement may help the child develop a sense of satisfaction in the completion of a task.

The Habit of Personal Growth

The final work habit with which we will concern ourselves here is the habit of personal growth. This is as much a frame of mind as it is a habit. It means that a person has the confidence—indeed, the desire—to attempt new tasks and to seek improved performance on old tasks. It is a habit that often differentiates good workers from poor workers insofar as advancement is concerned. It is a habit which adds excitement, interest, and vitality to life. And it is a habit which will become more and more important as we move into a period of increased job mobility at all ages, all levels, and all skills.

Some might call this characteristic "the pioneer spirit," because it's the kind of attitude which allows some individuals to welcome challenge, to push themselves toward new accomplishments, and to thrive on uncertainty.

Parents can help children acquire this attitude through a number of fairly common-sense approaches. Of course, the most important thing is not to discourage a child from attempting to develop and use new skills. It's so easy for parents to discourage a child with such comments as: "You can't do that. You're not old enough yet." Or "Not now. I don't have time to teach you how." Indeed, the child may not be "old enough yet," but attempting a new task may help him or her to learn that some tasks take practice and "growing into" before they can be mastered. And if the parent does not have time to teach a new skill at the moment, then he or she should make a definite appointment to do it at some later time. Many educators are concerned that parents not push their children into attempting tasks for which they are not ready, and rightfully so, but it is equally as damaging not to encourage the child to keep trying new skills and new tasks as part of the growth process. Certainly, the child will fail on occasion, but a good support strategy can minimize the negative effect of failure, so long as it does not occur too frequently. For example, a parent might say to the child: "Wow, you almost did it that time, didn't you? Let's wait a few days and try it again."

Another technique to support the personal growth habit is for parents to set the example themselves. This may require some extra effort at a time in life when one feels one deserves to relax a little and be comfortable, but it is an effort that can be as rewarding to the parents as to the child. It means forcing one's self out of the routine—out of the comfortable pattern—and into a new interest or a new challenge or a new task. It could mean developing new skills, such as taking music lessons, or learning about woodworking, or trying to fix a leaking faucet without calling the plumber. It could mean acquiring new hobbies, such as photography, or gardening, or tennis. It could mean simply changing traditional patterns, such as father fixing the Sunday dinner, or mother refinishing a piece of furniture, or the whole family selecting a new destination for the weekend outing. This process adds zest to living, and it sets a pattern that will allow children to experiment with new skills with confidence and without the self-conscious-ness which often accompanies the first awkward attempts at skill development.

Of course, if parents are to encourage personal growth on the part of their children, they must be willing to allow a certain amount of experimentation. Sometimes, the experimentation may not be pleasant, but so long as it is not dangerous, it should not be discouraged. For instance, a son may want to try baking a cake when he's eight or nine years old. The mess he creates may not be received with equanimity—and perhaps the cake won't turn out too well, either—but the child doesn't expect to make the finest cake on his first try; he simply wants to test out a new skill. Parents should get out of the way and let him try, making sure he knows that they are available for consultation whenever he needs them. As for the mess he creates, he should probably understand that part of the job is cleaning up after the cake is finished, although some might argue that the most important thing is that he is trying new skills, and that is worth a little mess in the kitchen.

As a part of encouraging personal growth, parents must also provide many opportunities for children to test out new skills and interests. Most of these "tests" will be experimental, but every child must search for that particular interest that motivates him or her. If not, the child will end up bored. Providing opportunities takes two forms. First, parents should make an effort to expose the child to many different types of activities, such as sports events, concerts, plays, and as many types of work situations as possible. It's always better for the child to participate than to merely be a spectator, but sometimes participation is not possible. This need not be a constant effort—and it should not take away materially from the child's own personal development time—but it ought to be worked into the family routine from time to time. Second, parents should provide some of the tools that make skill experimentation possible. No home should be without some kind of musical instrument, a few basic handicraft tools, paper and art materials, a few books, a flower pot and some seeds, or whatever other tools and equipment parents can provide. None need be expensive or elaborate, but they do need to be available for the child to experiment with. Even the greatest musical genius cannot play a tune on a television set. Parents might also consider occasional gifts that are skill related, such as jigsaw puzzles, models, art projects, handicrafts, food preparation "packages," and needlework kits. And don't discriminate based on sex. Daughters can learn from constructing model cars, and sons can learn from embroidering kitchen towels.

Some will object that this process places too much pressure on the child, that it will create a neurotic individual, constantly looking for new challenges, never able to enjoy one success before moving on to the next task. Indeed, that is a danger if parents become obsessed with the personal growth process and continuallly "push" their children into new challenges. We have all witnessed the example of the child who takes music lessons, dance lessons, special tutoring, swimming classes, and who participates in a whole list of self-improvement activities. Such a child has no time of his or her own, no time to experiment with new skills and interests, no time to become truly aware of self. We do not recommend that kind of programmed existence. Rather, we recommend simply that parents make available to their children a wide range of opportunities to develop, to grow, to experiment with interests, and to test new skills. The greatest value of the personal growth habit occurs when the motivation comes from within, from personal desire, not from parental direction. After all, parents lose much of their direct control over children during the middle teens, a time when the children still have most of their lives to live.

Finally, the key to the development of the personal growth habit is the ability of parents to assess the progress of their children and to be able to provide the proper challenge at the proper time. This is as true for the average child as it is for the brilliant child, as true for the "deprived" child as it is for the privileged child, as true for the handicapped child as it is for the "normal" child. (In fact, it may be even more true for the handicapped child, because parents have a tendency to "protect" handicapped children from challenging situations on the mistaken grounds that such children should not have to cope with the same challenges as "normal" children.)

This ability to assess the progress of children demands continuing observation, constant communication, and a certain amount of intuition. Parents can learn to detect signs of boredom by watching behavior patterns. The child who wanders aimlessly about the house, or who eats too much, or who watches television out of habit, or who teases brothers and sisters too much may be bored. He or she needs a new interest, a new challenge. To repeat, parents should not force the interest on the child but should make it available at the proper times. Parents can also learn a great deal about how their children feel by simply talking to them, or more properly, by listening. Listening involves "hearing" what the speaker *means* as well as what he or she *says*. It's a good idea, if possible, to establish a sort of routine communication time, a time when one parent and one child are alone for a few minutes so the child can sort of "debrief" about the events of the day. Tremendous insights into the child's self-concept can be obtained during these short communication sessions. So often, communication between parent and child is heavily one way, and at some point in the day parents need to stop being parents long enough to be friends. Child-to-parent communication is not an automatic thing. It must be developed over a period of years. It should not consist of "question and answer" sessions. Often, a few moments of silence provokes much more meaningful comment than even the most incisive question.

The habits we have discussed here are few. Obviously, we think they are important. However, parents may feel that other habits are more desirable for their children, and in that case they should devise their own strategies for instilling those habits in their children. As is the case with attitudes, children *will* acquire habits. Those habits can be good habits or bad habits, but they will exist and they will be difficult to alter. Ironically, most habits are acquired long before they are applied to critical situations. The worker who is bored with a job may have acquired the habit of boredom during the elementary school years, and he or she may be hard pressed to find *any* job which is not boring. On the other hand, the worker who acquired the habit of finding satisfaction in work early in life does not become bored with the job, and that applies to almost any job. He or she finds new challenges in the job or around the job to keep it interesting. And with added irony, the worker who finds satisfaction in the job is much more likely to have the opportunity to change jobs through promotion or other means than is the worker who is continually bored with the job to the point of performing poorly.

BROADENING CAREER AWARENESS

In addition to laying the foundations for good work habits, one of the things the school will concentrate on during the elementary grades is expanding the child's awareness of the world of work and the nature of our interdependent economic structure. We have talked about how parents can point out to children during the preschool years what various workers are doing in the child's environment—the mail carrier, the police officer, the grocery clerk, the truck driver, and so on. This same kind of awareness training is continued by the school, calculatedly increasing the scope of the child's contacts with the world each year. Teachers use field trips, film, guest speakers, and class discussion to help the child develop this awareness.

Parents can supplement the career awareness activities of the school by continuing their own program of orienting the child to the functions of workers. Routine trips to the grocery store, the doctor's office, the zoo, and visits to friends and relatives are all occasions for casual comments about the workers who build products or provide services. This is not a time for detailed discussions concerning career life styles, or training requirements, or specific tasks involved in the job. It is simply a time for building an awareness that many workers perform a wide variety of tasks in order to provide a wide variety of goods and services for the child and his or her family and friends.

Another benefit emerges as parents and the school introduce the child to a wider variety of workers. Instead of the child having just a few workers with whom she or he can "identify" in pretend play, the child will have a much broader base of make-believe friends with whom to play. Such identification allows the child to "become" different workers in a significant manner, even though it may be superficial, and the child begins to appreciate the skills which are required to perform such work, to understand the equipment needed in such work, and to realize the benefits which can be derived from such work.

These experiences which are coupled with the child's broadening awareness of careers and workers also allow parents to point out significant concepts regarding the world of work and the individual's relation to it. Some of those concepts are discussed below as an indication of the benefits which might be derived from a conscientious career awareness program.

Work and Workers Have Dignity

Children need to realize that regardless of the type of work that is being performed, there is a sense of dignity in all work. For example, work performed around the home is important to the health and welfare of the family. Such tasks as taking out the trash, washing clothes, dusting and cleaning, and keeping everything in its place and operating properly are vital to the health and protection of family members. When such tasks are not performed, the emotional climate becomes threatened. Understanding this principle is the beginning of an appreciation for the dignity of work.

The child can develop a sense of pride by taking care of his or her personal belongings. For instance, the child can wash and polish his or her tricycle, or keep toys in order and undamaged. Through the assistance of older family members, the child can participate in many activities which will promote a sense of pride and develop dignified attitudes toward work. Positive reinforcement occurs when the child hears such statements as: "Boy, doesn't that look great!" "I'm really proud of the work you did to help clean up the yard." "Look at how nice it is!"

Parents can help the child extend his or her understanding of the dignity of work to include all variety of jobs by calling attention to workers and the tasks they are doing as the family travels around the community.

Work Meets Personal and Family Needs

In a similar vein, the child should learn that work is an important part of the process of meeting personal needs and family needs. Parents should provide opportunities for the child to perform as many personal tasks as possible. The child should assume the responsibility for keeping his or her room tidy, for taking care of toys, and for cleaning up after the completion of such projects as coloring or fixing a sandwich. These personal work habits do not come automatically, as parents well know. However, through encouragement and by allowing the child to gradually assume more responsibility, parents can teach the child that work is part of taking care of personal needs. Parents are cautioned not to expect too much *or* too little of the child. He or she is capable of performing many of the tasks necessary to meet personal needs, and the child should be encouraged to do so. However, there are some things which are beyond the child's developmental capacities, and forcing a child to do such things can lead to failure and frustration, two things which parents want to avoid, since they tend to create negative attitudes about work rather than positive ones.

Work also is necessary to meet such family needs as food, clothing, shelter, and transportation. It is important for parents to instruct their children about these family needs and to explain the role that each family member plays in meeting the needs. The child can understand the concept that each family member makes a contribution and that certain family members have primary responsibility for satisfying specific needs. Parents should meet the challenge to sit down and organize the tasks to be performed around the home and to discuss who should perform the various duties and why. During such discussions, all family members gain insight as to the importance of one another in making contributions to the needs of the family unit.

A child who understands these relationships among individual capabilities, task completion, and group needs on the family level will be able to comprehend some of the complex relationships among workers in the community and the products and services they provide for the family.

Work Provides Rewards and Satisfactions

In addition to the personal pride and the conveniences

which are provided through working, a number of other rewards and satisfactions can be derived. It is important that the child become aware of the types of rewards that come from working. During the child's formative years, some discussions in the home should focus upon the ways people are rewarded for their work. This concept will become more meaningful if the child is personally rewarded for his or her work efforts with such things as additional privileges, money, or other compensations. The child might be given periodic rewards for continuing to do the jobs which he or she is assigned around the home or for accepting additional responsibilities. When the child comprehends how this concept of reward works and how it applies to him or her personally, the child will have a base from which to extend the concept within his or her own scope of understanding and strive for the acquisition of additional or different rewards as they are merited.

The intangible rewards of self-satisfaction which come from recognition and a feeling of accomplishment within one's self are probably more important than the tangible rewards discussed above. Often these intangible rewards take precedence over the monetary or privilege rewards, because the sense of self-satisfaction is a great motivator. Although some children tend to respond more easily to tangible rewards, they are nonetheless developing the need to have the intangible human needs met also.

Similarity of the Home to Other Job Settings

Children need to become aware of the fact that the activities they perform around the home are similar to the activities required in the world of work. The development of fine motor skills, gross motor skills, cognitive abilities, social interaction, emotional maturity, and other attributes begins in the home and continues into adulthood. Work around the home helps the child develop physical skills. Parallel to the physical skills are the social and emotional skills which require the child to interact appropriately with other family members and to cope with the factors which influence whether or not the child completes assignments.

Such "coping skills" include attention span, low level of frustration, "stick-to-it-iveness," the ability to be interrupted and then return to a task, endurance, and other behaviors which are required of workers on the job.

The child should become aware that the only difference between work around the home and the work performed by members of the family outside the home is the setting in which the work is performed. To a large degree, the same factors are present in all settings. Each work situation requires tools, equipment, workers, communication with others, and other common activities. This awareness develops as parents discuss their own work, the child's work, and the work performed by those in the community, and as parents make comparisons between tasks performed by those workers and the tasks performed in the home.

People Require Training for Most Jobs

Children must be trained to do the various tasks they perform—to operate a vacuum cleaner, to clean a sink, to make a bed. It is the same with all jobs in the world of work. No one is expected to perform work without adequate training, regardless of the level of difficulty the task may entail. In the home, this may require extra patience on the part of parents as they take the time to show the child how to perform certain tasks. Knowing the child's level of capability will decrease frustration and failure and will reduce the amount of time and patience required for skill training.

In addition to the specific skill, the child is learning that training is a requirement for work performance. As parents explain to the child that he or she becomes competent through a process of training, the child can transfer this understanding to the realization that those who perform work in the community have also been trained to do so. The child can also begin to understand—at a very basic level—that different jobs require different kinds of training and different levels of training preparation. This concept can be demonstrated within the home by explaining that certain family members perform certain tasks because they have learned how to do those tasks, and that the kinds of jobs the child does around the house will be influenced by the way he or she learns new skills through training as he or she matures.

The World of Work Is Filled with Variety

One of the easier concepts to teach a child is the fact that there are so many different kinds of jobs to be done. The home is an excellent laboratory in which to demonstrate this concept, because there are so many concrete examples of task variety within the home. Television provides another learning tool in this regard. Parents can guide discussions about the different characters who appear on television and the work roles they portray. Television provides a vast resource for such information. Not only can the occupations be identified, but the child can gain insight into the skills and capabilities which are required for various jobs. Parents can encourage the children to express their likes and dislikes about the various occupations they see, but parents themselves should avoid expressing value judgments about those occupations, particularly negative value judgments, because such statements are likely to condition the child's own attitudes and thereby restrict his or her horizons.

Getting Along with Others

In addition to the physical capabilities which come with maturity and the training which is necessary for skill development, an important component of the work situation is the ability to get along with others and to communicate effectively. Naturally, these abilities are developed and refined throughout a lifetime, but the earlier one learns and applies the rules for getting along with others, the sooner he or she will have acquired a necessary ingredient for success.

This concept can be approached on two levels. First, parents have the responsibility to teach their children to get along with other family members, and to point out the advantages of such behavior. Second, parents can make children aware of examples outside the home which demonstrate the effects of such behavior. For instance, a parent and child might notice two workers talking. The parent might suggest a possible subject of the discussion and ask the child his or her opinion. The parent might also ask what the child thinks would happen if the two workers did not get along with one another and could not communicate. That line of discussion might lead to a comparison with a recent event in the home where two family members had to coordinate a task through communication.

The Nature of "Products" and "Services"

The distinction between occupations which are "product" oriented and those which are "service" oriented is important because it explains so much about how our economy works and how tasks are interrelated. Every home depends on both products and services, and it is relatively easy to illustrate the differences by showing the child that some work around the home is product oriented and other jobs are service oriented. (Of course, some tasks are combinations of both.) Food preparation combines raw materials and labor to *produce* a consumable product. Serving the food and cleaning up the dishes are service tasks.

In this regard, the child's awareness of the vast numbers of workers upon whom he or she is dependent can be increased by playing a game at the table. Select an ordinary item—a can of soup, for example. Ask each member of the family to identify a different component of that product and to name the workers responsible for providing it. The number of occupations involved in producing such a product and providing it to the family is surprising—the farmer, the can manufacturer, the food processor, the truck driver, the grocer, and so on. Of course, that direct line represents only a small number of workers. Some family members will recognize that the farmer used a tractor which was sold and serviced by a tractor dealer; that the can manufacturer used raw materials from a zinc miner; that the food producer employed advertisers to help sell the product; and so on. There is no end to this exercise, but it does show how products and services are related and how each member of society depends upon countless others to do the work which makes life more satisfying.

Many other concepts about work can be learned in the home. We have illustrated only a few here. Others might include the changing nature of work roles through life, the relationship between geographic location and occupational opportunity, the importance of classification and organization, the value of planning and prioritizing, and the concept of cooperation for task achievement. The main thing is to be aware that opportunities for learning are continuously available in the home. Those learning situations occur by design or by accident, but they do occur. And those learning situations can be used to build positive values in the child, or they can be neglected. We believe that children benefit when such situations are used to create career awareness in the child.

SUMMARY

The career awareness phase of career education consists of healthy portions of self-awareness, together with an expanding awareness of the world of work. Parents can work with the school in this phase of career education by continuing and expanding upon the support mechanisms which began in early childhood. Just as nutrition, adequate medical attention, and opportunities to develop physically are important to the child, so is the need for a stimulating environment within the home critical to helping the child develop mental capacities, values, attitudes, and habits. This is also a period during which the child is developing his or her self-image, and the development of a positive self-image provides confidence and motivation which will serve the child well in school and in work.

Since the school is the child's first "job," parents will want to help the child develop good work values as well as good work habits. Parents can select their own set of values and habits to pass on to their children, but they should realize that lifetime work habits are developing, whether or not parents intervene. A carefully considered approach to habit development will benefit both the parents and the child.

In providing career awareness experiences for their children, parents should keep one caution in mind. The child's developing values and attitudes are influenced by his or her parents. Thus, if parents make disparaging remarks about specific careers or workers, the child is likely to attach negative values to those careers. In essence, that limits the child's ability to explore careers objectively, and it also essentially limits the child's freedom to select a career of her own or his own. A child cannot "project" herself or himself into a career which is surrounded with negative images.

ADDITIONAL READING

Bell, T.H., and Thorum, Arden R. *Your Child's Intellect.* Salt Lake City: Olympus Publishing Company, 1972.

Grant, Eva H. *Parents and Teachers as Partners.* Chicago: Science Research Associates, Inc., 1971.

Hoyt, Kenneth B.; Pinson, Nancy M.; Laramore, Darryl; and Mangum, Garth L. *Career Education and the Elementary School Teacher.* Salt Lake City: Olympus Publishing Company, 1973.

CHAPTER SIX

Career Exploration

The value of career education is increased if it "fits" naturally and normally into the developmental and need patterns of the children and youth it is intended to help. Accordingly, the preceding chapter dealt with career awareness and associated it with that time in the child's life—roughly, the elementary school years—when he or she is becoming aware of the world outside his or her immediate environment. At that early stage, the child's level of development does not lend itself to highly abstract or conceptual knowledge, but he or she becomes aware that there is a world outside the self, family, and neighborhood, and that one must begin to acquire certain knowledge and skills in order to be able to deal with that world. Career education seeks to add to that growing awareness of the world an awareness of work and workers and the functions they perform in society. It is also during these early years that work values and career stereotypes develop in children.

Somewhere between the ages of 10 and 15 years— roughly, the middle school or junior high school years—the child moves into another stage of development. The child begins to see himself or herself as a part of the world, as a

133

potential functioning component of the complex environment in which he or she lives. The child can still think only
in fairly concrete terms, using a thought process which
basically involves classification and relationship concepts.
Thus, he or she begins to look at the world from the
standpoint of: "Where do I fit?"

THE AGE OF EXPLORATION

As any parent of an adolescent youngster knows, this
stage of life is also accompanied by tremendous—often
traumatic—physical, psychological, and emotional changes.
Physically, the child goes through puberty, and no matter
how well prepared the individual may be, the physical
changes which accompany that process are unexpected and
often frightening, particularly since maturation rates vary
so widely during these years that the youngster may
sometimes feel "different" from his or her peers. Psychologi-
cally, the child must deal with "fitting" into life at the same
time that he or she is physically changing into a person who
is totally different from that comfortable body of the
childhood years. Emotionally, the child experiences new
feelings with relation to others and with relation to self. He
or she becomes concerned about appearance, and the
awkwardness or the acne of puberty magnifies that concern.
Most youngsters at this stage turn inward to the point
where parents and others criticize them for being self-
centered, for not thinking about the needs of others, and for
withdrawing from reality.
This turning inward is primarily a part of the activity
which so clearly marks this stage of development: exploration. The child turns inward because he or she must explore
this being who is himself or herself in order to find out
where it belongs. The child has a great need to classify, to
relate, to fit in . . . and in order to do so it is imperative that
he or she explore the inner self to learn what it is made of.
The unquestioning self-acceptance of childhood must be
replaced by a more critical self-knowledge.

The Exploration of Self

The child's intense exploration of self is inevitably accompanied by some exploration of the people, activities, and things which surround the child, usually in an effort to determine the youngster's own relationship to those components of the environment. One researcher identified ten developmental needs of adolescent youth which are part of the exploratory search:

(1) To achieve new mature relationships with peers

(2) To attain a feminine or masculine role socially

(3) To attain emotional independence of adults

(4) To accept one's physique and to be able to use the body effectively

(5) To reach an assurance of economic independence

(6) To choose and prepare for an occupation

(7) To prepare for marriage and family life

(8) To develop intellectual skills and concepts necessary for civic competence

(9) To want and attain socially responsible behavior

(10) To acquire a set of values and an ethical system as a guide to behavior (Havighurst, 1953)

The object here is not to defend or dispute individual items on Havighurst's list, but simply to give some indication of the range of problems facing the adolescent. All the problems are important; some are critical. No wonder adolescent youngsters often seem distant, confused, and troubled to their parents and others. Most of these problems are problems which the child has never before confronted, if for no other reason than that younger children rarely think in terms of long-range goals or future needs; they are almost totally oriented toward the present. But the problems faced by adolescents have lifetime implications. The mere thought of such long-range commitments may frighten the child or may appear to threaten the child's freedom.

Given this intense need for self-examination, education is meaningful and relevant to the child only to the degree that it provides information about himself or herself. For instance, the teacher of American history will be more successful if he or she can help students discover their own characteristics through the study of historical figures. One way to do this is through the use of simulation games where students assume the roles of others in order to discover their own reactions to certain historical situations.

This discussion of adolescent development is basic to understanding what is meant by "the career exploration phase of career education." It means more than simply exploring the world of work. It means looking at a wide range of job skills, career life styles, and work attitudes for the primary purpose of self-discovery. The object is *not* to have the student study a career for the purpose of deciding whether or not to pursue that particular career. The object is to explore various careers so the student can seek answers to such questions as: Do I have the kinds of skills necessary for that career? Can I acquire them? Is that the kind of life style I want to lead? Are my own work habits similar to or different from those of most workers in that particular career? How am I like that particular worker? How am I different? How would I react to that career situation?

In this way, career exploration becomes both a means to and a result of self-exploration.

The handicapped adolescent has the same self-discovery drive as his or her peers. The only difference is that in the case of the handicapped child the information learned in self-examination may be different from that learned by other youngsters *in one or more specific areas*. Both parents and schools must be careful not to precondition what the handicapped child may learn about himself or herself by establishing unnecessary restrictions around that child's exploratory activities. In addition, some handicapping conditions may require special assistance in order that the child might explore to the greatest extent possible. For instance, those with motor handicaps might require special transportation, the visually handicapped need leaders who can describe what occurs in the environment, and those with hearing handicaps need auditory assistance. The point is that whenever possible, such assistance should be provided in order to facilitate exploration. Self-discovery is just as concerned with learning about one's limitations as with learning about one's strengths.

Exploration of the World of Work

Career education at the middle/junior high school level is designed to help the student learn about himself or herself while exploring the world of work. In most cases, it includes a certain amount of testing, using standard test instruments—personality inventories, interest inventories, motivation assessments, and so on. Some educators question the meaningfulness of these tools, but in general they offer some insights for the individual involved in self-examination. Neither parents nor students should be intimidated by such testing.

Career education also involves a structured examination of the world of work. The complexity of the job market makes it unlikely that a person can adequately explore it without some kind of structured approach. The school is a logical place for such exploration to occur, because the school is a structured environment. However, that does not reduce the need for parents to assist their children in career exploration activities. That assistance is provided best by parents who understand the developmental stages through which their children are progressing, who appreciate the need for career education, and who are aware that career exploration is one avenue toward exploration of self. Parents can be helpful to their children if they remember these points:

(1) The adolescent years are marked by a great need to explore the self in relation to the environment.

(2) Only in very rare cases do youngsters select their lifetime careers during the middle/junior high school years.

(3) Youngsters frequently "experiment" with one or more occupations during this period, trying them on for "fit" in an effort to learn more about themselves.

(4) Frequent switching of interests is common during the adolescent years as the child struggles for more self-knowledge.

(5) Career education does not force a child toward a career choice, but merely provides a structured means for self-exploration using a career orientation.

(6) The adolescent has a strong need for peer approval, a factor which may influence the career interests expressed by the child.

(7) The child may seek out adult "mentors" who will also influence expressions of career interest.

(8) Peer influence and "mentor" influence will likely diminish as the adolescent's own self-concept begins to develop.

A good program of career exploration involves four distinct steps: organization, examination, research, and selection.

ORGANIZATION FOR CAREER EXPLORATION

Because the number of possible careers to be explored is so vast, it is impossible to explore all of them—or even a significant proportion of the total. Therefore, any proposal for career exploration must begin with some sort of classification or sorting of careers into manageable groups so that the student can approach the task by looking at large groups of related occupations instead of trying to deal directly with any single occupation. Thus, if the world of work consists of the entire planet, then these organized groups are the various continents waiting to be explored.

The number of groups and the method of grouping can be fairly arbitrary, so long as some sort of rational system guides the process. In the past we have frequently grouped jobs according to a horizontal or stratified system of classification. Jobs were grouped by level of training required, or level of expertise, or level of responsibility, or some combination of those things. Professional jobs were at the top level, followed by technical jobs, managerial jobs, skilled workers, laborers, and so on. The same system can also refer to "white-collar workers" and "blue-collar workers." (Many labor market statistics are still reported in this fashion, as indicated in Chapter 2.)

The horizontal or stratified system of classification creates a number of problems. First, the horizontal layers are not at all clearly delineated. Sometimes it's hard to decide whether a career is a professional career, a technical career, or a managerial career. Second, the differences between groups have markedly diminished. As reported in Chapter 2, differences in education, income, social status, and other criteria are not as great as they once were, and those differences continue to fluctuate. Third, horizontal grouping does not provide for functional relationships on either vertical or horizontal axes. The medical doctor and the musician fall into the same group, even though the functions in society are quite different. Fourth, horizontal grouping perpetuates the social stratification which diminishes the dream of equality for all citizens. It attaches implicit value judgments to various careers, value judgments which do not reflect meaningful value relationships. All jobs are valuable to society. In at least one very real sense, the doctor is no more valuable than the garbage collector who removes the waste which, were it left on the streets, would spread the disease the doctor must cure.

For these and other reasons, horizontal grouping is not often used in career education programs. A number of alternative systems have been proposed, and several different methods are being used with success in various parts of the country. One popular system is the "career cluster" system proposed by the U.S. Office of Education in the early 1970s. Although we are aware that the cluster approach is only one of several possibilities, it is the approach we have selected for this discussion because information concerning it has probably been more widely disseminated than is the case for any other single career exploration system.

The Career Cluster System

The cluster approach divides the vast number of careers which make up the world of work into areas (or continents) based on function. In the structure proposed by the U.S. Office of Education, fifteen functional areas (or clusters) were identified:

(1) Agri-business and natural resources

(2) Business and office

(3) Communications and media

(4) Consumer and homemaking education

(5) Construction

(6) Environmental control

(7) Fine arts and humanities

(8) Health

(9) Hospitality and recreation

(10) Manufacturing

(11) Marine science

(12) Marketing and distribution

(13) Personal services

(14) Public services

(15) Transportation

Each cluster contains all of the careers or jobs related to that particular function. Thus, the transportation cluster would include the airplane pilot as well as the baggage handler, the truck driver as well as the dispatcher, the ticket agent as well as the locomotive mechanic. Each cluster includes the entire vertical range of jobs within that cluster, from the professional to the laborer. And while some clusters cut across a fairly broad horizontal range of careers, each career within the cluster has some functional relationship to all other careers within that same cluster.

This organizational structure offers some distinct advantages, particularly for the junior high school student who is exploring the career world and his or her own relationships to it. The student can approach the cluster from at least two different points of departure: He or she may be interested in the cluster itself and in the function with which it deals, or the interest may begin with a specific career within the cluster. For instance, the student may be interested in transportation as a function and may want to explore some of the careers within that cluster. On the other hand, the student may have an interest in being a commercial airline pilot and may seek to broaden his or her understanding of that career by exploring its relationship to other careers in the transportation cluster. Since one major goal of career exploration is to facilitate self-discovery, the student begins "testing" his or her own needs and capabilities against those related to specific careers. The student finds that an airline pilot must bear an extremely high level of responsibility, must be able to operate on rigid schedules, must spend considerable time away from home, and must spend years in training and preparation before becoming a pilot. Perhaps the student feels he or she doesn't quite fit those requirements. That leads to the exploration of a related career which is just as important in the transportation of people or goods, but which may require a little less responsibility or a little less time for training and preparation. In the process, the student has learned a little more about himself or herself and has also learned some specific information about a number of careers, any of which he or she might find suitable.

The exploration may continue within the same cluster, or it may lead to another cluster, another list of careers, and another set of criteria which the student can beneficially use for self-evaluation.

One advantage to the cluster system, then, is that it leads to self-discovery through natural interests, while at the same time expanding knowledge of career opportunities. Another advantage is that the clusters are wholly integrated vertically. The primary determinant of clustering is functional; no job is considered any more important than any other job in performing that function. Built-in, arbitrary value judgments can be avoided. Careers and jobs can be examined not from the basis of where they fit in some hierarchy of value, but on the basis of where they fit functionally into society and what kind of "fit" they have for the individual. This should help to reduce the stereotyping of jobs by race, sex, and physical condition. Still another advantage to the cluster system is in its simplicity and flexibility. The fifteen clusters very nearly cover the entire range of economic activity, and yet they are flexible enough to allow for the rapid changes which are taking place in the labor market. It is relatively easy to grasp the structure of the cluster system, and most persons in modern society have had at least some experience with each of the clusters—a television experience, if not a real life experience.

Of course, the system also has its weaknesses. Some think it is *too* simple, that the individual clusters are too broad, and that it may mislead students into thinking that the career world is narrow. Two related weaknesses are that the clusters are not always easy to define, and many careers overlap from one cluster to another. For example, radio communication would seem to belong in the communication cluster, but radio is also important to the transportation cluster for scheduling, dispatching, and other operations. Accounting jobs can be found in many of the clusters. And it is difficult to draw distinct lines of demarcation between the marketing and distribution cluster and the communication or transportation clusters.

However, these strengths and weaknesses of the cluster system should not be measured against some theoretical or statistical concept but against the purpose for which the system was created. It was designed as a tool for students to use in career exploration and self-discovery. Despite its faults, the cluster system seems to provide a meaningful framework for that purpose. The cluster system offers a structure through which students can easily move from consideration of the entire world of work, to career clusters within the world, to specific categories of careers within each cluster, to specific jobs or job types—while at the same time exploring their own interests, needs, and capabilities.

What Parents Can Do

Parents can help their children during the career exploration stage by developing their own understanding of the career cluster system. The object for parents is not so much to learn about the details of the system as to learn why the cluster system is employed by schools and how it meshes with the needs of students for self-exploration. As parents talk to their children about work and work roles, they should begin to think of careers in terms of function rather than hierarchical level, and they should work hard to avoid the traditional stereotyping which has conditioned our thinking in the past. Parents often worry about the career choices of their children at much too early an age. As mentioned above, children rarely make long-range career decisions at the middle/junior high school age. But children do actively explore careers at that age for the self-interest reasons discussed above. And that kind of dual purpose exploration should be encouraged.

Such encouragement can be provided through a number of techniques. Special effort should be made to expose the adolescent child to a wide variety of work situations, including those in which the parents are employed and those in which relatives or family friends are employed. There is no reason to be reluctant about repeating activities and experiences which have been done before. It has been well established that "repetition is the key to learning," and that alone is reason enough for repeating experiences. But even more important is the fact that children develop so rapidly that old experiences continually renew themselves. The child who visits a parent's place of work periodically sees different things with each visit, because the child's own perspective changes with maturity. Part of this is due to the child's own development, and part of it is due to the fact that the school, through career education, focuses the child's attention to different stimuli as the years progress. The adolescent will likely have many questions to ask about various work situations to which she or he is exposed.

These are also important years to increase "hands-on" experiences for the child. Parents can make certain that children have the opportunity to perform—or try to perform—a variety of tasks which require personal effort. It is a time to test new skills and to experiment widely with new interests. In some cases, young persons of the middle/junior high school age can readily handle the responsibilities of part-time jobs or volunteer work. They can certainly "try out" different kinds of work during summer vacations from school. In fact, parents should encourage attempts at a variety of work experiences. The important thing at this age is not so much the job content—the specific tasks—as it is the variety of work settings. The child can learn a great deal about himself or herself by experiencing different work settings, such as outdoor labor, indoor office work, sales work, solitary work, creative work, laboratory work, repetitious work, and so on. Of course, no child can experience all of these things in one or two summers, but the point is to avoid the steady job, the one that invariably comes along each summer, the one in the family business, or the one that just happens to be convenient. Encourage the child to find hands-on experiences in a variety of settings, even if it means sacrificing a little in wages or in convenience.

Another thing which parents can do is to exert their considerable influence on the schools and other community institutions to provide work experiences for children. A number of programs have been tried in various parts of the country. Schools can provide various work activities for students, from assisting janitors and administrative personnel to meaningful activities in craft classes. Business and industry can become more involved in meeting the needs of students. In some communities, Job Service operates special employment programs for students during the summer. The organization contacts local businesses to inquire about student-level work, and helps students find work which is suitable to their needs and interests. In other communities, the local newspaper runs special help-wanted columns for summer jobs. In at least one community, the local chamber of commerce has become heavily involved with a program called BICEP, which stands for Business, Labor, Industry, Community, Education Partnership. The program seeks to establish an effective working relationship between the business community and the schools with regard to career education. Businessmen visit the schools as speakers and resource persons, lend materials and equipment, host field trips and, for those of the appropriate age, offer opportunities for work experience.

These are just a few of the ways in which parents can be involved with the career education of their adolescent children. Many opportunities will suggest themselves as parents begin to understand what career education is all about, and as they see how career education uses the cluster system as a tool to help young persons begin career exploration.

Examination of the Career Clusters

Career education provides a structure for the exploration of the world of work through the cluster system or some other meaningful organization. Career education also offers a structured approach to the examination of those career clusters in a way that is likely to be most beneficial to the student. Two critical considerations in examining the career clusters are the manner in which the examination is approached and the kinds of information to be examined.

The whole approach to the study of career possibilities must be non-threatening. Students of middle/junior high school age are easily threatened, both by the sheer bulk of information about the career world and by the fact that studying careers carries the threat of long-range commitment. The amount of available information about careers is so vast that it could easily intimidate a student, particularly when the student does not attach much relevance to such information. The numbers themselves are overwhelming— over 30,000 different occupations listed in the Labor Department's *Dictionary of Occupational Titles*. If the task of career exploration is approached strictly as an information-processing task, then few students will benefit from the exercise. (Indeed, the quantity of information is so great that few adult scholars approach it without considerable trepidation.) One way to reduce the threat of so much information is to group or classify the information into manageable divisions or units. Of course, that is one reason for the career clusters. Fifteen career clusters are much less threatening than 30,000 different occupations. And since students of middle school age have a tendency to sort things into categories, this approach fits into their own developmental stage.

Another way to reduce the threat of career exploration is to reduce or eliminate those components of information-processing which tend to be threatening; i.e., formal study and examinations. Career educators are not interested in having students learn and repeat the names of one hundred new occupations; career educators are interested in helping students realize that thousands of varied careers (and opportunities) are available to them. To express it another way, career education is more interested in expanding students' experience than in expanding their catalog of facts.

The potential threat surrounding the amount of career information is matched by the implications of that information. The process of studying careers carries with it the implication that one must choose an occupation. Most adolescents are simply not prepared to make those choices. They resist making any sort of long-range commitments, because they are busily involved in trying to figure out their own potentials and their current relationships. It's unlikely that a youngster who has lived only twelve years can think very seriously—or very meaningfully—about the next thirty or forty years.

Career education seeks to minimize the threat of commitment by concentrating on the self-exploration component of career exploration. The career educator is more likely to ask (in discreet terms), "What did you learn about yourself from watching the plumber at work?" than "What did you learn about the plumber's job?" Obviously, the student must learn something about the plumber's job in order to learn about himself or herself, but in turning the question inward, the educator uses the natural self-interest of the adolescent years as a motivational force to help students expand their cognitive experiences in the world of work. And as simplistic as it may sound, the approach seems to work, according to the testimonies of many teachers who have tried it.

In addition to the self-interest approach, educators use other techniques to help students during the career exploration stage of career education. One technique is the on-site examination, the field trip. Educators want students to see workers on the job performing tasks which are part of the job in order that students might see relationships among tasks, jobs, careers, and functions. In order of priority, the manner in which a career educator would like students to "experience" careers is: first, with hands-on experience; second, with on-site visits and observation; third, with movies and other audiovisual materials to show actual work situations; and fourth, with books or written materials. (Naturally, some areas of the country are limited in the amount and types of on-site visits which can be made, and secondary sources must be used. For instance, students in the plains states may find it difficult to make a field trip to a shipyard, but they can experience a shipyard on film.)

A technique being given increasing attention is that of providing hands-on experiences for students. This is more likely to be available at the high school level than the junior high school level, but it is certainly an important technique for self-discovery and career exploration. Many parents can remember their own experiences in various "shop" classes or "homemaking" classes, but those courses form only a small portion of the new "hands-on" emphasis. In many cases, such programs at the high school level include actual work experience on the job, either as volunteers or as paid employees, and the range of careers which have been included in work experience programs cuts across all of the career clusters outlined above. For many reasons, hands-on experiences in the junior high school are more limited, but each year the opportunities for such experiences expand as more and more schools emphasize the hands-on approach and as more and more materials for classroom application become commercially available. As discussed previously, parents can supplement these hands-on experiences by providing varied work opportunities at home, and by encouraging students to participate in volunteer activities or to seek part-time work.

A final technique used for career exploration activities is to invite resource persons from outside the school to visit the classroom. The object is not to have formal lectures but to make information available from the source. Often these resource persons can bring the tools of their trade to the classroom for students to examine. Typically, students undertake preliminary study and discussion of the specific occupation involved in order that they might be prepared to ask questions. Teachers attempt to secure wide representation from the various career clusters, and they try to avoid career stereotyping insofar as possible. Parents who want to be involved in the education process and to assist with the career exploration stage of career education should not be reluctant to let teachers know about their own career experiences and their willingness to share those experiences.

Exploration—whether of careers or of self—is most productive if it can be channeled in the most meaningful directions. For this reason, educators try to guide students toward the kinds of information which will likely prove most meaningful to them. In the case of career exploration, the most valuable information for students tends to fall into three categories: (1) the life styles of workers, (2) training and entry requirements, and (3) current opportunities and job market outlook.

Careers and Life Style

"Life style" is a catch-all term used by career educators to describe activities related to one's career or job which are not necessarily a part of that career. It includes such things as the normal daily routine, the area of residence, the type of after-hours activities, the motivating factors surrounding the job, the level of supervision, the degree of family involvement, the geographical location, the kinds of friends, recreational activities, degree of community involvement, and so on. Certainly, economic status may have something to do with life style, but it is usually not as great an influence as many believe. For instance, a truck driver and a college professor may earn approximately the same annual income, but their life styles are likely to be quite different.

The truck driver travels a great deal, spends many hours alone, must adhere to a rigid schedule, and is responsible for costly equipment and goods. The professor travels little—although perhaps more widely—spends most of the working hours interacting with others, operates within a fairly flexible schedule, and is responsible for ideas instead of materials. The truck driver may seek recreation in such solitary sports as hunting and fishing, may look to television and movies for entertainment, and may find that traveling makes it difficult to take an active role in community affairs. The professor may look to the interaction of such competitive sports as tennis and handball for recreation, may prefer concerts and plays for entertainment, and may feel a need for involvement in community affairs.

Naturally, these are merely hypothetical examples. A serious study of the life styles of the two careers may provide quite different information. And certainly, there will be many exceptions to any "typical" life style. The point is not that a person selecting a specific career must adjust to the particular life style of that career; the point is that by examining various life styles, a student can learn a great deal about himself or herself, about the advantages and disadvantages of different careers, and about the kinds of people who tend to be attracted by particular careers. The student who examines the life style of a park ranger and finds that type of outdoor, solitary living to be appealing has certainly learned something about her or his own likes and dislikes. Conversely, the student who knows he or she prefers solitude can learn through the study of life styles that careers in politics or sales work will not be personally satisfying, no matter what other appeals those careers may have.

The study of life styles provides important indicators for those youngsters seeking identity. Parents and friends can help by increasing their own awareness of life styles, and by talking about careers as much in terms of life styles as in terms of duties, tasks, and abilities required. However, it is important to avoid making judgments about life styles. One life style is not necessarily any better than another; it is only different. A life style that is satisfying and meaningful to one may be dull and offensive to another. Most young people will eventually draw many elements of their own life styles from the life styles of their parents, but in the process they will want to examine and experiment with other life styles as part of the self-discovery process. Since children must select life styles based on their own needs, parents should avoid attaching value judgments which will simply add confusion to the already difficult task of selecting a career and a life style.

Training and Entry Requirements

Closely related to the examination of life style in career exploration is the examination of training and entry requirements for various careers. Most careers have well established "rules" for entry. Some of the rules are set by government. For example, in most states real estate brokers must obtain a license from the state which requires some sort of examination to demonstrate familiarity with real estate laws and finance. Some of the rules are set by labor unions. For instance, entry into the building trades unions often requires a period of apprenticeship, and successful pursuit of a career in one of those trades in many locations implies union membership. Some of the rules are set by professional or trade associations. For example, attorneys are licensed by the state, but the examination which governs the issuance of such licenses is administered by the state bar association. And some of the entry rules are set by tradition. For instance, it is traditional—but not always necessary— that those wishing to become college professors must first obtain doctoral degrees. One may argue with the reasonableness of these rules—and a few may even circumvent the system—but for the most part the rules have developed over a period of years and represent valid attempts to protect either the workers or society or both.

Because these training and entry requirements are such an integral part of most careers and the life styles associated with them, the examination of training and entry requirements is an important part of career exploration. The student who is interested in becoming a physician but who does not like school and does not do well in school should be aware that medical training requires up to ten years of post-high school education. The student who is examining himself or herself in relationship to a career as an airline pilot should include as part of the self-examination a consideration of his or her response to the many years of training required in less glamorous positions preparatory to assuming the role of captain for a major airline.

In addition to the type and length of training required for entry, the kinds of related information which might be useful to the student's own self-discovery process includes such factors as: specific skills or talents required, the geographic location of training facilities, whether or not training is available on a part-time basis or at night, the entry requirements for training institutions, the likely geographic location of entry-level positions, and the cost of training.

The Job Market and Employment Outlook

Still another area of information which might be examined during the career exploration stage is information about the job market and about the employment outlook in specific careers and career clusters. Students of middle/junior high school age do not need much information about the job market, but sometimes such information can be useful. For example, the student who has an interest in noise abatement may be encouraged by the fact that employment opportunities in that field will likely expand greatly during the next few years. (This example may be somewhat romantic, since adolescents appear to have more interest in noise creation than in noise abatement.) The student with an interest in mechanics may be able to channel that interest toward a growing specialty rather than a dying one if he or she knows something about the outlook for job opportunities in various mechanical fields.

However, parents, teachers, and students should remember that the labor market changes constantly. The outlook will certainly be different by the time the junior high school student is graduated from high school or from post-high school institutions. The study of labor market trends can be useful, but any in-depth study of job opportunities at this stage is probably superfluous. Even the study of relative numbers of workers and the competition for job openings is probably not helpful at this stage. Students need support and encouragement much more than they need the facts of statistical probability. If they are to be successful in their exploration of self, they should not be discouraged by the establishment of artificial boundaries to that exploration. The young lady who dreams of being an anchor woman for television network news should not be discouraged from examining that career avenue simply because the odds for success are so miniscule. Career education's primary goal for that young lady is to help her learn more about herself through career exploration. She will have time to learn about the realities of the job market later. Besides, the chances that she will continue to pursue a career selected in junior high school are about as small as the chances that she will land that network news position. The adolescent years are years of exploration, not years of commitment.

The same is true for all aspects of the career exploration process: The goal is not to force the youngster into narrow fields of consideration but to keep the exploration broadly based, to encourage the examination of all career clusters and many specific careers, to spread before the child as many opportunities for self-discovery as possible. This whole process is actually a prelude to decision making. In the terminology of the computer age, it seeks to "expand the data base" in two directions at once. The first and most important direction is that of self-knowledge. The second direction is that of knowledge about career opportunities, and it is a natural byproduct of the career education approach to self-discovery.

Research Into Specific Careers

We have implied above that examination of the career clusters inevitably leads to a certain amount of research into specific career opportunities. The process of narrowing from career cluster to general field within the cluster to specific occupation within the field is unavoidable. Most of us—especially junior high school students—prefer to deal with specifics rather than generalities. Many career educators resist this tendency on the part of students to restrict their own career exploration activities to narrow fields, feeling that such restriction limits the potential for self-exploration. Certainly, this is a valid point of view, and every effort should be made to keep the exploration broadly based. However, the specifics are bound to be more exciting, more accessible, and more meaningful to students than the generalities. The most realistic stance might be to simply resist the tendency to narrow, not to prohibit it.

Students who want to study specific occupations can profitably do so, so long as the primary goal remains one of self-exploration. Other students can benefit through class discussion and similar "sharing" practices. Some educators who encourage students to research specific occupations require that students select at least two different occupations from two different career clusters. One positive value to be achieved from research into specific occupations is that it provides a subject for research which is relevant to student interests, and while they are learning about the occupation itself they are also learning something about simple research methods. They may also be required to write a paper or deliver a verbal report to the class, both of which are additional learning experiences.

The important thing for parents and teachers to keep in mind is that whatever research is assigned should be directed primarily toward the student's own process of self-exploration. Whatever the student learns about a specific career should be turned inward to produce some scrap of self-knowledge. While this may sound complicated, it is not, because the major thrust of the student's intellectual curiosity at this age is toward attempts to classify himself or herself. All the parent or teacher must do to facilitate the process is to allow the student sufficient leeway so that the natural impulse may operate. Avoid emphasis on the acquisition of "facts" about careers; stress the importance of the students' personal reactions to work situations and job-related activities. This can probably best be done by emphasizing the three categories of information discussed above: (1) the life style associated with the occupation or career, (2) the training and entry requirements for the occupation, and (3) the job market outlook for the occupation. (As mentioned earlier, the job market outlook is the least important of the three categories, and it should be considered only in a general sense.)

The main effort in asking a youngster to do research about a specific occupation should be to encourage the student to extend her or his efforts beyond the normal information gathering activities of home and school. Every youngster sees many workers in work situations during the course of daily activities. A child involved in a good career education program will begin to see those workers from a different perspective. He or she will notice the clothing (uniform) worn by workers, the nature of individual tasks being performed, the ratio of physical to mental effort, the amount of interchange with others, the degree of supervision imposed, the conditions of the work environment, and the satisfaction—or lack thereof—evidenced by the workers.

Of course, thousands of occupations are not easily observed. They take place inside factories, or in office buildings, or in other special facilities which students are not likely to visit. Both parents and teachers can help students expand their career exploration horizons by encouraging the use of four simple teaching techniques: personal interviews with workers, reading, hands-on experience, and visits to work locations. A number of good film introductions to occupations are available in schools and libraries, including at least one series based on the cluster system and titled "The Working Worlds."

The value of having resource persons visit the classroom has been discussed above. In addition, if students are doing research about careers, part of the research should certainly be person-to-person inteviews with workers involved in those careers. Those interviews should occur at the place of work, if possible. Guests in the home may prove to be rich sources of career information for young members of the family. A few minutes of discussion about work and life style is not an imposition on any guest. It is a good way to involve young members of the family in the conversation, and guests often consider it flattering to be asked about their work.

Reading material is another good source of career information. Most libraries are expanding their resources in the career field in response to the popularity of career education. Some school districts are establishing career information centers, where they gather and catalog a wide range of such materials. But reading about careers need not be confined strictly to books and articles designed for career information. Novels, magazines, and newspapers are all full of information about careers and life styles, once the reader is able to recognize that information.

By the time children reach the adolescent years, they have already acquired a considerable amount of hands-on experience with work. Most have grown up doing "chores" around the house, and many have participated in other types of work experience. Those experiences should be expanded as part of the career exploration process. Obviously, children cannot "play" with complex equipment. But they can experience the "feel" of various tools. They can work with a parent on household accounting or income tax preparation. They can change a tire or replace a worn-out washer in a leaking faucet. In the process of interviewing workers for career research, students will often find an opportunity to try their hand at a task. All these hands-on experiences expand the young person's knowledge of his or her own interests and capabilities at the same time that they expand his or her knowledge of the world of work.

Finally, the value of visits to work locations cannot be overstated. Even though the adolescent child may appear bored or indifferent on such occasions, his or her whole orientation is toward absorbing the new experiences and new sensations which are an inherent part of moving about in the environment. Field trips have become an important part of career exploration in most schools. The keys to a successful visit are: (1) orientation before the trip in order to provide some guidance about what to look for, and (2) some sort of discussion following the visit to bring out student impressions of the experience. From the standpoint of career education, the important things to consider are the individual tasks involved in the job, the functional relation-ship of the job to other careers and to a career cluster, the life style of the workers, the work environment, and the attitudes of workers.

CAREER SELECTION

The subject of career selection is included here only because it is a natural byproduct of the career exploration process. As has been emphasized previously, any career selections by the student of middle/junior high school age are purely tentative. Several studies have indicated that even though students may have selected careers prior to entering high school, those choices have a high probability of changing before high school graduation. Career decision making and career preparation activities are more likely to occur during the high school years or later. In fact, there is some evidence that most firm occupation decisions occur as late as the mid 20s. (Those two subjects are discussed in the following chapters.) Career exploration is a prelude to decision making and career preparation, and if exploration is extensive the chances for good decision making are improved, as are the chances for career success.

With the complete understanding that most career selections by adolescents are tentative, we nevertheless strongly advocate that teachers and parents support the child in those decisions. The decisions will probably change from time to time, and some youngsters may not make any decisions at all, but the child who does make a career selection is likely to be serious about it. He or she is testing his or her own commitment to ideas and to goals. The youngster is looking for indicators of personal characteristics and may use career selection as a tool for that search. Wise parents avoid making judgments about career selections or about the youngster's ability to participate in specific occupations. Instead, parents should ask questions which might lead to self-knowledge: Do you know someone in that line of work? Can you tell me about the kinds of tasks involved in that occupation? How does one acquire training for that job? Which part of the work do you think you would like most?

Parents and teachers should show interest in the career selections of middle/junior high school students. Positive responses will encourage the youngster to study the occupation more thoroughly and to examine his or her own reaction to that occupation more seriously. Parents can also learn a great deal about their own children by watching the career selections made by the child and by encouraging communication concerning those selections. If every selection is met by skepticism or negative value judgments, the child will soon learn not to communicate. On the other hand, if selections are greeted with encouragement and support, the child will probably gain more benefit from the process itself and will likely share future decision-making activities with parents and others.

A youngster has a better chance of making good lifetime career choices if he or she has the help of others during this important self-exploration period. The flexibility of the modern job market indicates that career selection is a process which will be repeated several times during each person's life. Patterns established during the adolescent years will repeat in later years. Career exploration and career selection coupled with self-exploration is a meaningful pattern for career development.

SUMMARY

Career exploration is the second stage in the career development process. It fits naturally into the middle/junior high school years, because its goals are harmonious with the natural developmental patterns of children. The middle/junior high school years are characterized by self-exploration, and career education couples that need for self-knowledge with a structured system for exploring the world of work. Thus, career exploration becomes a tool for self-exploration.

One possible approach to the structuring of the world of work is the career cluster system. This allows youngsters to explore careers from a functional point of view and avoids some of the problems inherent in traditional hierarchical methods of structuring. The cluster approach seeks to eliminate divisions based on "status," as well as career stereotyping based on sex, race, or handicapping conditions.

In a typical career exploration program, youngsters learn to organize the world of work into functional clusters, they examine each of the clusters in ways that are non-threatening, they do some research into specific occupations, and they may or may not select personal career goals. The purpose is not to learn specific information about each occupation so much as it is to learn about one's self in relation to various careers. For this reason, career exploration is concerned with three kinds of information: life styles of workers, training and entry requirements for occupations, and job market outlook for general career types.

Career selections made during the middle/junior high school years are subject to considerable change. Most youngsters are not goal oriented at that age. However, the selections are important to the youngster as part of the self-exploration process, and they deserve support by parents and teachers.

ADDITIONAL READING

Evans, Rupert N.; Hoyt, Kenneth B.; and Mangum, Garth L. *Career Education in the Middle/Junior High School.* Salt Lake City: Olympus Publishing Company, 1973.

Flores, T., and Olsen, L. "Stability and Realism of Occupational Aspiration in Eighth and Twelfth Grade Males," *Vocational Guidance Quarterly* (1967), vol. 16.

Gribbons, Warren D., and Lohnes, P. *Emerging Careers.* New York: Teachers College Press, Columbia University, 1968.

Havighurst, Robert J. *Human Development and Education.* New York: David McKay Co., Inc., 1953.

Hollender, John. "Development of Vocational Decisions during Adolescence," *Journal of Counseling Psychology* (1971), vol. 18.

Hoyt, Kenneth B.; Evans, Rupert N.; Mackin, Edward F.; and Mangum, Garth L. *Career Education: What It Is and How to Do It.* Salt Lake City: Olympus Publishing Company, 1974.

Inhelder, Barbara, and Piaget, Jean. *The Growth of Logical Thinking from Childhood to Adolescence.* New York: Basic Books, Inc., 1958.

Osipow, Samuel H. "Implications for Career Education of Research and Theory on Career Development." Paper prepared for the National Conference on Career Education for Deans of Colleges of Education. Columbus, Ohio: Center for Vocational and Technical Education, Ohio State University, 1972.

Super, Donald E., and Overstreet, P. *The Vocational Maturity of Ninth-Grade Boys.* New York: Teachers College Press, Columbia University, 1960.

CHAPTER SEVEN

Decision Making

Throughout most of history and for most individuals the problems of career decision making have been few. There were a limited number of careers from which to choose; social, geographic, and skill mobility were minimal; and most persons had career choices "imposed" on them from outside forces. This was especially true of women. However, the picture has changed considerably, as discussed in previous chapters. Today, an extremely wide range of career opportunities is open to virtually every individual.

This may be both a blessing and a curse. It is indeed fortunate to have so many choices, but it also can become extremely confusing and frustrating trying to decide which of all these career alternatives to select. And complicating the circumstances even more is the rapidly changing nature of the world of work. What is true today with regard to career opportunities may very well change in the near future, and so an intelligent choice today may prove to be an unfortunate choice by the time the necessary skills are acquired. But while unemployment rates are high among all workers, they are especially high among young people who are unskilled and unprepared to enter the work force. Thus, education and training are vital if one wants to be employed. But the question is: What kind of education and what types of training ought one to pursue? That requires a decision. Each step along the road to a career requires decisions, and never before has it been more difficult to make them or more crucial to have effective decision-making skills.

THE IMPORTANCE OF MAKING DECISIONS

In a sense, maturation is a process of learning to make independent decisions. An infant makes no decisions; every act is a reaction to a stimulus. A mature adult makes decisions constantly: what to wear, what to eat, how to use time, how to react to various individuals and various situations, how to act, what to think about, when to think, how to think. The pressure of decision making is never totally absent from the mature adult's consciousness. (Even when one decides not to decide, one has made a decision.)

What happens between that no-decision state of infancy and that constant-decision state of maturity? We learn how to make decisions. We learn it whether we want to or not. Learning to make decisions is as inevitable as growing old. The question is: Do we learn good decision-making techniques or bad decision-making techniques? In fact, the question may be even broader than that, because no decision-making technique can guarantee "right" decisions. The goal is to reduce the number of "poor" decisions and to increase the likelihood of productive decisions. Thus, the real secret to decision making is not so much how one makes a decision as what one does with the decision once it is made. It is a matter of developing sufficient confidence in one's own decision-making ability so that one can make intelligent (not necessarily "right") decisions easily, can act on those decisions with commitment, can accept the problems occasioned by "poor" decisions without feeling personally threatened, and if necessary can commit to a revised decision with the same confidence as in the first instance.

The transition from the childhood state of total decision-making dependence to the mature state of decision-making independence is a slow and gradual process. It takes place over many years. One author maintains that the process begins the first time the child says "No" to his or her parents—and all parents know that the word "no" is one of the words children learn first. Until that time, the child is but an extension of his or her parents, existing at their will and by their command. The first "no" is a sign of beginning independence, a signal that an individual has arrived in the house, and that the new individual is beginning the process of separating his or her own will from the will of parents. It is a good sign, even though it may be difficult for parents. It is the beginning of what management consultant Peter Drucker calls "organized self-obsolescence." It is a sign that parents should *begin* the long process of phasing themselves out of the child's life insofar as decision-making dependence is concerned. This should not be a threatening prospect for parents, for it is a process that will take many years to develop fully. When the process is completed, parents will not be left out of the child's life but will merely enter into an important new role, one that is different from the dependence role of childhood but just as essential to the mature adult the child has become.

This transition can be less painful and much more effective if there is a decisive, planned approach for children to start very young to assume responsibility for decision making, with that responsibility increasing as the child grows. It is comforting to parents to know that decision making can be taught as effectively as any other skill. And since decision making is an underlying foundation of virtually all behavior, the development of good decision-making skills will contribute immeasurably to whether a person has a successful, happy life.

Career-related Decisions

We are concerned here with those decisions which are related to career development and career activity. While they may constitute a small portion of the total number of decisions made during a lifetime, they are decisions which are important beyond their numbers. In fact, career-related decisions will certainly establish preconditions for many of the other decisions an individual must make. That is one of the primary characteristics of decision making—that no decision is totally independent, that each decision is conditioned somewhat by decisions made previously, and that future decisions will be somewhat preconditioned by decisions made in the present. In other words, decisions are like building blocks: Each new decision rests on decisions constructed earlier, and attempts to seriously alter earlier decisions may cause whole sections of the structure to collapse.

This concept has tremendous implications for parents. By the time a young adult reaches the stage of making serious career decisions, he or she will have declared independence from the decision-making influence of parents. But the foundations for those critical career decisions will have been laid by decisions made early in childhood, at a time when parents had great influence over the child's decisions.

Figure 5 shows a highly simplified graphic presentation of this process by comparing it to travel down a path with many intersecting alternatives. As the child grows, he or she makes decisions about which paths to follow. Literally thousands of alternative paths are available; the illustration shows only a few key junctions. The kinds of work attitudes and values the child "decides" to accept in early childhood determine to some extent the kinds of work habits the child can choose during the elementary school years. The "choice" of work habits preconditions the way the child will look at the world of work during the career exploration phase, since that phase involves self-exploration as much as it does career exploration. The careers which interest the child in high school are conditioned by how well those careers mesh with the child's own work values and habits. Success—if defined to include happiness—is determined to a great extent by how well each of the decisions along the path "fits" with all of the previous decisions. Some observers call this "congruence theory," but it seems more appropriate to call it "common sense."

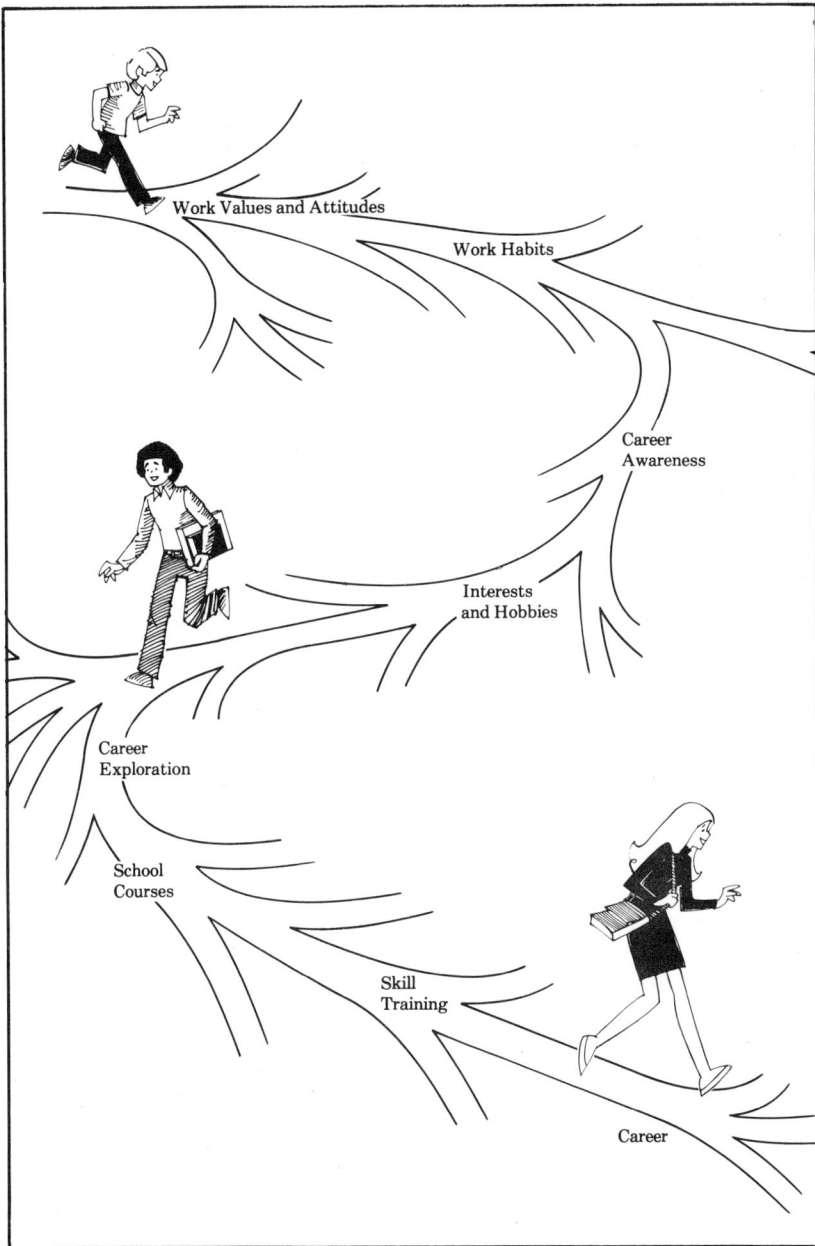

FIGURE 5. Independently made career decisions
are conditioned by career-related
decisions made earlier in life.

The reader will also recognize the fact that as the child moves along this path of career-related decisions, the degree of direct influence from parents diminishes. Parents directly influence work value decisions, almost to the point of imposing them on children. On the other hand, parents have little direct influence over the career plans of high school age children. Parents may serve as advisers or counselors, but they can rarely make direct career decisions for their children. The path in the illustration, then, also represents a growing independence in the decision-making process, as well as the child's increasing skill in decision making.

Remember that we said earlier that an important part of decision making was the self-confidence of the decision maker. Couple these two concepts, and you can begin to see that parents can significantly affect the decision-making skills of their children by beginning decision training early and by encouraging children to develop independence in decision making. Imagine these two situations. In the first instance, the eight-year-old child comes to her father and laments: "I don't have anything to do. None of my friends are home. What can I do?"

The father makes a decision based on his own needs: "Clean up your room. It's a mess."

For the sake of making a point, assume that the child does what she is told. She cleans up her room and is no longer bored ... for a few minutes. Then she must return to her father for further instructions, because she has gained nothing in the transaction insofar as decision making is concerned.

Another child approaches her father with the same lament. She's bored and doesn't know what to do. The second father takes a moment from what he is doing and replies: "Well, let's see if we can think of something."

The two discuss the problem for a few minutes. They develop a list of five acceptable activities, including going out to play alone, cleaning up the room, reading a book, playing with crayons and paper in the house, or taking a nap. Then the father says: "I'd like it if you would clean up your room, but all those other things would be fun, too. Why don't you pick one?"

Assume once again that the child decides to clean up the room. When she is finished, the father takes time to compliment her on a good job. She then has some other alternatives she can pursue without bothering him again. More importantly, she has made a decision. She has selected from alternatives. And she feels good about her decision. She has acquired a little of the self-confidence that she will need to make other decisions, many of them more important than what to do on a lonely afternoon.

Which child has a better chance of making good decisions when father isn't around to pose alternatives and to "influence" the results?

The example illustrates how parents can help their children acquire decision-making skills. It also illustrates some of the factors involved in decision making. A decision is the selection of one course of action from among several alternatives. If a person has no choices available or is unaware of choices, there is no decision to be made. Before a person can set about making a decision, he or she must be aware of its necessity and importance and must be aware of the nature and condition of the alternatives.

The Right to Choose

To develop effective decision-making skills, each child should have some freedom to choose. The child should have alternatives from which to choose, should understand what the alternatives are and what they imply, and should have the freedom to do things in his or her own way. The child should also take responsibility for the decisions and the actions that follow. That means that the child must be given the authority which goes with decision making. Finally, the child must receive recognition for those things he or she achieves as a result of making adequate decisions.

However, just as each of us learns to exercise independence and autonomy, we must likewise understand that we are subject to certain sources of authority which provide both control and direction. This is true in the family, in school, and in life, as well as in the world of work and every other phase of our society.

For example, each home has certain chores which must be done in order to have harmonious family life. The completion of such chores usually requires some combination of individual decision making and direction by authority. One family met together periodically to discuss the various work tasks and to decide upon an allocation of responsibilities. They began by making a list of the necessary tasks. The list included such things as:

Wash breakfast dishes

Wash dinner dishes

Make beds

Clean bedrooms

Vacuum or clean carpets

Put away clean clothes

Prepare breakfast

Clean bathrooms

Take out the garbage

Mow the lawn

In family council the list was presented for consideration, and it was made clear that everyone was expected to do a share of the work. Through discussion, everyone decided that making beds and cleaning bedrooms was the responsibility of whomever occupied the bedroom. Other jobs to be done were to be chosen by the various family members. It was also jointly decided how long a person would have a given job so no one was "stuck" with a particularly undesirable job indefinitely. Age and ability were discussed, and the relative difficulty of the jobs was assessed. After each person had a reasonable time to consult with other family members, to think over the various jobs, and to decide upon her or his choices, each was allowed to make requests. Obviously some negotiation was needed, but a prime factor was for each family member—especially the parents—to listen to each child and the reasons for making choices.

When the decisions had been made and agreement reached as to who would perform which tasks, each child was given freedom to decide how and when to do the work, so long as it met the family needs. The responsibility for following through on commitments was also left to the person involved, but there were obvious natural pressures which developed. For example, if the person who was to prepare breakfast or to put away clean clothes did not follow through, family members were quick to let them know about it. It is important to note that parental involvement was necessary, not only to provide motivation in whatever form needed to encourage completion of assignments, but also to praise and appropriately reward excellence in performance.

For most parents, the goals for their children include the following:

(1) *To develop competence*—learning to reason things out, learning useful skills, developing the ability to make a contribution to the world

(2) *To learn to manage emotions*—to control anger, hate, and other impulses; to feel and show love and concern for others at appropriate times; to establish satisfying relationships with friends, family, employers, and fellow workers

(3) *To develop autonomy*—learning to stand on their own two feet, to think for themselves and to set and accomplish goals of personal meaning (Chickering, 1969)

Central to the capacity to grow in these ways will be the degree to which the child has learned decision-making skills. Each person is the sum total of the decisions he or she has made.

For most children, decision making is likely to be impulsive, emotional, and short sighted. Children alternate among a variety of moods, and they seem least likely to seek help precisely at those times when they need help the most. In other words, children tend to react to situations rather than acting upon situations. Reactive decision making is quite normal and natural for children, since they are still in the process of developing the capacity to see situations in context, to consider the events which led up to the situation, and to assess the long-term implications as well as the short-term results of various alternatives. In fact, for very young children it is difficult to imagine that alternatives other than the reactive impulse actually exist, let alone to consider the merits of those alternatives.

But for most parents, the fact that children make impulsive decisions can be disturbing. They wonder how a child who can't even be trusted to take out the garbage on schedule will ever be responsible enough to help make correct decisions about the world's food problem, or about which occupation to select, or about how to vote in a national election. Of course, one doesn't trust a child to make those decisions; one trusts a mature adult who has developed some decision-making skills. And every child will develop those skills as part of the growing process. Some will develop better decision-making skills than others, just as some will develop better carpentry skills than others. The important thing for parents to remember is that they have all the resources necessary to help children effect a positive transformation from reactive decision making to considered decision making. Parents need only to understand something about the process and institute some sort of plan to support the transformation.

COMMON PROBLEMS IN DECISION MAKING

Children need opportunities to make decisions and to carry those decisions to conclusions with the accompanying results. As we said above, this necessitates freedom to choose, and that means children will make some mistakes and experience some failures, together with the successes. Some parents tend to be too protective. They have a tendency to say "No" to their children unless they can think of some strong justification for saying "Yes." This often will have a stifling effect upon children insofar as concerns their ability to become creative in the decision-making process. Routinely saying "No" seems to give children the message: "You made a poor choice. You don't have good judgment."

In order to reverse this tendency, parents must make a decision themselves. They must consciously decide to avoid saying "No" unless there is a strong reason to do so. This means that before giving their own decision, parents must take a little time to think about whether "Yes" or "No" is the appropriate answer. In other words, parents must also avoid the reactive decisions. When that time comes, there need not be an ensuing power struggle. Instead, the parent needs to try to see the child's point of view, and at the same time help the child to see the parent's point of view. The two parties should try to agree in as many aspects as possible, not allowing one point of disagreement to blow the whole issue out of perspective. Then the parties will need to follow the process which is a vital part of career choice and decision making for every person; namely, optimization. This means a series of manipulations and compromises to bring the optimum solution. There is in this process the element of deciding while also being subject to certain societal rules. There is also the element that each time you make a decision you gain some things and give up others. The person must ask: "Is the reward or payoff I get for making this decision worth more to me than what I am giving up?"

Becoming Aware of Decisions

Like it or not, we are thrust into decision making as a way of life. Unfortunately, people often are unaware that this decision making is taking place. To become consciously aware of what is happening is a major step—aware in terms of the choice to be made, the context in which the choice will be made, and the payoffs.

Decisions often will bring disappointments, hurt feelings, failures, pain, and misunderstanding. As we experience the agony of defeat or the humiliation of failure, we are thrust into a decision-making mode. This may be in the form of deciding to succeed next time or some other future time, to immediately fight back in either offensive or defensive ways, or to give up and withdraw. Such devices as rationalization, pretended or real disinterest, self-justification, or renewed determination and participation are evidenced. In any case, a decision is reached by the participant to behave in a specific manner. This must be recognized.

This same process holds true with regard to career-related decisions. Some decisions will bring disappointment, forcing the individual into a new decision-making situation. The individual must then find a way to "live with" the earlier decision, either through self-blame or through some justification rationale. Parents can provide early support mechanisms to ease the difficulties which come with disappointment. First, parents can treat the decisions their children make with full respect, so that the child begins to develop the self-confidence necessary to overcome occasional mistaken decisions. Second, parents can give their children sufficient decision-making opportunities so that they experience disappointment during the early years when there are supportive backup mechanisms available, and so that they learn to deal with those disappointments as easily as they deal with the successes. Third, parents can help children build their own backup mechanisms by providing them with a sufficiently wide range of interests so that no "loss" is ever cataclysmic. These interests have their foundations in early childhood, and it is during that period when parents should ask themselves questions about the following items.

Artistic creative pursuits—Should the child invest time and effort in learning to play an instrument, learning to sing, learning to dance, learning to draw or paint, learning to write well, learning to express herself or himself publicly, or learning to create using manual crafts? Skill in one or more of these areas could pay off in one's later career in terms of confidence, social relationships, poise under stress, and so on. There is also some evidence that artistic activity can increase one's creativity, which could add immeasurably to success in certain careers.

Athletic activities—Should the child participate in organized sports? If so, which sports? How much time and money should be invested? Career-related benefits from athletics might include learning teamwork, learning perseverance, and setting and reaching goals. One family recognized a flair for gymnastics in their four-year-old son, and the parents enrolled him in a private instruction program. They provided encouragement, but allowed him to decide whether or not to continue. Part of their agreement was that he use a small amount from his allowance to help pay for the lessons. Important lessons in deciding how to use one's resources were thereby taught.

Service pursuits—What opportunities exist in the neighborhood or family for the child to learn service to others, unselfishness, compassion for the disadvantaged, and respect for others? Organized youth programs often provide opportunities for service, or alert parents can instigate projects on their own to encourage children to reach out to help others. Deciding to use time in these activities can be a source for learning important lessons in responsibility for others, which is the essence of leadership. And capacity for leadership is a vital ingredient in career advancement.

Social activities—What kinds of social interactions will be best for the child? Will she or he become confident in social situations before meeting a prospective employer? What opportunities will come up for learning to plan and implement social activities with others, which involves myriad decision-making opportunities?

Hobbies—In *Lives in Progress*, Robert White describes the actual case history of a man whom he called Hartley Hale. At an early age, Hartley demonstrated great interest in creating and inventing with his hands. He failed in an attempt to construct a perpetual motion machine, but he succeeded in building model airplanes and radio sets. His enthusiasm and precision in working with his hands were later expressed through a successful career as a surgeon, using his hands to reconstruct human anatomy and to design orthopedic appliances for handicapped persons.

This hobby might have expressed itself in any number of ways, from automotive mechanic to electronic engineer. Another possibility is that the hobby might not be expressed as part of one's vocation, but would be a rewarding and rejuvenating aspect of one's leisure time.

The point is that one's choice of hobby almost always provides clues to one's interests, which is one important component of deciding which career will be most rewarding. Another valuable aspect of pursuing a hobby is that it offers practical experience in decision making. The child must decide how much time and energy to give to the hobby, how to obtain the necessary resources, how to get help from others. . . . The list is endless, but each item has its career decision counterpart.

Money—As in other areas of life, in the area of a decision making, money is a vehicle of learning. The common saying that money burns a hole in some people's pockets is probably true to some degree of all of us, including children. Having money calls for action in doing something with it, which is to say that it calls for decisions. Those decisions involve how to obtain funds, as well as what to do with them. Parents can help by making sure children learn about the various sources and uses of money.

Work experience—The importance of decision making in this area is crucial in two ways: In helping to decide later which career to pursue, and in gaining practical experience in the decision-making process. The process of deciding which job to take is similar to deciding which hobby to pursue, but there are more constraints placed on the decision. The job must be something within the child's ability and must be a currently available opportunity. Upon taking the job, the child quickly learns that if he or she has chosen something within his or her interests he or she will be happier than if the choice was outside the area of interest. Work experience also requires the child to make daily on-the-job decisions that affect performance.

One woman who now is a successful professional recalls as a child the necessity of deciding whether to work part time after school in a grocery store. Her parents wisely decided to allow her to make the final decision, but took advantage of the opportunity to discuss with her other ways in which she might use the time and to suggest the restrictions which working would put on her, as well as to discuss the monetary advantages and work experience advantages. They also suggested that she talk to a neighbor who was a successful lawyer about the decision in order to obtain a different perspective.

Her final decision, which she made after several days of deliberation, was to turn down the job, to work during the summer to earn extra money, and to use the time to pursue extracurricular activities at school. The experience thus gained in work with student government, the school literary magazine, and athletics was not only an enjoyable use of time, but it tipped the scales in her favor when she applied for a scholarship to college.

When to Help and When Not to Help

Central to success in training a child in decision making is the ability to recognize whether or not the child needs help and how much help to offer. At one extreme, offering too much help is stifling; at the other extreme, not offering enough help is negligence.

An example that comes readily to mind would be the opportunity to help a child learn to play a musical instrument. The overbearing parent, without consulting the child, would decide for the child whether or not he or she even wanted to learn to play. The parent would decide what kind of instrument the child should play and would arrange for the lessons. The child would not be given a chance to participate in the decision process. On the other hand, the negligent parent would simply not be aware of the opportunities available for music lessons or instruments or would not recognize the child's desires or talents musically.

These are extremes, and most parents would fall somewhere in the middle, where there is room for a broad range of approaches, depending on the child. The moderate parent would be alert to the advent of the decision on the part of the child whether or not to learn to play an instrument. The decision will come at different times for different children. Some might be interested at age seven, others at age seventeen, and others not at any age.

One possible parent strategy might be to expose the child to different instruments and their uses. A visit to a music store that sells various instruments, combined with listening to different concerts (preferably live), might be a good combination. The next step would be to get an instrument into the child's hands for awhile, perhaps on a rental basis so the child can try it. Other than arranging for instruction and providing some encouragement, the parent's task would be to help the child decide how much of a commitment he or she would want to make.

This is not the only possible approach. Some children have thanked their parents in later years for making them practice the piano when they were younger. Others have vowed they will never touch a piano again because of the way their parents made them practice. The approach depends on the child's needs, and sometimes a heavy hand is needed in the beginning. The important thing is that the child be made aware of alternatives, and that the child be allowed to change his or her mind if the decision later appears to be wrong.

Paradoxically, a child needs parental help both less often and more often than most parents think. By less often we mean that many times a parent will be tempted to jump into the situation and make the decision for the child in order to save her or him the excruciating pain of choice. This temptation becomes especially acute when the child seems to be tending toward the wrong decision. In most such situations, the best thing to do is stand back and let the child experience the consequences.

It is a truism that experience is the best teacher. Making decisions for the child is in effect robbing her or him of experience and retarding decision-making growth.

Allowing the child to gain the experience of making decisions for herself or himself—and knowing the consequences—is analagous to saving money in the bank. Saving money involves making a small sacrifice now (going without the luxury of having parents make decisions for her or him) in order to be able to enjoy the strength later on of confidently and wisely making her or his own decisions.

On the other hand, the child needs parental help more often than parents think in the sense that there are countless ways parents can turn situations that seem to have nothing to do with decision making into actual decision-making learning situations. Skill in doing so will provide repeated opportunities for growth.

Developmental counseling theory, which is concerned with how normal people grow and develop in decision-making skills as well as in other ways, provides instructive insight in this regard. The research associated with this theory suggests that the process of growth is not simply a function of learning or simply a function of normal maturation processes. The growth process also depends on a third variable, the environment. Growth occurs as the child learns and matures and interacts with the environment. The parent can be of help more often by being aware of the readiness of the child to learn, of the current level of maturity of the child, and of the way the environment can be structured to increase learning and maturity. The opportunity to structure the environment may come up more often than most parents think, allowing them to help more often than they might think.

STEPS IN THE DECISION-MAKING PROCESS

Research has shown that an effective procedure for decision making consists of four basic steps:

(1) Clarify the problem

(2) Consider the alternatives

(3) Choose and use one alternative

(4) Evaluate and revise

Step One—Clarify the Problem

John Dewey has said: "A problem well stated is half solved." Even if Dewey may be overstating the case, he helps us see the importance of accurately understanding the problem to be solved.

One of the major deterrents to effective problem solving is the tendency to pass judgment, make a decision, and embark on a course of action before the true nature of the problem is understood. Peter Drucker says that the effective decision maker always assumes that the event that clamors for attention is a symptom, and that the best procedure is to find the root or generic problem so as to avoid spending time solving the symptom alone. An example of this would be for parents and a child to assume that the decision to be made is what classes to take in school. Upon further scrutiny it becomes evident that the root or generic problem is choosing long-term goals so that the symptomatic problem of deciding on this semester's classes is to help prepare the child for life and not just to fill up a schedule.

If the base or root problem is found, then many subsequent problems which are symptomatic will be seen in perspective and in relation to this generic problem. The decision made will not be so difficult, and a routinized procedure can occur. For example, if the choosing of classes for a given semester is seen as crucial in career preparation, then each succeeding semester's choices are made with that in mind. Being able to understand problems to be solved or decisions to be made in root terms enables one to generalize from one to many situations and thus routinizes what may be otherwise time-consuming and frustrating dilemmas.

Step Two—Consider the Alternatives

It is important to generate as many alternatives as possible and to clearly consider all the advantages and disadvantages in order that acceptance or rejection can be done effectively. "Brainstorming" either alone or with others is a commonly used technique here. Creative and original approaches are useful to consider, as well as the traditional tried-and-proven approaches. Consulting with others who are in a similar circumstances also is useful and effective.

While generating various alternatives is important, one should not become so involved as to go on *ad infinitum* seeing other ways or ideas and deferring progress toward the narrowing process of settling on the decision.

Step Three—Choose and Use One Alternative

Making the decision or settling on one alternative can occur in many different ways, any of which can be effective.

A logical comparison of alternatives can be made by listing them on a sheet of paper and then rating each of them in various categories, such as likes, practicality, chance of succeeding, financial rewards, acceptance by others, and so on. Another approach is to ask others to rate the alternatives and then react to their responses.

In the final analysis, consideration must also be given to how the individual concerned feels about the choice. Although at times logic may tell one the choice should be one thing, the final decision might well be something different because the person cannot *feel* comfortable about it otherwise. Some good questions to ask oneself are: If I make this decision what are the things I get? Do I feel good about them? What things will I have to give up? Am I willing to give them up? If I have to live with this decision for a long time, am I willing to do so? How does this decision fit with my present life style? How will my loved ones accept this decision, and how do I feel about that?

There are no fool-proof decisions. Thus, every decision contains an element of risk. We grow through risking, through trying new things, and parents are in a key position to encourage sensible risking. If a child is considering a decision where there is an element of risk involved, the parent might wonder: What would be the chances of succeeding in this choice? Do all concerned understand the risk? Are all concerned willing to take the risk? Would it be better to find another alternative with a lower risk factor? Will this decision benefit my child?

Drucker notes that " . . . the most time-consuming step in the process is not making the decision but putting it into effect." Unless a decision has "degenerated into work," it is not a decision; it is at best a good intention. This means that, while the effective decision itself is based on the highest level of conceptual understanding, the action to carry it out should be as close as possible to the working level and as simple as possible.

But while implementing the plan is difficult, it also can be the most exciting part of decision making. The idea is to crystalize a specific plan making it very clear what is to be done and why. The plan must be realistic and do-able, taking into account the realization that new behavior is usually difficult and awkward. With any plan, there will almost surely be some false starts and some failures. Too often people tend to try a plan, and if something goes wrong they give up. It is the "all or nothing" syndrome. One must learn to accept partial successes or even temporary failures as victories. Successful people realize that final success is usually built upon many minor successes and failures. It is for this reason that a successful plan must include not only a long-range or ultimate goal but also intermediate goals, short-term goals, and mini-actions. One must include room for growth and for variations, modifications, and adjustments. The key is to be flexible, but not wishy-washy.

Probably the most important element of all in implementing the decision process is to truly decide—to be committed. One must confidently feel: "This is my decision, and now I will do it?" Then one must act according to the decision, even if at first it seems clumsy.

Step Four—Evaluation and Revision

After carrying out the plan, it is important to look realistically at what has happened and see if the decision was good or bad. Questions to be asked may include: What has happened as a result of this decision? Did I do what I said I would? Why, or why not? Do I need to change the decision, revise it, or abandon it?

OTHER METHODS OF DECISION MAKING

A word is in order here about alternative methods of decision making. The foregoing four-step process might be called the scientific decision-making process. Indeed, it is an application to the decision-making process of the same scientific method that has successfully produced the enormous array of technological advances that fill modern life with desirable alternative choices. Obviously, it is not the only method of decision making that might be appropriate in a given situation. When making selections from a restaurant menu, one may quite appropriately wish to choose rather impulsively, although even in that case rudiments of this four-step process will be present.

Another approach is to use the group to advantage. An example of this is found in decisions by consensus, with accompanying give-and-take compromise.

Some people simply try to avoid making a choice and decide not to decide—which, of course, is a decision. This may be an excellent course if the time is not right for a decision or if the information is not yet available. On the other hand this can result in decision by default, thus losing control of the vital right to choose.

APPLYING THE DECISION-MAKING PROCESS

Let us return to the four-step process and consider a practical application of the method. Suppose a parent is trying to decide how best to help a child get some practical work experience. The following demonstrates the use of the steps in the decision-making process for this particular problem:

(1) *Clarify or identify the problem.* Parent and child could find an appropriate time and place to talk over the child's desires to have more spending money. "We both know you would like to have more money to buy some of the things you want. Can we agree that it would be better if you earned it on your own rather than just having me hand it over to you? What are some of the other considerations?"

Another subject for discussion might be the nature of the job. Work experience *per se* is good, but even better is work experience under proper supervision, in a type of work environment that will furnish some positive learning experiences, in lines that are compatible with the child's manifested areas of ability and interest, or in lines that are generalized or applicable to future career goals. Of course, the child's desires may be quite different from the parent's. For example, a job which allows associations with the peer group and which has influence with them may have much more importance for the child than some other rational considerations.

(2) *Consider the alternatives.* Together, parent and child generate alternatives such as: Do work around the home, examine job openings listed in the want ads, check openings at the local job service, talk about places where other youth of your acquaintance are working, call friends who are employers and inquire from them, check with the school counseling or placement office, consider creating a job from some hobby or recognized skill area, call employers who have jobs related to interest areas.

(3) *Choose and implement one alternative.* Together, parent and child can discuss the alternatives, weigh the advantages, and risks, and assess the probable outcome. This may take a while, and several discussions may be needed. Although a great deal of parental input is often in order, the final choice should be the child's.

Once the decision has been made, then comes the exciting but difficult aspect of planning and implementation. This is the translation of ideas to action. There are few jobs more demanding than the job of finding a job. Generally, the child not only will need encouragement and praise, but also will need structured plans about where to go, who to see, and what to say.

The circumstances will vary with each situation. Parents can take an active role, an advisory role, or an observer role. Often, a blend of all three is what occurs. Planning should consider not only getting the job, but succeeding in it as well. (More information on this step is provided in Chapter 11.)

(4) *Evaluate and revise.* This step is important whether the child is successful in obtaining the job or not. It will help for future reference to realize just what happened in relation to the kinds of efforts made. If the effort to find a job proved unfruitful, it is especially vital to understand what went wrong, lest the child be filled with self-doubt about personal worth and gain a negative attitude toward the world of work. A revised plan which allows for a more efficient approach to job finding may be needed. Use of other resource people may be desirable, and parents should not see this as a

personal failure if they need to call upon others for help. Instead, it should be regarded as wise parenting.

Time pressure is a very real element in decision making. The child needs to know *now*, not next week, whether or not to buy the car, take the job, try marijuana, sign up for the class, go to the meeting. Adding to the problem is the omnipresent reality that possible outcomes are seldom clear cut. The decision is often not what is right or wrong, but which of the two rights is preferable or which of the two wrongs is less undesirable.

Lest the parent resemble a firefighter, rushing around putting out fires—and always wishing for a bigger fire extinguisher—a few rules of thumb are in order:

Rule of Thumb 1—Let the fires burn a while. Take a close look to see whether the flames are real or simply imitations. Does the child really need to decide *right now* whether or not to commit to the project? Would waiting tend to clarify the situation?

Rule of Thumb 2—Let the one who started the fire put the fire out whenever possible, but keep a close watch. Learning decision making comes through using one's own resources to the fullest extent possible, making the decision to the greatest degree possible on one's own, and living with the consequences. The amount of freedom left to the child is a function of her or his level of responsibility. A five-year-old might be incapable of deciding whether or not to go to kindergarten, but the same child might be responsible enough to decide what to get baby sister for her birthday. Beware of rushing in and solving the child's problem, depriving her or him of the opportunity for growth.

Rule of Thumb 3—Carry a huge fire extinguisher, but use it as little as possible. Knowing that someone is ready and willing to help is possibly more important to the child than the actual help. Showing interest in the child's decisions and expressing willingness to help will aid the child in gaining the confidence to go ahead.

The key parental role is to help the child from a point of complete dependence to a point of independence. This is accomplished to a great extent by even greater free agency made possible by effective mastery of decision making.

SUMMARY

In applying the techniques outlined above, parents need to remember that decision making is a lifelong developmental process. Parents can expect a child to grow gradually in skill as he or she is confronted with increasingly difficult tasks. One role of parents is to help the child as he or she progresses so that the child accepts responsibility for decision making when he or she is "ready" for the particular decision-making situation, but does not attempt to make decisions which are not appropriate to the child's age or stage of development. For example, it would be absurd to expect a five-year-old to decide from among a number of part-time employment opportunities outside the home. However, that is an appropriate decision for a sixteen-year-old youngster.

Below is a list of decisions which parents might expect children to make at particular age levels. However, we emphasize that this list is meant primarily as a sequential guide. Children vary greatly in their rates of development, and parents must determine the "readiness" of their own children for these decision tasks on the basis of observation and not on the basis of chronological age.

Beginning at age 2:

> Choice of friends
>
> Choice of food
>
> Choice of play activities

Beginning at age 4:

> Choice of clothes

How to spend money

Choice of bedtime songs

Choice of television programs

Arrangement of room

Work assignments in the house

Which drawer in which to put things

Choice of bedtime stories

Choice of toys

Beginning at age 6:

Use of after-school time

Helping plan vacations

Response to homework

Hobbies

Planning family activities

Beginning at age 8:

No new categories of decisions but a general readiness to be more accountable and responsible for own actions and decisions

Beginning at age 10:

Decisions to join organized athletic teams such as little league

Choice of music participation in school

Choice of adult role models (i.e., choosing adults they wish to model themselves after)

Beginning at age 12:

Choice of part-time work on limited basis (paper route, mowing lawns, babysitting)

Involvement with organizations such as scouting

Response to junior high school environment

Limited choice of classes

Tentative career in terms of abilities, interests, and values with emphasis on interests and values

Choice of which talents and abilities to develop

Beginning at age 14:

Dating companions

Wider range of choice in school classes

Involvement in extracurricular activites, including school athletic teams, musical groups, debate and drama groups, service clubs

Beginning at age 16:

Driver's license opens up new range of options

Opportunity for more extensive part-time work

Choice of emphasis in school: college prep, vocational, or non-school options (leaving school)

More realistic tentative career choices; more emphasis on abilities

Beginning at age 18:

Marriage

Choice of full-time work or further career preparation

Choice of geographical location

ADDITIONAL READING

Bolles, Richard N. *What Color Is Your Parachute?* Berkeley, Calif.: Ten-Speed Press, 1975.

Campbell, David. *If You Don't Know Where You're Going, You'll Probably End Up Somewhere Else.* Niles, Ill.: Argus Commmunications, 1975.

Chickering, Arthur W. *Education and Identity.* San Francisco: Jossey-Bass, 1969.

Clark, Jay, and Simon, Sidney B. *Beginning Values Clarification*. San Diego: Pennant Press, 1975.

Coser, Lewis A. *The Functions of Social Conflict*. New York: Free Press, 1956.

Drucker, Peter F. *The Effective Executive*. New York: Harper and Row, 1967.

Dyer, William G. *Insight to Impact*. Provo, Utah: Brigham Young University Press, 1976.

Haldane, Bernard. *How to Make a Habit of Success*. Unity Village, Mo.: Unity Books, 1960.

Kirschenbaum, Howard, and Simon, Sidney B. *Readings in Values Clarification*. Minneapolis: Winston Press, 1973.

Maslow, Arthur H. *The Farther Reaches of Human Nature*. New York: Viking Press, 1971.

White, Robert. *Lives in Progress*. New York: Holt, Rinehart, and Winston, 1966.

CHAPTER EIGHT

Career Preparation

A third stage in the career education process is the career preparation stage. In one sense, career preparation is something that begins in childhood and continues throughout life, but in the sense in which the term is used by many career educators, it encompasses those final steps that are taken as one makes the transition from the life style of a member of the student population to the life style of a member of the work force. In other words, career preparation is the process of getting ready to walk out of the school doors and into the work place.

The most basic characteristic of the career preparation phase is that it is filled with decision situations. That is why we prefaced this chapter with the chapter about decision making. As the student prepares to make the transition from school to work, he or she must decide what classes to take, when to look for work, how to look for work, whether to continue in post-secondary education or training, where to seek that type of training, whether or not to marry, when to marry, what career field to pursue, and on and on. For the student, it seems to be one decision after another, most of which have long-range implications. It is a difficult period for a young person whose previous decisions have been pretty well limited to short-term considerations.

However, at some point during the high school years, most young persons move into the developmental period which education theorist Jean Piaget calls the stage of "formal operations." The child—now a young adult—begins to think in the logical framework necessary to deal with concepts over a period of time and to understand the connection between today's events and tomorrow's consequences. But such a change does not occur overnight. It may take years. And in the meantime, the normal adolescent can be expected to suffer the joy and the pain of what some have called "the wonderful age of absolutism"—the age where the individual is convinced that somewhere there is one and only one "best" answer to every problem. This is simply an overlapping of the early stage of self-concern with the more mature stage of "formal operations," and it represents the natural kind of insecurity adolescents experience as they become more and more aware of the fact that eventually they are going to have to take care of themselves and assume responsibility for their own lives.

Career development theorists describe a child progressing from some kind of "fantasy" stage and moving developmentally through a series of stages until a point is reached which has some degree of stability of occupational choice and progression. In other words, the child moves from the "fantasy" stage to a "realistic" stage, or from "awareness" and "exploration" to something which might be described functionally as "maintenance and progression."

One thing upon which most career development theorists seem to agree is that the senior high school years do *not* include the period in the life of an individual when final and firm occupational decisions are expected to occur. Instead, these theorists picture the late adolescent years as a period of tentative occupational choice. In most cases, the establishment of firm career patterns seems to be reserved until at least the age range of the middle twenties. Of course, this is not to say that the students wouldn't like to make firm choices, or that they could not do so if their environments were more conducive to decision making. It says only that the making of firm occupational decisions does not seem to be an expected part of normal career maturation for persons between fifteen and eighteen years of age.

Given those facts—that high school youngsters feel a need for single, absolute answers to every question, and that those same youngsters will likely not find the final answers to their career questions for five or ten years—imagine what a disconcerting period of time it is for the growing young adult! Such a person can find answers for all the great problems of the world . . . but can't find an answer about his or her own career. It's a difficult time, and it's no wonder that parent-child relationships are often strained during this unsettling period.

Career education can't eliminate all parent-child conflicts, but it can help the individual student through the difficult transition from school to work. It attempts to reduce the difficulty of transition in a number of ways. First, it helps the student establish perspective with regard to the world of work and his or her potential role in that world. Second, it gives the student a better understanding of the decision-making process, including both the potentials and the limitations of that process. Third, it emphasizes the nature of career planning and indicates to the student the benefits which might be derived from careful and conscientious planning activities. Fourth, it provides skill training in areas which are vital to a successful transition, including basic academic skills, general vocational skills, good work habits, and job-seeking, job-getting, and job-holding skills. Fifth, it offers a support base for the vital decisions the student is making during the transition period.

THE IMPORTANCE OF PLANNING

We mentioned the importance of planning in an earlier chapter as one of the work habits parents can help their children acquire. It also has application for the subject of career preparation. Perhaps the importance of planning can best be illustrated by recalling an incident from Lewis Carroll's *Alice's Adventures in Wonderland.* Alice has wandered about, confused, for some time, when she meets the Cheshire Cat. Alice asked the Cat: " 'Would you tell me, please, which way I ought to go from here?'

" 'That depends a good deal on where you want to get to,' said the Cat.

" 'I don't much care where—' said Alice.

" 'Then it doesn't matter which way you go,' said the Cat."

In other words, if you don't know where you are going, any road will get you there.

Too often in career development we don't know where we are going, and so it doesn't matter which road we take. That's when we let someone or something else make decisions for us; we lose control of our lives. And when we finally get to where we are going, we find it is a place called "If Only"—*if only* I had gone on to trade school; *if only* I had taken a vocational course in high school; *if only* I had studied harder; *if only* I had learned to be a plumber; *if only* I had looked ahead a little; *if only*. . . .

If only we would all do a little more planning in life, we wouldn't find ourselves asking so many "if only" questions.

Business leaders have developed the process of planning to the point where it is a science. Indeed, the subject of planning is taught in every business school. But it has just as much application to individual lives as it does to business and other organizations. Planning offers three fundamental psychological benefits. First, it establishes priorities for the individual so that he or she is not confused by the overabundance of available alternatives. Freedom is wonderful if it has some sort of direction; it is meaningless if it leads to running in circles. Second, planning motivates the individual, since it provides a goal and a reason for action. One usually walks a little faster when heading for a specific destination than when simply wandering. Third, good planning builds in that unmatchable sense of satisfaction which comes from accomplishing what one sets out to do.

Steps in the Planning Process

The process of planning is relatively simple: One defines a goal and then sets out to achieve it. But it requires other

considerations. For one thing, most goals must be achieved
one step at a time; they do not happen all at once. Therefore,
the good planner analyzes the steps which must be
accomplished along the way to the goal. Those steps become
objectives, and as each objective is reached, it indicates
progress toward the goal and it also provides a bonus of
satisfaction due to achievement. Finally, the good planner
uses the objectives to measure progress toward the goal and
to assess how well the plan is working. This means that
objectives must be measurable kinds of things, such as
acquiring a diploma, learning a skill, applying for a job, or
being accepted into a course of training. It also means that
the objectives usually include a time element or a deadline.
Thus, the wise planner can periodically examine his or her
progress to see if the plan is on schedule, and to determine
whether or not adjustments are required with regard to the
major goal, or the objectives, or the schedule. Flexibility is
one mark of good planning, because it is a lot less traumatic
to fail to achieve an objective than to fail to achieve the
major goal. One can save considerable pain by recognizing
early that the goal has been set a little beyond reason, and
by using that information to modify it to more reasonable
dimensions. That turns a failure into a success, because the
plan has succeeded even if the original goal has not been
attained.

But how does planning fit in with the concept
mentioned earlier that high school students rarely make
more than simply tentative career goals? It would seem that
one concept might conflict with the other. However, one
must remember that planning is a skill which can be
learned just as playing the piano can be learned. One doesn't
begin by playing a concerto. One begins with simple
exercises, and then practices those exercises until sufficient
skill is acquired to move on to the next level of challenge.

The same is true of planning. Skill in planning is
acquired by stages. One begins with simple, short-range
planning and works up to those goals which have lifetime
implications. A young child may help in planning a birthday
party a week hence. With parental assistance, the child lists
objectives—issue invitations, prepare games, arrange facil-

ities, prepare food, purchase favors—and assigns each objective a deadline day. An older child might plan for events two or three months ahead. For example, if little league football tryouts are in August, the child might set some skill objectives and work out a training program to achieve those objectives in June. By the time the child reaches high school, he or she is probably able to think concretely about events or goals two or three years ahead. Obviously, those goals cannot be final and permanent, though they may, in some instances, turn out to be career goals. They can certainly be career-related goals based on the self-exploration (and the career exploration) which occurred during the middle/junior high school years. For example, the child may have discovered in junior high school that he or she enjoys working with "things"—materials, machines, and other objects—rather than working with ideas. The youngster can use that self-discovery to set certain goals for the high school years. He or she may decide that one goal would be to be able to take apart and repair an automobile engine. That is not a career goal—it doesn't involve lifetime commitment—but it *is* a career-related goal. The objectives might include the completion of a course in physics in order to understand how the engine works, to complete a course in mathematics in order to learn to deal with machine-part tolerances and with size designations for nuts and bolts, to find a part-time job in a garage to acquire some hands-on experience, and so forth. There is also nothing lost if a youth fixes upon what he or she considers a final choice and then later experiences a change of mind. There is value in the experiences of planning for and disciplining oneself to pursue a goal. There is even value in learning at some point that the goal is undesirable.

Success Brings Satisfaction

If the plan is well designed, the youngster periodically achieves objectives on the way to the major goal, and each time an objective is achieved it brings satisfaction and a chance to assess progress. The youngster has some direction and can use the plan to help establish priorities with other activities. And incidentally, the youngster makes progress in school, because he or she recognizes that school—at least a part of it—is something more than a way to spend time on the road to graduation.

At the same time the high school student is beginning to practice long-range planning, he or she can continue to polish skills in short-range planning. For instance, a young person may decide it would be a good idea to have a summer job. The goal then becomes the acquisition of a job. Parents or a counselor can help develop a plan which includes the various steps necessary to find a job—the need to do some research about possibilities, the need to write letters of inquiry, the need to prepare a resumé, the need to appear for personal interviews, the need to consider time schedule and travel requirements, and so on. These become the objectives, and the student can begin his or her quest of the goal. Obviously, the student who has never before searched for a job will need to understand that employers begin planning their own summer hiring early in the spring.

Parents can also help their children learn about planning by continuing to act as role models, by communicating their own planning activites to their children, and by giving children some planning responsibilities for family goals. Children should be allowed to enter into the discussion and planning—including defining their own related objectives—for such family activities as vacations, major purchases, job changes by parents, and self-improvement needs. Parents may find that the benefits to be gained by such a practice will go far beyond simply teaching children how to plan.

BASIC ACADEMIC SKILLS

The need for certain skills is common to almost all occupations and to all citizens who must somehow function in society. For instance, it is difficult for those of us who read to contemplate the problems which must confront an illiterate person. The illiterate's world must be severely limited to familiar road signs, packages, forms, and sensory stimulation. And thoughts must be limited to the inadequate language of spoken communication. When one cannot read, one's view of life must be very narrow, indeed. Imagine the frustration which must attend the inability to read a road sign, or a road map, or an application form, or a label on a can, or a letter which comes in the mail, or a title on the television set, or the washing instructions on a clothing label.

The situation is just as difficult for those who have not acquired other skills which we might label "academic skills." As a minimum, those basic skills include communication skills, computation skills, and social skills.

Communication skills include reading, of course, but they also include the ability to comprehend what has been read, the ability to write a simple sentence, the ability to carry on a meaningful conversation, and the ability to listen. Few occupations remain which do not require communication skills, at least to some degree. Prospective employees must be able to write letters of application, to read application forms, and to converse with others during employment interviews. Many jobs require the submission of periodic written reports which employees must be able to accomplish with relative ease as one of the tasks associated with the job. The complexity of modern machinery frequently requires that operators be able to read instructions, either in instruction books or on the machinery itself. Communication between employer and employee—in both directions— has expanded tremendously in recent years. Employers have found that communication can be facilitated most effectively with printed materials, and so they issue letters, bulletins, employee magazines, booklets, newsletters, and a variety of other communications. The employee who cannot read and digest those materials is at a severe disadvantage. Likewise, the employee who cannot effectively communicate his or her concerns to the employer has limited potential for advancement and for satisfaction on the job.

Computation skills are similarly important to the worker in modern society. The ability to deal with numbers pervades all aspects of our lives. Family budgeting, wise purchasing decisions, simple banking transactions, comparing values . . . all depend on basic mathematical skills. But those skills are often even more important in the work place. Many workers must deal with prices, quantities, tolerances, production quotas, and other numerical concepts on a daily basis. And while the electronic computer has greatly simplified many computation procedures, it has geometrically expanded the instances of the use of numbers as part of our language, particularly in the business world. Literally everything and everyone has a number, or is a number, or can be treated as a number . . . not necessarily because business is "impersonal," but simply because the computer handles numbers much more efficiently than it handles some of our traditional language concepts. (Human beings can deal with "green widget" much easier than they can deal with "108-385-6663-7," but for the computer the opposite is true.) One can hardly imagine a day—or even an hour of a day—in which he or she does not make use of numerical skills, beginning each morning when one looks at the numbers on the alarm clock to see if there is time for five more minutes of sleep.

Social skills are more difficult to describe—and probably more difficult to learn—but they are no less important. They are difficult to describe because they include such a wide range of concepts, behaviors, and activities. They are important because so much of what we do every day is somehow related to others. Most jobs require some social skills, if for no other reason than to obtain the job in the first place. Even work which is purely mechanical (i.e., working with "things") usually requires the ability to deal with fellow workers, or with supervisors, or with customers. Few of the tasks we perform are "lonely" tasks; most involve some sort of cooperative effort.

Of course, one of the basic functions of education is to help students acquire communication, computation, and social skills in preparation for occupational use, as well as for use in other of life's activites. Indeed, many educators feel strongly that these and other skills taught in the academic classroom contribute greatly to the quality of life. Proponents of career education share that conviction. We would add only that by helping students to understand the relevance of these skills to career pursuits, educators can significantly increase the motivation of students to acquire the skills. Thus, one of the effects of career education is to actually encourage students to acquire skills which will add to the quality of life in all the things they do.

How Parents Can Help

The education system should not be called upon to bear the entire burden of helping students acquire these skills. Parents can—and do—serve an important role in the process. The role of parents during this stage of development is not to teach—in the pedagogical sense of that word—so much as to augment the teaching which occurs in the school by providing supportive experiences and activities. Students at this age have a growing desire to participate in and understand the adult world. Therefore, parents should begin to accept children as equals in discussions of their own problems and activities. Since we are concerned here in particular with motivating children to acquire the skills necessary to prepare for entry into the occupational world, we will concentrate on that area of activity.

The most effective way for parents to emphasize the importance of academic skills is by simply calling attention to the use of those skills in their own lives and in the lives of their children. For instance, if a child is considering whether or not to sign up for a mathematics course in school, a parent might point out how often he or she used mathematics during that day—in grocery shopping, in balancing the checkbook, in figuring a bill for a customer, in determining the size of the tip at lunch time, in estimating some cost factors on the job, and in a variety of other situations where academic training in mathematics helped to make the day easier. Then the parent might ask the child to talk about a few of the ways in which he or she uses numerical concepts on a regular basis. Another example would be in making it a point to talk about tasks on the job which require the skills learned in the academic classroom. This can be fairly subtle. One can talk about reading a communication from an employer or about preparing a written report without making the discussion a didactic lesson about the need for studying English. Perhaps an even more effective way to emphasize the importance of academic skills in the work place is to ask the high school age child to use those skills in assisting the parent. For example, the parent might ask the child for some help in writing a portion of a report for work, or the parent might ask the child to check the computation on an expense account, or the parent might ask the child's opinion about a particular problem with a subordinate. The question might be phrased in such a way as to call upon subject matter the child is studying in school. For instance: "I'm really having trouble with Mary Watkins. She seems to resent everything I say to her. I know you're studying social adjustment in your psychology class. Have you run across anything that might give me a clue about what to do?"

Obviously, this accomplishes two purposes. It not only emphasizes the importance of academic training, but it also lets the child know that his or her opinion is respected.

Basic Skills in Work Situations

Finally, work situations around the home offer frequent instances where academic skills can be called upon. Repair work requires computation skills to figure how much of each type of material to purchase. Applying fertilizer to the lawn requires knowing the square footage of lawn area in order to purchase the proper amount of fertilizer. Painting requires an estimate of the room area in order to buy the proper amount of paint. Completing the tax form requires the ability to read, as well as computation skills. Parents should ask high school age children to help with these and other problems in order to impress upon them the fact that academic skills are important in all kinds of career applications.

Social situations provide another opportunity for parents to help emphasize the importance of academic skills. Youngsters of high school age frequently identify with family friends as being "ideal" models. Often these identifications are short-lived, but they can be very strong. Parents who observe such attachments can call attention to particular skills the individual has or, preferably, can ask the individual to point out how he or she uses various skills in occupational situations. Parents should try to include their teenage children in at least some of their own social activities. We do not advocate constant family "togetherness" at this stage of development, but children should have the opportunity to become acquainted with as many adults as possible. At times, this may be awkward for both children and parents, but it is a relatively easy way to help children develop social skills and expand their knowledge about various career opportunities.

One important group of career activities which is common to all members of society are those activities associated with citizenship. These include such things as voting, participating in community discussion of issues, paying taxes, understanding rules and regulations, and so on. Each of these activities requires basic academic skills, and each requires the ability to apply those skills with some intelligence. Once again, parents who find ways to include their children in these kinds of activities are helping the children use the skills they learn in school and, more importantly, are helping the children to understand why academic skills should be acquired. The child who hears and participates in dinner table discussions about issues, candidates, taxes, and other responsibilities of citizenship— no matter what the point of view—will likely bring to the schoolroom a greater motivation to learn about those subjects. Teenage youngsters are eager to be a part of the adult world; if they understand that academic learning makes entry into that world easier, the desire to learn is increased.

As a final—but important—point regarding skills learned in the academic classroom, we should like to note that there is not necessarily a direct relationship between school grades and the acquisition of skills. We do not believe that only students who earn 'A' grades are learning the skills. One goal of the education system is to teach those skills to every student, and grades often reflect factors other than skill development.

GENERAL VOCATIONAL SKILLS

Career preparation also includes the development of such general vocational skills as organizational skills, manipulative skills, and thought-process skills. Just as with certain of the academic skills, these skills have application for a broad range of occupational pursuits. Most work situations require one or more of the abilities associated with general vocational skills. In fact, about one-third of the occupations in the U.S. economy require no more formal training than that already obtained by any normal high school graduate who also knows how to drive an automobile. Another one-third of jobs require no more formal training than this for entry, but they may indeed require formal training on the job.

Children begin to develop general vocational abilities as early as the preschool years, and by the time they reach high school age they should be able to make some assessment concerning their own interest in these skill areas and their individual level of development. This self-assessment is part of the process of career preparation, and it is important to making good career decisions. For example, the student who has acquired considerable manipulative skills and who has high interest in that type of activity would do well to consider work which has some mechanical component, whether it's repairing the transmission in an automobile or fixing a cavity in a tooth.

Organizational skills are those skills which involve planning, organizing, arranging, scheduling, and so on. These are skills which we all must use frequently. When one schedules an appointment for a specific day and time, one is organizing time. When one plans a budget or pays the bills, one is organizing finances. When one arranges clothing in a drawer or tools in a tool box, one is organizing materials. When one assigns duties and responsibilities to members of the family or some other group, one is organizing people. We use our organizational skill so frequently that we sometimes forget that it is an acquired skill and that we have learned it over a period of many years. It involves the ability to judge time requirements adequately, the ability to establish priorities, the ability to categorize materials according to type or function, the ability to break a larger task into its component smaller tasks, and the ability to grasp sequential relationships.

Manipulative skills are necessary for any situation in which one must work with tools or materials in the physical sense. Writing words with a pen or pencil is a manipulative act. Changing a sparkplug is a manipulative act. Scrubbing a floor is a manipulative act. Digging a ditch is a manipulative act. Manipulative skills are motor skills; they always involve the use of muscles. The muscles are used to manipulate objects, whether they are the tiny objects in a watch movement or the timbers in a roof truss. Once again, the development of these skills begins at an early age when a child learns to button a shirt, or play with toys, or assemble a jigsaw puzzle, or play a musical instrument. The high school age youngster is near to full maturity with regard to physical growth, muscular development, and coordination. Thus, it should be possible during the career preparation stage to fully test out those manipulative skills, to put them into practice in a variety of situations, and to make some fairly accurate assessments about level of development and interest.

Thought-process skills obviously involve dealing with ideas. They include the ability to "process" concepts, the ability to analyze problems, the ability to create a new thought from a disparity of existing ideas, and the ability to think something through in a rational fashion. Thought-process skills are just as important to a mechanic who must figure out why an engine does not work as they are to the business woman who must figure out why a particular employee isn't motivated to work more efficiently. Of necessity, children learn some basic thought-process skills early, but since they cannot deal well with concepts involving long periods of time until late adolescence, it is not until the high school years that these skills really begin to take form in the most sophisticated sense; i.e., dealing with ideas that are abstract, long range, and highly complex.

Most high schools today offer students a variety of opportunities to "experiment" with these general vocational skills as part of the career preparation process. For instance, the number of vocational classes being offered in high schools has increased dramatically over recent years, together with the variety of such courses. At one time, the only vocational classes offered were "shop" classes and "homemaking" classes. Now students in many schools can select from courses which range from "Bachelor Living" to "Medical Technology." School vocational laboratories are equipped with modern tools, and the quality of vocational instruction is usually high.

Work Experience

Some schools offer work experience programs to students. In these programs, students actually go out on the job for part of the day and gain the training that is available only on the job site. Such programs are also available in a variety of fields, ranging from production work to medical assistant. Schools sometimes "tailor make" programs for specific students or for the specific occupational structure of the area. One of the great advantages of work experience programs is that they attempt to coordinate the experience in the work place with the education program.

Part-time jobs offer another way for students to develop general vocational skills, as well as to gain work experience. Each student must make his or her own decision about whether or not to take on a part-time job during the high school years. The advantages of such an experience are that it provides work experience, it gives the student a sense of independence, it provides financial support and the accompanying experiences with handling money, it offers training in planning and scheduling, and it helps develop a variety of skills. The disadvantages are that it takes time and effort away from school and school activities, it creates an early dependence on the money earned, it may provide a rather narrow view of work experience, and it interferes with certain self-development activities. The needs of each student are different, and the decision must be an individual one. The primary thing to remember is that learning experiences should almost always have priority at this stage of life. The question is where learning is most likely to take place—in the classroom, on the job, or in some other setting. Often, an acceptable compromise is to forego the part-time work in favor of a full-time job during the summer months.

Hands-on Experience

All of the above activities provide hands-on experiences in work-related situations. Several other activities can also provide hands-on experiences which are just as meaningful as those mentioned above. The school itself provides many opportunities which are work related, such as committee work, work with theater groups or athletic teams, work on the school paper, assistantships, and other activities. Volunteer work is a rapidly growing field, and a wide variety of volunteer assignments are available in every community, including hospital work, political activities, social services, and environmental enhancement projects. Such volunteer work can be very useful in the development of general vocational skills.

Hobbies offer another avenue for the acquisition of skills. It is not unusual for interest in a hobby to lead to occupational roles. The young person who collects stamps or other items is developing organizational skills. The individual who builds model trains or airplanes is improving manipulative skills. The adolescent who designs and "throws" pottery is working on both manipulative and thought-process skills. Hobbies are an excellent way to test skills and to test interests, and we recommend that wherever possible parents go "the extra mile" in encouraging the hobby pursuits of their children. This may mean setting aside a closet for a photography darkroom, or providing a work room for sewing projects, or ignoring the grime that goes with a torn-down automobile, or tolerating the confusion of weekly practice sessions for a music group, or making a special weekend trip to search for a certain type of rock formation. Whatever the problems caused by hobby activities, parents should remember that such activities usually provide opportunities for growth which will have lifetime benefits. There are few better ways to "experiment" with a range of interests than through hobbies.

With regard to all of these skill-development practices—vocational classes, work experience programs, part-time jobs, and hands-on experience—parents should do their best to encourage participation by their children. Unfortunately, our society is so much oriented toward the traditional types of academic pursuits that both students and parents often neglect the development of general vocational skills. This is an inadvisable oversight for two reasons. First, these general vocational skills have many applications in situations which are not job-related, such as in home repair work, in hobbies, and in simply understanding how things work. Second, it no longer makes much sense to force a youngster into a specific occupational pursuit simply because it has more "prestige" than some other occupation. The traditional patterns of stratification are breaking down so that all work has prestige value. The more important consideration is to find a type of work which the individual enjoys and from which she or he can derive satisfaction. Besides, it is a good idea to participate in a variety of academic and vocational experiences if one is to develop a good understanding of one's interests and abilities.

GOOD WORK HABITS

We have already discussed in some detail how children develop work habits (Chapters 3 and 4). Since it is difficult to change behavior patterns once they are established, it is important that the foundations for good work habits are provided in early childhood. The earlier in life that good work habits are adopted by the child, the more likely they are to be retained. Parents continue to influence the work habits of their children through the high school years, using the same strategies which were employed earlier.

First, parents serve as role models for their children. The adolescent continues to observe the way parents react in work situations and the kinds of work habits parents exhibit. He or she watches the way parents use their time and the attitudes parents have toward their work. Often, the teenager may be critical of the work habits of parents, but that surface criticism may simply be an attempt to mask what is a growing tendency to employ the same kinds of work habits. At this age, if parents can arrange to take their children to work with them, it should be for more extended periods of time so that the child can actually observe the parent at work and not just observe the place of work.

Second, parents assist in the development of work habits by helping their children to pattern their behavior along satisfying paths. Of course, it is up to parents to decide which values they wish to use to govern the patterns, but parents do have influence over their children, and they can use that influence to direct children into certain behavior patterns. For example, parents can remind their children about their responsibilities and about the need to schedule adequate time for various activities. This should be a supportive type of influence rather than "nagging" or dictatorial directives. There is considerable difference between making a decision for a child and simply letting the child know that he or she *must* make a decision.

Third, parents should continue to make certain their children have success experiences in many areas of life. This means encouraging children to test their skills in new ways, and then following through with enough support so that the child feels the satisfaction of success. This is especially true in the field of work and work-related experiences. If the child does volunteer work or has a part-time job, that activity is as important to the child as the parent's work is to the parent. The child experiences success—or failure—on the job, and he or she is anxious to share those experiences and to receive support for them.

Some of the skills related to good work habits are developed primarily during the high school years. Those skills include prioritizing, allocating, limiting, and accomplishing. The ability to establish priorities for tasks is an important skill, because it is so necessary for choosing from among the great variety of demands upon time that are part of the maturation process. In high school, one begins to realize that time is limited, that opportunities for use of that time are limitless, and that one must somehow choose those uses of time which are likely to be most valuable. Social demands, study demands, family demands, personal demands . . . all compete for the time available, and one soon learns that it is impossible to do everything. Thus, it becomes necessary to say to one's self that while all of these things may be important, some are more important than others. This is difficult for high school age students, because the natural tendency at that age is to deal in absolute terms rather than relative terms. Something is either right or it is wrong; there are no "in-betweens." The process of establishing a ranking of priorities is difficult to grasp because it says that some things may be more right than others, but that few are totally wrong. In other words, it may be good to spend time going to the Thursday night basketball game, but it may be "more good" to study for the Friday mathematics examination. That concept is difficult for high school age students to grasp, but it is part of the prioritizing skill. (Keep in mind that in some instances the basketball game may be more important than the examination.) Of course, the high school student should begin to establish a few long-range priorities related to career interests and life style, and to act upon those priorities.

The establishment of priorities eventually leads to the allocating of resources. Each of us has a limited amount of time, a limited number of talents, limited interests, limited financial resources, and so on. We allocate those various resources to the things which have priority for us. This is another of the many decision-making situations with which high school students must learn to deal. It means concentrating on those things which are most important at the expense of those things which are somewhat less important. Acquiring this skill often creates frustration for high school students, because they are not used to thinking in terms of long-range priorities. All of their lives, they have allocated their efforts to the satisfaction of immediate needs. It's difficult to change that pattern, and learning to do so may require a number of years. It's easy for parents to become impatient with the process.

Allocating personal resources is a skill closely related to the skill of limiting personal needs. No one can do all the things she or he wants to do. Each of us must limit our needs and desires, based on our system of priorities and on our assessment of our own resources. Once again, this is a decision situation, and the decision of necessity will be made, either by the individual's own conscious processes or by some outside forces. However, limiting is a skill which can be acquired through experience and practice. The problem is always to tread a rather narrow line between limiting one's desires so severely that one fails to accomplish anything, and not limiting one's desires enough to avoid the debilitating frustration which can come from trying to do too much.

The use of these skills—prioritizing, allocating, and limiting—is a necessary part of the education process at the high school level. The student is required to make many decisions at that age level which involve these skills. Parents can help by supporting the decisions their children make—no matter what they might be—and by pointing out the connection between what the student does in high school and what the student will do in work situations. The work habits which show up in high school are the same work habits which will govern performance on the job.

JOB-SEEKING JOB-GETTING, AND JOB-HOLDING SKILLS

One final group of skills are the concern of the career preparation stage of career education. Those skills are what might be called the "transition" skills. They are the skills used to move into the work force and to remain there as an employed worker rather than an unemployed statistic.

In the days when the world of work was less complex, the transition skills were not nearly so important as they are today. In those days the individual just found an entry level job with the help of friends or relatives, usually in the home town. The job was often determined by factors beyond the individual's control—i.e., location, industrial base of the community, socioeconomic status, level of education, parent's work experience, and so on—and the individual didn't worry much about career choice, or training, or life style, or personal needs. Now job hunting and employment practices are much more complex, and a whole new set of skills are required. Those skills are job-seeking skills, job-getting skills, and job-holding skills.

Finding a Job

Job seeking today requires some knowledge of the labor market and the various sources of information which are available. Because of the complexity of the labor market, a number of specialized agencies have been developed whose job it is to help workers analyze the job market, analyze their own capabilities and seek out those jobs which seem most appropriate.

State employment agencies—now called "Job Service" in many locations—operate in thousands of communities throughout the nation. The agencies are operated by the various states under the sponsorship of the federal government. They are designed to assist both workers and employers, and they perform a number of services. The Job Service solicits employers to learn about job openings in the area. Those jobs are listed, usually in a public place where job seekers can examine the listings, and the materials are kept up to date insofar as possible. The percentage of job openings in an area that are listed with the Job Service varies according to the occupational structure of the area and the employers' confidence in the local office, but the proportions are reasonably high for some occupations, and some employers are required by law to list their job openings. Trained representatives of the Job Service interview workers who are seeking jobs and attempt to match the worker's needs with the available jobs. The agency also provides testing for job seekers to help determine aptitudes and interests. The trained personnel know a great deal about the local labor market, and they can provide considerable information to the job seeker. All of the services offered by Job Service are free of charge.

All high schools and colleges have counselors who help students with personal problems, selection and application to college, and to a lesser extent, career choice and job seeking. Those schools most involved in career education have developed career resource centers with extensive occupational information and with counselors specialized in vocational guidance. Some high schools and most trade schools, vocational schools, colleges, and universities operate placement services. These are usually staffed by trained personnel who understand the labor market and who can deal with the individual needs of the job seeker. Some school counselors have excellent information about post-secondary training institutions. They can help students decide where to go for the specific kinds of training they desire, they can provide information about entrance requirements, and they can assist students in making applications for such training. In some schools, the school placement service makes arrangements for students to take "examinations" which indicate aptitudes and interests, and counselors help students interpret the results of such inventories. Some school districts have instituted district-wide placement centers, centrally located facilities where students can go to find out about job opportunities, to participate in counseling activities, and to obtain help in their job-seeking and job-getting activities. These placement centers provide more comprehensive services than the individual school placement services. Both the school placement service and the Job Service provide similar services to the job seeker. The main difference is one of emphasis based on the clientele served. The school placement service is designed primarily for the needs of the student population. Thus, it concentrates on entry-level jobs and on post-secondary training opportunities. The Job Service is available to all citizens, whatever the level of occupational interest.

Labor unions are another possible source of job market information. Some craft unions (those that represent workers in a particular occupation rather than a whole industry) perform a number of valuable services, including worker placement in many instances. For some occupations in some areas of the country, union membership is a requirement for entry into the occupation, because employers hire all of their employees through the union. This is particularly true for the building trades, but it also applies to other trades and crafts. Those labor unions can provide a great deal of information about labor market needs, entry requirements, and training possibilities for their particular trades. Local unions are listed in the telephone directory.

Another source of information for the job seeker is the private employment agency. Most cities have one or more such agencies, and some are associated with national organizations, which may be an advantage when seeking work outside the local area. These agencies charge for their services. An advantage of such agencies is that because they charge for placements, they have an added incentive to find jobs for workers and workers for jobs. One disadvantage may be that some such agencies have only limited listings of job openings. Private employment agencies frequently specialize in specific types of workers (i.e., professional, secretarial, and so on) or in specific types of employers (i.e., manufacturers, publishing industry, medical workers, and so on).

The "Help Wanted" section of the newspaper classified advertising provides some job market information in most areas. Generally, the information supplied about the job is limited and some ads may even be misleading. However, the help wanted ads are often the most readily available source of information and a good place to start the search for a job. The job seeker can then probe more deeply once having contacted the employer placing the ad.

All of these sources are valuable to the job seeker. However, they all have one serious limitation: They have no control over the supply of jobs. Employers do, and they have their own choice of recruitment methods. The successful job seeker is the one who is most aware of the methods employers use in recruiting personnel and taps into that system.

How Employers Find Employees

Figure 6 is a representation of the way that most employers conduct their search for employees. As the employer recognizes the need for added personnel and begins to broadcast the availability of a job, the first resort will generally be internal—who should be promoted or transferred to that job. The employer often feels obligated to current employees, besides which they are a known quantity, whereas new employees are always somewhat of a risk. If the job cannot be filled from that source, government statistics show that the next most prevalent source of recruits or jobs is through the informal grapevine of friends, relatives, and acquaintances. Such new employees are familiar or have been vouched for; at least, if one is satisfied with current employees their friends and relatives are more likely to be satisfactory than a random choice.

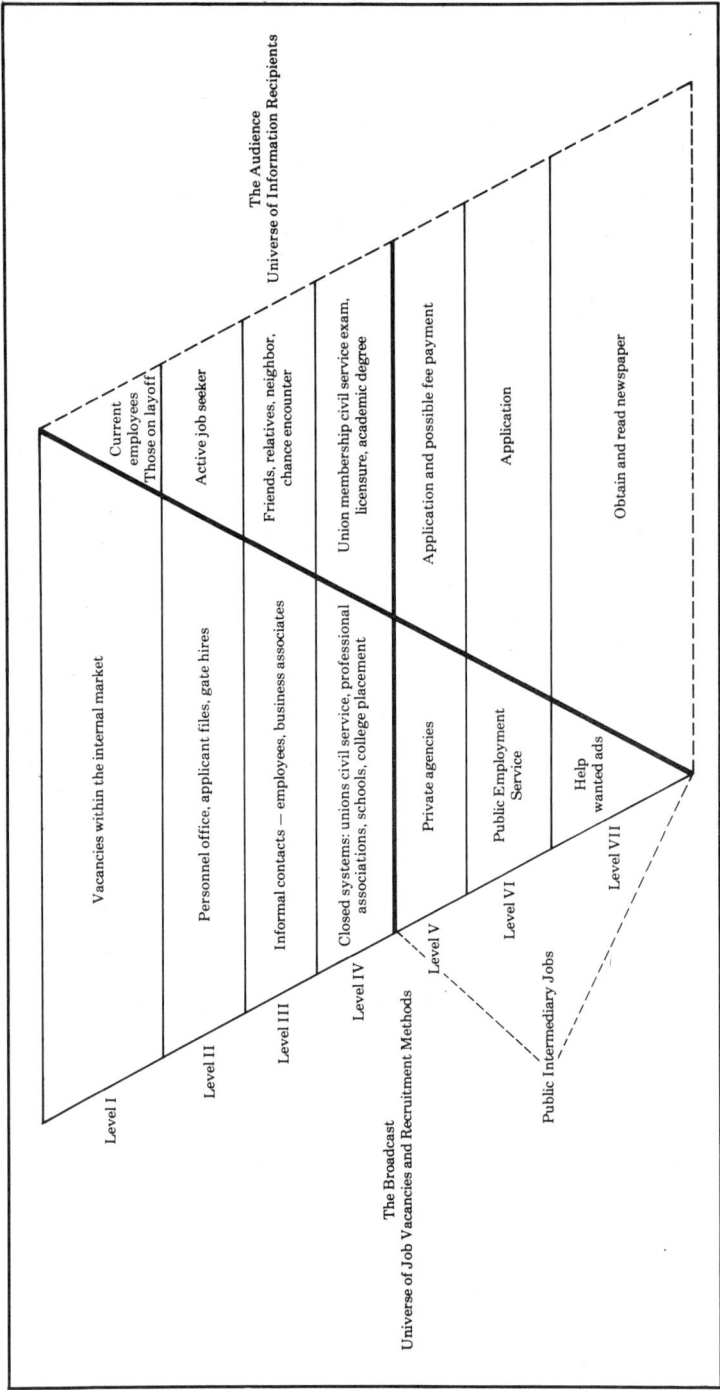

FIGURE 6. The "Recruitment/Job Search Model" illustrates how employers find employees in the labor market.

If those sources do not fill an employer's needs, the next most used source is from among those who have submitted applications at their own initiative. These are generally assumed to be more ambitious than those who have not shown that initiative. A large group of jobs are filled from limited access sources such as union and professional association members, those with licenses or special academic credentials, and through merit system examinations.

Only after all of these sources have been exhausted do employers generally open their jobs to the intermediaries serving the general public—the newspapers, the public employment service, and the private employment agencies. While the latter are generally useful as sources for jobs, the job seeker must recognize that the jobs will have been picked over by applicants at earlier stages in the recruitment process. Only the hardest to fill jobs will be left. Some may have been hard to fill because of the unique skill requirements, others because of low pay or undesirable working conditions.

The wise job seeker and the wise parent aiding a job-seeking youth will look for ways to tapping into earlier stages in the recruitment process. The very best approach to job search is to let the maximum number of interested persons know of the desire for a job. Get every friend, relative, or casual acquaintance acting as agents, watching for job opportunities, and spreading the word of availability. Then apply to all of the placement agencies as well for maximum exposure. Both parent and youth should see the value of becoming aware of the maximum number of job opportunities and then choosing those with the most long-term promise, given the youth's objectives, rather than grasping the first job offered.

One of the things which career education is trying to do is to help students know about these various sources of information so that the student can make use of such sources in job-seeking activities. Part of the career preparation stage is for students to learn how to go through a job search. They learn where to look for job market information, how to compare available jobs with their own abilities and interests, and how to analyze a job for future potential as well as current value.

Obtaining a Job

At least as important as job market information is to be taught job search skills. Each youth needs to be taught how to seek a job, how to prepare a résumé, how to fill out an application, how to impress an interviewer, and how to follow up on an opportunity, as well as how to do a job once obtained.

Once a potential job has been identified, the next step is to obtain the job using the three basic tools of the job seeker—the résumé, the application form, and the interview. (Obviously, these tools require the use of communication skills and social skills.) In most career education programs, students learn how to write a letter of application and a résumé, usually in an English class or some other communication class. The point is not so much the actual letter or résumé they produce—although those may be good writing exercises—as it is in learning what goes into a letter and a résumé, and why those things are important. In trying to obtain a job, students should remember that often all the employer has available to assess the individual is the letter or the résumé. Those items represent the student in the initial stages of the job transaction. Students are taught to consider what it is the employer is looking for in those items and to make certain that material is included. Since many students will eventually be applying for positions some distance away, it is important that they be able to carry on adequate correspondence.

Some schools also have students go through sample job application forms in order to see the kinds of questions which might be asked. A number of schools have used simulation exercises for the application and the interview. In these cases, students act as personnel managers and as job applicants. They have the opportunity to ask the questions and simulate the responses which might be realized in the real-life situation, and it provides a chance for the student to experience the job-getting experience from both points of view. Teachers sometimes ask a personnel manager from a local company to visit the classroom, to discuss the kinds of things she or he looks for in an interview, and to explain the importance of personal appearance to the interview situation.

To some parents, this process may seem far removed from the traditional concepts of education. To others, it may seem as if the school is trying to push the child into the job market. However, remember that career education is responding to a need. The complexities of the labor market demand that this type of orientation take place somewhere along the line. It has been assigned to the career preparation stage of career education—the high school years—because that is a key point in the transition from school to job. For some students it will be the last opportunity to learn these vital skills. Other students may use these skills only in pursuit of part-time or temporary jobs until they have completed many more years of post-secondary training. But all students will have a chance to learn the fundamentals of job search and job application if they attend a high school where career education is a part of the curriculum.

Nonetheless, parents are in a better position than the schools to help with the all-important informal pursuit of jobs. The parent has access to a wide circle of supervisors, subordinates, fellow employees, business acquaintances, friends, relatives, political representatives, places of businesses from whom the family buys . . . all of which are potential sources of employment for the youth. In each case, the parent can inquire, can vouch for the youth, and can then work with the youth in developing the diligence and competence necessary to keep the job.

Holding onto the Job

The final set of transition skills—job-holding skills—are much more difficult to pinpoint. They include a wide variety of abilities, some of which are learned in early childhood and some of which are acquired during and after high school. Certainly, intelligent decision making is one of the skills necessary to holding a job. And once the selection of an occupation has been made, then one must acquire the specific skills necessary to hold a job in that occupation. This may mean additional training and education in the high school or in such post-secondary institutions as trade schools, vocational schools, apprentice programs, colleges, or universities. The array of these institutions in most communities may appear confusing at first, but the parent can help the youth make some sense of them. The starting point has been mentioned: The recognition that about one-third of U.S. jobs require no formal occupational training, another one-third require no pre-entry training but the new hire must be taught on the job, while a final one-third must have occupational training before being hired. Exactly which jobs in which categories varies from place to place, making it impossible to provide a simple list that would be valid everywhere. Some exploration of the local scene is necessary. Observation and inquiry will expose the norms in each community. Retail clerks, service station attendants, assembly line workers, delivery drivers, and similar jobs hardly ever require training. For those, appearance, grooming, and demeanor are the criteria most likely to lead to being hired, and diligence and dependability are the key to retention.

In your community do most secretaries and other clerical personnel learn their office skills in the high school or in a post-secondary institution? It's best to follow the norm. Do local metal trades employers depend upon the high schools, the post-secondary vocational schools, or their own company training program for new employees? In general, if the training schools are available and of good quality, employers will prefer their graduates. If not, they will train their own new employees for occupations which do not require a long duration of training. Two years of specialized training would be ample for a number of occupations for which employers have become accustomed to the products of four-year institutions and will not accept less as long as the latter are available. For many occupations, a four-year college or graduate school is dictated by the extensive theoretical and technical content.

Some occupations will require a license or membership in a union or professional association in one location, but not in another. For many skilled crafts, the "ports of entry" will vary by location among vocational school training, learning the trade informally, union memberships, and apprenticeship. In areas where the particular craft is largely unionized, apprenticeship is the general preferable route, since it involves union membership as well as training and because apprentice trained craftsmen are more likely to rise to supervisory status. Before seeking training in a school for a craft such as plumbing, electricity, sheet metal, carpentry, or machinist, it is well to check to see what success past graduates have had in gaining entry to jobs in that field.

In fact, the best test of any school is the ability of its graduates to find employment in the occupational areas for which they have been trained, giving due consideration to the state of the local economy at the time. Public schools can be depended upon to be reputable but not always competent. In most larger communities there are profit-seeking proprietory trade schools specializing in various occupations. Most of these are also reputable, not just their publicity brochure, that the majority of their graduates are in fact placed in training-related occupations and are not retrained by the employers once hired. The most dependable testimonials are those obtained personally from the students and employers themselves.

Unfortunately, there is no single, easily accessible place in any community where one can obtain unbiased information on the most effective means of preparation for any particular occupation or an inventory of training institutions relevant to each occupation. School and employment service counselors can be helpful, but ultimately the prospective student with parental guidance will need to make personal inquiry and exploration.

But getting the training and getting the job are only the start of preparation, not the end. At some point, one must learn what it means to take a job—that to do so requires a certain amount of commitment. One must be to work regularly and on time; one must work with some diligence; one must be concerned about the quality of work; and so on. These are skills, or habits, or attitudes which are learned by applying them to all kinds of activities, from work around the home, to school work, to certain types of play activity. The same is true for another type of commitment which is part of holding a job—the commitment to continue growing, to work at polishing old skills and developing new ones, to keep looking for opportunities to improve.

All of the skills we have talked about here are part of the career preparation stage of career education. Parents play vital roles in the development of these skills in their children. First, they can teach the skills in the home through example and precept, beginning in early childhood. Second, they can provide many opportunities for children to develop, test out, and experiment with the various skills. Third, they can give continuing support to the efforts of the schools to build these same skills in their children.

SUMMARY

Career preparation is the final formal stage of career education, and it involves the development of the many skills necessary to make the transition from school to work. Those skills include the basic academic skills, general vocational skills, the skills associated with good work habits, and the job-seeking, job-getting, and job-holding skills. Closely related are the skills of planning and decision making.

In almost every case, these are not skills that one can learn easily, the way one learns to ride a bicycle. Instead, these skills must be acquired over a period of many years. They require continual practice, beginning with simple applications and working up to the more sophisticated applications associated with entering the world of work, where such skills often mean not only the difference between success and failure, but also the difference between a working life filled with satisfaction and one filled with frustration and unhappiness.

Because the acquisition of these skills is a long-term proposition, the role of parents and the home is vital. Parental influence provides the continuity which bridges the years from early childhood to high school graduation—and beyond—in a way which no school system can duplicate.

ADDITIONAL READING

Erickson, Erik. *Identity: Youth in Crisis.* New York: W.W. Norton and Company, 1968.

Haldane, Bernard. *Career Satisfaction and Success.* New York: American Management Association, 1974.

Holland, John L. *Making Vocational Choices: A Theory of Careers.* Englewood Cliffs, N.J.: Prentice-Hall, 1973.

Hoyt, Kenneth; Evans, Rupert; Mangum, Garth; Bowen, Ella; and Gale, Donald. *Career Education in the High School.* Salt Lake City: Olympus Publishing Company, 1977.

Johnson, Miriam. *Counter Point: The Changing Employment Service.* Salt Lake City: Olympus Publishing Company, 1973.

Mangum, Garth L.; Becker, James W.; Coombs, Garn; and Marshall, Patricia (eds.). *Career Education in the Academic Classroom.* Salt Lake City: Olympus Publishing Company, 1975.

Roe, Anne. *The Psychology of Occupations.* New York: John Wiley and Sons, 1956.

Walsh, John; Johnson, Miriam; and Sugarman, Marged. *Help Wanted: Case Studies of Classified Ads.* Salt Lake City: Olympus Publishing Company, 1975.

CHAPTER NINE

The Handicapped and Career Education

Career education is as much for the handicapped child as it is for any other child. Much of what has already been said in this book applies equally to the handicapped child. However, with such a child there is a need to give special consideration to the early development of self-confidence, to the improvement of self-awareness, and to the continuing assurance of self-worth. The handicapped child and his or her parents need to have full understanding of the child's individual differences, and that process requires additional thought, time, and effort—in the early years to develop positive values and expectations, in the career awareness stage in order to explore the areas of careers for the handicapped. Parents need to determine realistic goals, and they need to know how those goals may be met. Parents also need to be creative and skillful in constantly seeking new and better ways to help their handicapped child learn about and prepare for the world of work.

In support of career education for the handicapped, the Bureau of Education for the Handicapped in the U.S. Office of Education has identified as one of its five major objectives the goal of making certain that by 1977 every handicapped child who leaves school has had career education training that is relevant to the job market, that is meaningful to his or her career aspirations, and that is realistic for the child's fullest potential.

This is an admirable and ambitious goal. According to the U.S. Office of Education, in 1974 there were approximately seven million youngsters in the nation who were handicapped, including one million of preschool age. Thus, during the latter part of the 1970s, approximately 2.5 million handicapped young persons will leave the public school environment. One observer predicted in 1974 that of that group, five hundred and twenty-five thousand (21 percent) will be either fully employed or will enroll in college, one million (40 percent) will be underemployed or employed at the poverty level, two hundred thousand (8 percent) will be in their home community and will be idle much of the time, six hundred and fifty thousand (25 percent) will be unemployed or on welfare, and seventy-five thousand (3 percent) will be totally dependent and in institutions.

The challenge to all of us—parents, educators, and society itself—is to alter those figures so that a much higher percentage of the handicapped can enjoy the fulfillment and the satisfactions which come from employment. The challenge is especially important to career education.

Career education is vital for the handicapped if they are to be prepared for meaningful, productive employment and meaningful, productive lives. The prospects for those who enter the labor market without adequate preparation are grim, both for the individual and for society as a whole.

The goals of career education for the handicapped are the same as those for any other individual: to prepare the student to make wise career choices and to develop marketable skills which are appropriate for entry into the chosen field. The overall goal is one of self-fulfillment for the individual. Kenneth B. Hoyt, director of career education in the U.S. Office of Education, has frequently called attention to the need for more effort directed toward the handicapped:

Handicapped persons are as deserving of whatever benefits career education has to offer as are any other individuals. To date, few career education programs have made the kinds of special efforts necessary to make career education a reality for handicapped persons. It is hoped that these remarks may stimulate both those in career education and those working in the field of the handicapped to work together to correct this lack of attention. The need to work is a human need of all. Handicapped persons are human.

THE ROLE OF PARENTS AND THE HOME

We have stressed the importance of parents and the home to the concept of career education. If anything, that importance is even more pronounced in the case of handicapped children. The reason for this is not that career education offers any more challenge or less promise to the handicapped child, but simply that the handicapped child needs more individual attention than other children, and parents can do a great deal to provide that attention. Keep in mind that we do not refer to attention of a patronizing sort; we mean that the handicapped child needs help in self-assessment, in developing self-confidence, and in making contact with "real world" work situations which are relevant to his or her handicapping condition. This often requires special effort on the part of parents.

Parents of handicapped children also need to make special efforts with regard to their own self-concept. It is not unusual for parents of handicapped children to develop strong feelings of guilt, as if they were personally responsible for the child's condition; or to play the role of the martyr, sacrificing everything for the child's well being; or to seek anonymity for themselves and the child. None of these feelings are proper or healthy. They will not help the child, and will in fact make it difficult for the child to develop to his or her full potential. The first order of business for parents who have such feelings is to deal with them by seeking counseling or other professional help. To take such a step early, when necessary, is probably the best thing a parent can do for his or her handicapped child.

While we are on the subject of counseling and professional help, we would like to mention that considerable help of this nature is available to the handicapped through government agencies, schools, and private organizations. Parents of handicapped children should certainly identify these sources of assistance very early in the child's life and should not be reluctant to seek the counsel of persons specially trained to help the handicapped. In the field of career education, the handicapped child and his or her parents need counseling services at a much earlier age than the normal child. This is because the child's special condition may define certain needs with regard to career potential. The counselor can help identify those needs and can provide guidance about how parents can help the child develop interests which are compatible with those needs. A counselor can also provide suggestions and support for parents, and can help parents find information and services which may be of considerable value.

Most educators agree that all children—whether handicapped or not—go through certain stages of development in a certain order. Furthermore, those children who do not experience the various stages in proper sequence are likely to have learning problems later in life. Career development is no different than other forms of development. The handicapped child must go through the stages of career development and career education in exactly the same sequence as all children. Those stages are discussed thoroughly in preceding chapters, and the information presented there applies no less to handicapped children than to others. However, there are some special activities which parents of handicapped children can use to augment career education.

Work Attitudes and Values

The most serious problem facing the handicapped child with regard to work attitudes and values is to develop self-awareness. This rather general term means basically that the child must develop an appreciation of his or her own value as a human being, and of his or her own potential as a contributor to the well-being of other humans. We often interpret that potential as the potential for meaningful work. (Of course, we recognize the important fact that for some severely handicapped children the very act of being contributes substantially to the well-being of others.) In the case of the handicapped child, self-awareness means being as aware of the "sameness" which exists between himself or herself and other children as he or she is aware of whatever difference may exist.

In most handicapped children, the handicapping condition affects only one or two facets of the individual, leaving all other faculties unimpaired. The child with a motor handicap still has a mind eager to absorb knowledge and think creatively. The child with limited mental ability has a fine, strong body. The blind child can hear and think and smell and touch and walk about. Unfortunately, this is a difficult concept for non-handicapped persons to understand; they think that a specific handicap has some sort of general effect. Accordingly, as the handicapped child develops work values and attitudes, he or she must also develop an understanding of the specific limitations dictated by the handicapping condition and of the potential not affected by that condition. This understanding, and the self-confidence which goes with it, must be constantly reinforced by parents, because the child will have to convey that message to friends and associates throughout his or her lifetime.

For this and other reasons, it is vitally important for the handicapped child to begin very early the development of positive attitudes about work and about his or her relationship to work. The child must learn early that there are tasks he or she can perform, and that while those tasks in some instances may not be so comprehensive as tasks performed by others, the tasks are nevertheless rewarding and satisfying.

In other words, the child must have the confidence to want to attempt a variety of tasks, together with some understanding about which kinds of tasks are likely to lead to frustration. In this respect, the handicapped child is no different from any other child, and we recommend parents use the same types of support strategies suggested in Chapter 4. Of course, these should be modified where necessary to take into account the child's specific handicapping condition, but remember that parents of handicapped children are more likely to ask too little of their children than they are to ask too much. Whenever possible, let the child set his or her own limits instead of imposing limits from the outside. This will lead to a higher level of self-awareness.

Certainly, the handicapped child should learn the value of work by accepting duties and responsibilities around the home, the same as every other member of the family. The child should participate in planning sessions and in work assignment discussions. When the child wants to do tasks which may require limitation because of the handicapping condition, deal with the problem openly and directly. It does no good to avoid the subject or to pretend it doesn't exist. For example: "Sure, Jimmy, you can do the vacuuming this week. But because you can't see, we'll have Alice work with you until you get the feel of it. Okay?" Or: "You know, Sally, I'll bet you'd do a terrific job of taking out the garbage. But there are two flights of stairs out to the yard, and that would be hard for you in your wheelchair. Why don't you bring all the trash baskets to the kitchen, and I'll take them out for you. And I'll trade you my job of folding the laundry in return."

As we said in Chapter 4: "The important thing to remember is that the parent must be responsible in influencing the child, keeping foremost in mind the need to free the child to become what the child chooses to become."

Career Awareness

During the career awareness stage—approximately the elementary school years—the same kinds of special efforts discussed above should certainly continue. In addition, there are some other career education activities which become increasingly important.

The child has a great need to associate with other children of the same age group, to see what they are doing, how they are acting, and what interests they are developing. This process of social interaction is vital, even though it may at times be painful. The patterns of interaction established during these years will stay with the child through life. If the child learns to withdraw, he or she will continue to withdraw in later years. If the child learns to feel ashamed of his or her condition, that feeling will limit activities throughout life. On the other hand, if the child learns to deal openly with the handicapping condition and expects others to do the same, that will set a positive pattern which will help resolve many problems as the years go by. Certainly, the social interaction will inevitably bring some ridicule and some pain, but parents can help the child to realize that the problem is not with the handicapped person but with those who do not understand.

We know that some children are not mentally capable of dealing with these abstract concepts. Nevertheless, they should not be denied the benefits of social interaction. Parents simply have to work a little harder to reach the child *at the child's level* to help him or her comprehend the actions of others. Once again, professionals trained in the field of exceptional children or special education can often provide sound advice for the particular situation.

Another special effort which should be made by parents of handicapped children during the career awareness stage is to make certain that the child's experience includes opportunities to become aware of other handicapped persons in work situations. This means visiting work places where handicapped workers are employed, inviting handicapped workers to the home, and bringing in older students (perhaps of high school age) who are handicapped for the child to meet. In one community, parents got together and developed a directory of places where handicapped workers were employed. They organized field trips on their own, and they updated the directory on an annual basis so it could be circulated to other parents of handicapped children.

None of the above should be interpreted to mean that handicapped children should not also become aware of non-handicapped workers. The experiences described above should be *in addition to* the regular career awareness experiences described in Chapter 5. Handicapped children need to learn about how many different kinds of workers contribute to the well-being of the family and how many different kinds of jobs are necessary to society. The very fact that the world of work is so diverse will help the handicapped child understand that differences among people are universal in nature, whether one is speaking of physical differences, of intellectual differences, or of differences in interests.

Career Exploration

It seems quite likely that by the time the handicapped child reaches junior high school age—the stage of career exploration—he or she will be more advanced than the non-handicapped child in terms of self-awareness and self-concept. At least, the handicapped child has probably been working toward that kind of self-knowledge for many years longer than the non-handicapped child. Therefore, career exploration activities by the handicapped child will likely be somewhat more concerned with trying occupations on for "fit" than will be the case for the non-handicapped child. In other words, as the child looks at each career cluster and at each occupation within the cluster, he or she will be directly concerned with whether or not he or she might be able to function within that occupation.

This concern will probably lead the child to ask a great many questions. It will be a period when the child first begins to wonder what kind of work he or she can do, and what kind of work setting will be best, and what kinds of social adjustments will be necessary. If the questions are not verbalized, they will certainly be internalized. It may be a period of frustration and confusion. Parents may find that they don't have all the answers for the child's questions. Once again, we feel that the services of a professional counselor can be extremely helpful. The school system should have counselors who understand the occupational concerns of handicapped students and who can answer the questions of students and parents. If the local junior high school or middle school does not have such a counselor, parents should write to the state board of education or to appropriate government agencies until they find someone who has the necessary skills. It is extremely important that the child, first, be able to verbalize the questions which are troubling him or her, and second, be able to find adequate answers to those questions.

In addition to the above, parents should continue to augment the career exploration activities of the school with some special activities of their own. The support strategies discussed in Chapter 6 are also applicable to parents of handicapped children. The child should have an opportunity to see handicapped workers in a variety of work situations and to converse with those workers about such things as job satisfaction, life style, and skill preparation. Parents should work with school teachers to make certain that when audiovisual material is presented and when resource persons are asked to visit the classroom, the handicapped are represented. (Films and other materials are available from various government and commercial sources.) The main objective is to make certain that as the handicapped child explores the world of work, he or she fully understands that work can be as much a part of his or her life as it can for anyone else.

Finally, parents should continue to provide the child a variety of hands-on work experiences and skill development experiences. Parents should encourage the child to try new tasks, to develop self-confidence, and to thoroughly define whatever limitations are created by the handicapping condition, as well as whatever potentials are unaffected by that condition. Some frustrations are inevitable, but continuing support by parents and others can turn the frustrations into valuable learning experiences.

Career Preparation

Some of the career preparation activities discussed in Chapter 8 may be more difficult for the handicapped youngster than for non-handicapped persons. This is particularly true with regard to part-time work and such programs as work experience. Undoubtedly, opportunities will expand in these areas in the near future, but current opportunities are limited. However, the fact that some opportunities are limited does not reduce the importance of the overall career preparation stage of career education. The young person still needs to learn about decision making and planning, and about the job-seeking, job-getting and job-holding skills which are so integrally a part of entry into the labor market.

The handicapped youngster certainly needs to know how to plan for career activities and how to make decisions related to those plans. He or she also needs to know about how to find a job and how to keep it. The techniques are similar for all those who want to find work, but those techniques include a few special activities for the handicapped. For instance, the handicapped youngster should become aware of the various protections which exist under the law and of the historical foundations of those protective laws. (Some of that information is covered below in a general way.) The handicapped youngster also needs to know about various training institutions, scholarships, and support mechanisms which are available to him or her. This information is available through the school counselor or through appropriate government agencies.

As mentioned in Chapter 8, the things which youngsters need most during the career preparation stage are information, skill development and practice, opportunities for new career-related experiences, and challenges designed to increase self-confidence. This should be a time of increasing independence for all youngsters, including the handicapped. They should be testing out their abilities to make sound decisions, testing out their skills, and testing out their capabilities for leading independent lives. Parents must make opportunities for this type of development, and they must be strong enough to avoid unnecessary intercession into the child's activities.

During recent years, the U.S. Office of Education has encouraged a number of exemplary programs in career education for the handicapped. The majority of these programs to date have been concerned with career preparation activities, since there is an immediate need to move handicapped students into the work force in order to prepare the way for others who are currently in the other stages of career education. Parents who are interested should make certain local school administrators are aware of these exemplary programs. Descriptions are available from the U.S. Office of Education or from the Council for Exceptional Children.

The challenge facing parents—and facing society—is to make certain that no handicapped person is denied entry into the labor market and meaningful work within that context solely because of some handicapping condition. Career education can help to meet that challenge, and we strongly believe that parents of handicapped children should consider career education to be an ally in the pursuit of equal opportunity. Much has been accomplished in recent years, as evidenced by the discussion which follows, but much remains to be done.

DEVELOPMENT OF THE RIGHTS OF THE HANDICAPPED

One cannot fully understand how career education relates to the handicapped or why the principles of career education are more important now than ever before to the handicapped child unless one first considers the hurdles which have had to be overcome in the quest for equal rights for the handicapped. With a little historical perspective, those who are concerned about the rights of the handicapped can understand how important career education might be in securing appropriate employment opportunities. We are currently experiencing a period of positive attitude change toward the handicapped, both in terms of self-image and in terms of public image, a period of significant advances in educational and scientific technology for the benefit of handicapped persons. Public awareness of the problem has increased markedly—and continues to increase—and it has, in turn, influence practices in the labor market to the advantage of the handicapped.

But those advances did not come without a struggle, and we can profit from an examination of the development of rights for the handicapped. Progress has occurred over many years and has gone through several different stages, as illustrated in Figure 7.

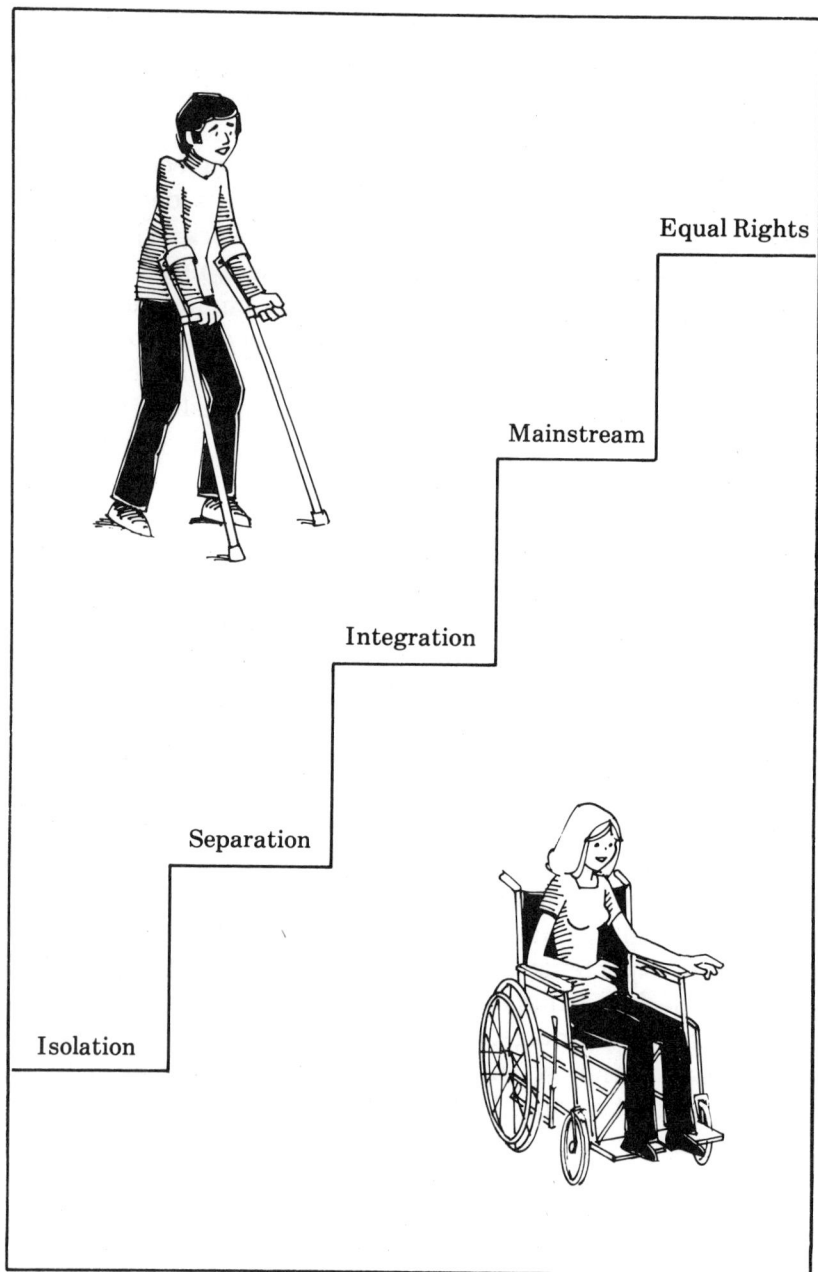

FIGURE 7. Treatment of the handicapped by society has progressed through a fairly distinct series of steps.

Historical Attitudes

In years past—and even today, to a lesser extent—the handicapped child was *hidden* from society because he or she was "different." The child was not permitted to mingle with other children in the neighborhood or to appear within the mainstream of society, except when extenuating circumstances necessitated such exposure. Even such unavoidable appearances were usually painful to both the child's parents and the child. Parents of a child with a handicap felt guilt and frustration; they were often subtly or outrightly rejected by relatives, friends, and other members of the community. Other children in the family were also ostracized, because their peers feared contact with them.

Not only was there a very real physical isolation of the handicapped child and his or her family, but there was also an emotional and psychological isolation. The child's handicap condition was seldom discussed inside or outside the home. The family usually felt that they must endure the "burden" alone. There was no one with whom to share the daily emotional pressure or the long-term heartbreak and frustration. Visitors seldom ventured into the home, and the complexities of family management and financial responsibilities constantly threatened the existence of the family unit. The forced isolation of one family member interfered with social activities of all family members, and brothers and sisters of the handicapped child could not look forward to such normal activities as dating, employment, and marriage without experiencing discrimination because of their handicapped sibling.

The handicapped person had even greater problems in trying to enter the work force. In fact, few of the handicapped could find any type of employment, except perhaps where a family enterprise provided some work or where the tasks involved were so menial as to be shunned by others. The thought of a handicapped person living a productive and rewarding life was so unusual that no one made an effort to find employment for the handicapped. Even family members did not encourage the handicapped to perform work in the home. Consequently, the majority of the handicapped population remained inside the home, existing in idleness and dependency.

It was a period of prevention—preventing the handicapped from realizing any kind of self-fulfillment by imposing environmental and attitudinal barriers. Unemployment was the accepted condition for the handicapped person.

Many of these same feelings exist today, but not to the same extent that they did prior to the 1950s. And as is the case today, those early conditions were based on fear and ignorance. Little was known about the causes and effects of various handicapping conditions, and even less was known or understood concerning the social and emotional implications. The ignorance created superstition and doubt and fear, which led to the isolation of the handicapped. And of course, the isolation created more ignorance and superstition and fear. It is a vicious cycle as old as human kind, but in this case it led to severe restrictions on the rights of a significant segment of the population—the handicapped.

The Topsy-turvy Period

Whenever conditions change remarkably, the change is preceded by a period of adjustment characterized primarily by confusion and a series of false starts. Such a topsy-turvy period with regard to treatment of the handicapped began in the late 1950s. To some extent, it is still with us.

During the past two decades, a movement developed to identify the handicapped in our population and bring them into the educational setting, particularly those who were less severely impaired. But in each case, the handicapped were treated as a separate group, to be segregated from others. Thus, a limited number of handicapped children entered the school system under some rather unusual conditions. Parents had to provide transportation for the handicapped child, or in some situations separate buses made the rounds through the district to collect only handicapped children. (In some cases, this meant that children spent as much time on the bus as they did in the classroom.)

The practice created new frustrations and fears among parents, educators, and children. Parents who had previously kept their handicapped children isolated were expected to suddenly remove the protective shield with which they had encompassed themselves and their children. This was often a traumatic experience. Few were prepared to cope with the situation brought about by this "new" educational concept, because there were still so many unknowns.

Teachers and school administrators were equally unprepared. They were able to anticipate some of the problems which confronted them and the handicapped students in their new environment, but they were not prepared to manage some of the more complex circumstances which arose. For example, the teacher had to assume responsibility for dispensing medications to some children, and it compounded the complexities of the daily schedule. In many instances, teachers had not been trained in the management of exceptional children, and in order to develop their competencies, teachers attended in-service training or evening classes. The combination of new experiences in the classroom and the demands of training outside the classroom frequently left teachers exhausted and reduced their classroom effectiveness.

It was not difficult for parents and educators to conceptualize how such programs for the handicapped *should* operate or how the individual children *should* be managed, but there were no precedents upon which to build. The programs were essentially experimental, and most of the information obtained was obtained through the awkward experiences which took place in the classroom or at home, often at the expense of the handicapped child. The period was also marked by a certain amount of secretiveness between school administrators and parents. There was little parent involvement in the programs, either in planning or in direct participation. Reports and evaluations were kept from parents so that they did not know exactly what was going on with regard to their children.

In addition, although some handicapped children were beginning to be served through public education, and although a superficial mingling of the handicapped and the non-handicapped emerged, this period of separation proved to be devastating to many parents and to their handicapped children. Admission to the programs was selective, and many courageous parents brought their handicapped children forward only to have them rejected by the programs. Parents could not understand how educational opportunities were being provided for some handicapped children and denied to others because they did not "fit" into the system. Such experiences tended to promote even greater feelings of hopelessness and frustration.

Children were not the only ones who were having problems. During this same period, a national "Hire the Handicapped" program was underway. The slogan appeared on billboards, in newspapers and magazines, and on radio and television. But relatively few employers actually did hire handicapped persons. Often, the hiring of such individuals was merely a token move, not accompanied by a real sense of moral responsibility or by a real commitment to provide a meaningful job for the handicapped employee. Handicapped workers realized they were suffering from the same problem as their younger counterparts in the school system. It was a problem of acceptance, and it arose not so much from their own handicapping condition as from the attitudes of employers and fellow workers.

The problem occasioned a number of studies, and researchers found that handicapped workers were, indeed, good employment prospects. They had the same abilities to perform many jobs as did non-handicapped workers, they were often more dependable workers than the non-handicapped, and they tended to take pride in the work they did.

Armed with this kind of information, a new emphasis began to form. In the past, the premise had always been that the handicapped person could not function within a given environment because of his or her own inability. The new perspective moved away from emphasis upon the person and focused on the influence of the environment as the factor which causes most of the problem. A person cannot function in an environment which does not allow that person to exercise his or her capabilities. Thus, handicapped workers, as well as parents of handicapped children began asking a more meaningful question: Are the barriers which prevent the handicapped child or worker from attaining his or her highest potentials *within* the individual, or is the individual a victim of barriers created by the environment *without*?

All of these changes had a significant effect on the status of the handicapped in the labor market. Prior to this "topsy-turvy" period, the handicapped were simply not employed, but during this time they became grossly *under* employed; that is, they entered the work force to some degree, but almost always in positions which were below their capabilities. Part of this was due to a lack of skills occasioned by previous restrictions on access to training. Also, little effort was made by employers to accommodate the special needs of the handicapped with regard to architectural barriers and working conditions. The handicapped were hired only if they "fit" into the company's existing program in much the same way as young handicapped persons were admitted to the school only if they "fit" into the school setting.

The period can be viewed with some ambivalence. It included steps forward, as well as steps backward. In many instances, the handicapped person was humiliated by barriers which actually exaggerated the differences between the handicapped and the non-handicapped. In some respects, the separation which existed in school and in the work place widened the gap because it called attention to the differences rather than emphasizing the sameness between handicapped and non-handicapped. This polarization is still prevalent in many educational and employment settings throughout the United States.

However, it cannot be denied that there were many positive outcomes which occurred in favor of the handicapped when the period of isolation shifted into a period of separate educational rights and some employment. For example, the level of public awareness of the problem rose considerably. Through observation and research conducted regarding the handicapped child in school and the handicapped person at work, much information was obtained which enhanced the image of the handicapped. This information pointed to the great potential strengths within the child and the adult if they were only given the opportunity to develop their skills and capabilities.

Also, during this period a more humanistic approach to the acceptance of the person with a handicap began to appear. The public began to accept more responsibility and concern for the handicapped child. This general shift in attitude was triggered by court action in response to parent complaints against state and local school systems, by increased contact with the handicapped, by the effective actions of professional organizations and parent groups, and by the response of legislators to the obvious needs of a significant population group. Certainly, the battle had just begun, but positive results were evident, and there seemed to be increasing promise for the handicapped.

The Current Status

Beginning in the late 1960s and continuing to the present time is an era of accelerated activities designed to enhance the image of the handicapped child and to provide more opportunities for them. Interest in education for the handicapped has reached new heights, and as a result of this interest, many exemplary programs have been developed and numerous research studies have been conducted. These studies consistently underscore the basic proposition that handicapped children can make exceptional gains if their handicaps are identified early and if they receive educational services attuned to their special needs.

In 1968 the enactment of the Handicapped Children Early Education Act authorized the establishment and operation of model early education projects for handicapped children. Many of the features of programs developed under the act have been replicated in other programs throughout the United States and abroad. The programs repeatedly show the remarkable developmental growth these children can experience, and the variety of skills they can acquire.

Such programs also provide much of the information needed concerning the child with a handicap. Prior to this time, little was known about the management and education needs of the child, the capabilities of the child, or what intervention techniques would be beneficial for the child. Using the information obtained through these programs, both parents and educators are better able to deal with the problems. Also, the studies point to a need for more investigation of the traditional norms and functional levels of the handicapped child, and the desirability of setting new challenges related to the higher capabilities of the handicapped child. As a result, some handicapped children are reaching levels of educational attainment never before thought possible.

Researchers now feel there is no strict dividing line between children whose needs are special and those whose needs are normal. All children have needs, but the needs of some are more extensive than those of others. The special child usually has more needs than other children, they occur more often, and they tend to interfere with everyday life and performance. In fact, the director of educational services in the U.S. Office of Child Development, Dr. Jenny Klein, has advanced the proposition that handicapped children are more *like* other children than they are different. Therefore, it is a mistake to conceptualize great differences between the normal child and the handicapped child. The handicapped child is first of all a child, with all of the feelings, interests, and attitudes of other children; the handicapping condition is just one aspect of the child's total picture of strengths and weaknesses.

The key concept to come out of the turmoil was the concept of "mainstreaming," which meant that instead of isolating handicapped children or segregating them from others, they should be integrated into the regular classrooms and should participate with their non-handicapped peers in a wider variety of academic and social activities.

Just as the handicapped child was becoming more visible in the education system, his or her adult counterpart was beginning to make small gains in the labor market. The passage of the Rehabilitation Act of 1973 made it illegal for firms which do a minimum amount of business with the federal government ($2500 per year or more) to discriminate against handicapped individuals in employment. More than two million business organizations and public institutions were affected by the act, and many of them implemented affirmative action programs to stimulate employment of the handicapped. Firms which did not comply with the provisions of the act had complaints filed against them, and during the first four years following passage of the act almost 500 complaints were filed.

While progress has been slow, it is accelerating. The vigor of enforcement is increasing; employers are beginning to understand and appreciate the handicapped worker. The imaginary impressions and stereotypes of the past are being replaced by more accurate and positive observations as employers gain experience with handicapped workers. The same is true of relations with fellow employees. Because they were denied opportunities to develop such skills in the past, many handicapped workers lack some of the social interaction skills and abilities necessary to cope with the work environment, an environment which imposes a variety of demands upon the handicapped person which she or he has never experienced before. In the past, other workers were also denied the opportunity to interact with handicapped workers. Fortunately, both groups are learning, and the next generation will have the advantage of having spent years together in the nation's classrooms, and so all of the interaction skills will have been learned by the time that group enters the labor force.

Another positive change during the period has been the active development of career education and vocational training for handicapped high school students and for post-secondary school adults. Most of these programs were non-existent during the 1950s and early 1960s. They provide training for the handicapped and help them acquire the skills necessary to compete in the labor market. The fact that more and more handicapped individuals are receiving training prior to placement has influenced the variety and levels of employment available to the handicapped, and it will continue to have an even greater impact in the future.

Dropping the Barriers

At this point, there seems little question that the barriers to educational and employment opportunities for the handicapped are being gradually diminished. But much remains to be done. Figure 8 indicates the kinds of barriers which must be dealt with if the handicapped are to be fully accepted into society. Those barriers are of two types. Obviously, the physical barriers make it difficult for the handicapped to move around freely in their environment. Those barriers include problems in architectural design— stairways, for instance—problems with transportation facilities, and problems with machinery and tools designed for the non-handicapped. But even before significant changes can be brought about to diminish those physical barriers, there is a need to change the more intangible barriers, the attitudinal barriers. Perhaps it is a result of the suddenness with which the handicapped have gained visibility, or perhaps it is from some other cause, but among the major barriers between the handicapped and the non-handicapped are the feelings members of each group have toward themselves, as individuals, and toward each other as members of society.

The management strategies used in bringing the handicapped forth from the rooms of their homes to the mainstream of society and in elevating them to an equal level in the societal structure are very complex. Underscoring these strategies is the premise that the level of equal rights which the handicapped can obtain is directly predicated upon the degree of attitude change which occurs among both the handicapped and the non-handicapped populations.

Change in Attitudes

In order for more positive attitudes to develop, there must be drastic changes in the image of the handicapped. Philosophically, many parents, educators, administrators, legislators, employers, and others offer lip service to the advocacy of equal rights for the handicapped, but the full implementation of that concept is still in its infancy.

We have stressed in other chapters of this book the importance of the family and the home in building attitudes and values in the child. If anything, that importance is even more pronounced in the case of the handicapped child. The

BARRIERS TO THE HANDICAPPED

Attitudes

Physical

- Self

- Family Members

- Peers

- Community Members

- Educators

- Legislators

- Employers

- Transportation

- Architecture

- Machinery

- Tools

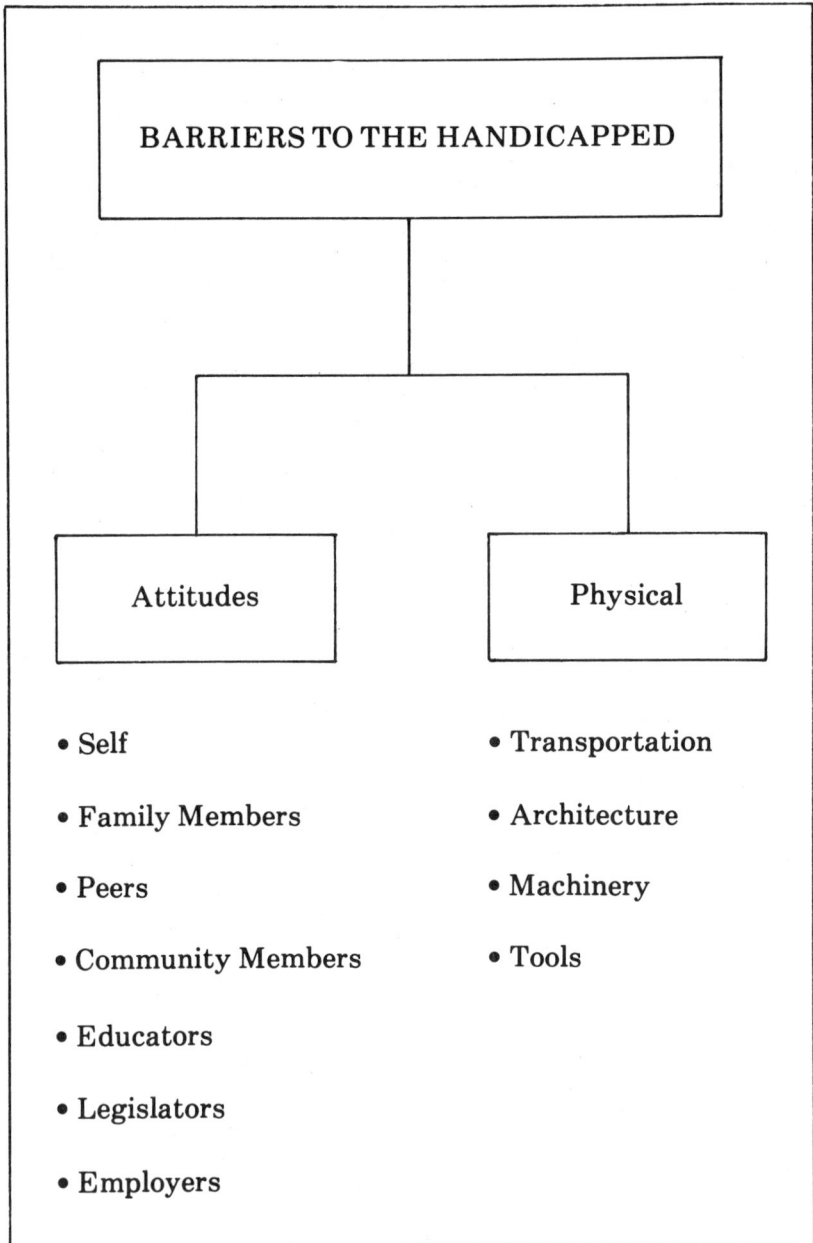

FIGURE 8. The two major types of barriers which must be dealt with if the handicapped are to be fully accepted into society.

image the person with a handicap has of herself or himself, and the perceptions that person has of the attitudes of others toward her or him, is heavily dependent on the family. Leo Buscaglia has stated the position eloquently. Referring to the handicapped child, he wrote:

> For the most part, unconsciously, the child will learn about the world outside and of life from each person in his family. If they are fearful, he will learn to fear. If they are suspicious, he will become so. If they are optimistic, he will know optimism. If they love, so will he. This, of course, is an over-simplification of the process of personality growth and development—but in general, we *learn* to be human and the family members are our first teachers.
>
> To some degree each family member tells each other who he is and whether or not he is likely to succeed, even before he has come into contact with the larger society outside of his home.

Typically, parents and other family members still view the handicapped child as needing more extra protection than is required, and in many instances they see themselves as the major caretakers of the child for life. This is basically a negative attitude. It concentrates on the weaknesses and limitations of the child, not on the child's strengths and potentials.

This tendency toward negative attitudes is fairly general. For example, in one instance neighbors were surprised to learn about the independent life style of a mentally retarded married couple, who left their home daily to ride the bus to and from work. Neighbors worried about how the couple managed their affairs. No one noticed the positive aspects, such as the fact that the couple's yard was one of the most attractive in the neighborhood, or that the couple's productivity on the job and their record of attendance was higher than non-handicapped fellow workers. In another deplorable example, a local library board requested the termination of an employee when the board learned the individual was educably mentally retarded, even though the employee had a record of successful performance of duties over a period of two years.

These kinds of unsupported attitudes must change, and there is indication that they are changing.

The Scene Today

The decade of the 1970s is undoubtedly one of the most significant periods in the history of the civil rights of the handicapped. Much of the activity is the result of legislative action at federal and state levels. For example, Public Law 93-516, The Vocational Rehabilitation Act of 1973 as amended in 1974, states: "It is of critical importance to this Nation that equality of opportunity, equal access to all aspects of society and equal rights guaranteed by the Constitution of the United States be provided to all individuals with handicaps."

The U.S. Office of Education is committed to assuring equal educational opportunities for all handicapped children. Efforts of the Office of Education in meeting this commitment are coordinated through the Bureau of Education for the Handicapped. Among the objectives designed to implement this priority are: (1) to assure that every handicapped child is receiving an *appropriately designed education*, and (2) to assure that every handicapped child who leaves school has had *career education training* that is relevant to the job market, meaningful to his or her career aspirations, and realistic to the individual's fullest potential.

Another significant legislative action took place in 1975 with the passage of Public Law 94-143, the Education for All Handicapped Children Act. This act was the result of over four years of intensive legislative development, including extensive hearings conducted by both the U.S. Senate and the U.S. House of Representatives. Among the findings of the Congress were: (1) there are more than eight million handicapped children in the United States, (2) the special educational needs of such children are not being fully met, and (3) more than half of the handicapped children in the United States do not receive appropriate educational services which would enable them to have full equality of opportunity. The purpose of the act is stated in the text:

It is the purpose of this Act to assure that all handicapped children have available to them. . . . a free appropriate public education which emphasizes special education and related services designed to meet their unique needs, to assure that the rights of handicapped children and their parents or guardians are protected, to assist states and localities to provide for the education of all handicapped children, and to assess and assure the effectiveness of efforts to educate handicapped children.

In addition to education and employment, another area in which the handicapped are receiving attention is in the area of leisure activity. Both government and private organizations are working to assure availability of public recreational facilities to the handicapped, to develop special leisure activities for the handicapped, and to encourage the handicapped to participate in a variety of recreational activities.

As was indicated earlier, there has never been such a time as the present insofar as growing opportunities for the handicapped are concerned. With the implementation of recent laws, and with a growing increase in the awareness of the need for equal rights for handicapped persons, much more can be expected to happen in the near future. As always, major responsibilities must be assumed by the parents of handicapped children. All education, including career education, begins at home, and the parents of handicapped children must continue to be effective teachers.

THE CHALLENGES OF TODAY AND TOMORROW

If the handicapped child is to fully benefit and to be assured of the type of employment which will provide him or her with the greatest self-fulfillment, parents must assume responsibility for three major roles. First, they should participate actively in local parent and professional organizations which serve as vehicles to transport their desires and concerns to public officials who are responsible for securing the rights of the handicapped. Through such membership, parents will be better informed about their own rights and about the rights of their handicapped children. The strength of numbers and the organized approach can move many obstacles. With few exceptions, the laws which are now in effect can be traced back to the outcries of parents. Parents must become involved in the movement which has now begun, the movement to guarantee to the handicapped child full participation in education, including career education and the resulting opportunities for career realization.

Second, as part of the mainstreaming movement, parents must make a conscious effort to provide opportunities for their handicapped children to participate with non-handicapped peers in a variety of settings. Laws can be enacted, architectural barriers can be removed, modes of transportation can be modified, and technology can provide machinery adaptable to the handicapped, but until *attitudes* of both the handicapped and the non-handicapped are significantly changed to reflect a more positive image, the aspirations of the handicapped cannot be fully realized.

Third, parents must be sincerely positive in their attitudes toward the career prospects of their handicapped children, and they must transmit those positive attitudes into a supportive and reassuring but realistic environment.

The challenge to parents of handicapped children is to provide those children with opportunities to interact with others on a regular basis in order to develop a more adequate understanding of strengths and weaknesses. Parents must gain insights into the capabilities of their handicapped children, and then place those children in situations where they can demonstrate those capabilities. The non-handicapped children with whom today's handicapped children associate will some day be the fellow employees, the employers, the educators, and the public officials who will have direct influence over the opportunities available to the handicapped population. We know that progress depends on the development of positive attitudes among both handicapped and non-handicapped populations. We also know that those positive attitudes will not develop so long as suspicion and misunderstanding exist. Handicapped individuals do fare for themselves when they are given appropriate opportunities. For this reason, parents should be insistent that, where appropriate, their children attend a preschool where they can learn to interact with other children, and where other children can learn to accept and befriend those who may be handicapped. Many preschools accept handicapped children at the present time. If parents cannot find such a preschool, they might consider taking action to encourage the establishment of such a school in the vicinity. Reports coming from such integrated settings are positive and encouraging to parents of both handicapped children and non-handicapped children.

Insofar as career education is concerned, parents of handicapped children should consider the suggestions offered in this book and modify them according to each child's interests and capabilities. Since children need role models, parents should consciously seek out older handicapped persons who may serve as such models for their children. Handicapped adolescents and adults may be located in area high schools, in universities, or within the community.

The progress made by the handicapped over recent years gives promise of even more progress. The handicapped have become—and will continue to become in increasing numbers—contributing taxpayers in our society. They have become home owners. They have become active in civic affairs. They have become participants in all community activities. Most important, recent progress has proved that the handicapped can lead happy, useful lives.

Career education offers another avenue for the handicapped to gain a sense of accomplishment and to acquire realistic, effective preparation for full participation in the work force and in society.

SUMMARY

Career education has as much application for handicapped children as for the non-handicapped. All children must go through the stages of career development described in this book, and so parents of handicapped children should provide the same kinds of support activities as the parents of normal children, although they must tailor those activities to meet the special needs of their special children. The role of the parent in providing career education is no less critical for parents of handicapped children than for other parents; indeed, it may be more critical because such parents must deal with their own attitudes, with the attitudes of their handicapped children, with the attitudes of the peer group, and with the attitudes of society in general.

The struggle to obtain equal treatment for the handicapped with regard to education and employment has been a long and painful struggle, and it is by no means completed. However, significant advancements have been made, and the handicapped can now expect the advantages of education—including career education—and the opportunity to find meaningful employment.

ADDITIONAL READING

Becker, Wesley C. *Parents Are Teachers*. Champaign, Ill.: Research Press, 1971.

Braddock, David L. *Selected Readings in Early Education of Handicapped Children*. Reston, Va.: Council for Exceptional Children, 1974.

Brutten, Milton; Richardson, S.O.; and Mangel, C. *Something's Wrong With My Child*. New York: Harcourt Brace Jovanovich, 1973.

Buscaglia, Leo. *The Disabled and Their Parents*. Thorofare, N.J.: Charles B. Slack Co., 1975.

Hoyt, Kenneth B. *Career Education: Contributions to an Evolving Concept*. Salt Lake City: Olympus Publishing Company, 1976.

Lake, Thomas P. *Career Education: Exemplary Programs for the Handicapped*. Reston, Va.: Council for Exceptional Children, 1974.

_____. *Selected Career Education Programs for the Handicapped*. Washington, D.C.: Department of Health, Education and Welfare, Publication No. (OE) 73-05501, 1973.

Siegel, Ernest. *The Exceptional Child Grows Up.* New York: E. P. Dutton & Co., 1974.

Thorum, Arden R. *Instructional Materials for the Handicapped.* (Revised ed.) Salt Lake City: Olympus Publishing Company, 1977.

Verhoven, Peter J., and Goldstein, Judith E. *Leisure Activity Participation and Handicapped Populations: An Assessment of Research Needs.* Arlington, Va.: National Recreation and Park Association.

Weiner, Florence. *Help for the Handicapped Child.* New York: McGraw-Hill, 1973.

Wynn, Suzan. *Mainstreaming and Early Childhood Education for the Handicapped.* Washington, D.C.: Wynn Associates, 1975.

CHAPTER TEN

Career Prospects

A major message of career education to parents is that one need not await an "appropriate" time for occupational choice before beginning to help a child prepare for a career. Willy nilly, that process starts the moment of birth in the messages the child gets from his or her daily environment about the role of work in life. Nevertheless, at some point occupational choices must be made, deliberately or by default, either in anticipation of preparation or at the point of entry into a job. Thus, there is value in being aware of the need for occupational choice long before one is made. Children and youth are not generally good at abstract concepts. To them, work is simply a task that they do or that someone else does. They develop their work values and career awareness through actual work roles and through observing the occupations in which people are engaged. As they begin the process of exploration, they must identify ocupations consistent with their preferred life styles. One need not be concerned with premature choices. All young people go through a string of "what I want to be when I grow up" choices. However, work and careers become more meaningful concepts as children begin to visualize themselves in future occupations and as they conceive of themselves preparing for those occupations.

The rapidity of occupational change in a modern technological society has become a cliche. Change is more rapid than in the distant past but perhaps not as accelerated as many believe. Educators, as well as parents, sometimes remark: "Why speak of career education when we don't even know what jobs will be available?" Educators might be reassured and parents might be better prepared to help their children through an exploration process if they had some idea of the occupational outlook.

Generally, projections are made of the number of jobs likely to be available in various occupations only five to ten years into the future. Current projections extend only to 1985. Those detailed projections are prepared at a national level by the Bureau of Labor Statistics and at the state and local level by the state departments of employment security and occasionally by universities. The *Occupational Outlook Handbook* and *Occupational Outlook Quarterly* are available in the offices of most school counselors, at the local offices of the state employment service, and at most libraries. This is the best source of national data, while the state employment service office is the place to inquire for local data. These sources do not generally project the outlook for employment on various occupations in precise numerical form. Such data is available from the same agencies for those with such need. However, the youth and the parent or counselor are only interested in whether an occupation is growing or declining, and how fast, and whether openings are likely to be available from expansion or from replacement as others retire, die, or quit. The exact numbers are meaningless.

Beyond 1985, the outlook becomes more "iffy," but knowledgeable observers can identify long-run trends. Even though a particular occupation may disappear over the long run, few are so specialized that the skills acquired cannot be used in some other occupation. A ten-year outlook gives ample time for redirection, as long as one is alert to the prospects.

This chapter identifies those occupational areas that look promising as far ahead as one can see. It also explores the kinds of preparation required. This does not mean that a youth should not choose an occupation that is not within this list. It does mean that if he or she chooses a declining or static occupation, the competition will be tougher. Even in declining occupations, openings occur from turnover, retirements, deaths, and other factors. If one wants in badly enough, is sufficiently capable, has the right contacts, and is patient enough, it is generally possible to be successful, but one should know the odds.

OCCUPATION OUTLOOK BY PREPARATION REQUIRED

Between 1975 and 1986, all employment in the United States was expected to increase by 20 percent. Therefore, any occupation growing by that amount is proportionately stable. It is worth looking at the occupational categories expected to grow more rapidly than that average. Figure 9 provides an overview of the types of jobs which will be growing or declining. Various occupational groupings are organized by the amount of education generally considered necessary for entry to them.

Occupations for People without a High School Education

There is a difference between the amount of education actually required to do a job and the amount an employer may require because it may be considered necessary for promotion or simply because people with that education may be available. Although there are a variety of occupations available to individuals with less than a high school education, the occupational requirements and expected earnings are quite varied. For example, most of these occupations are geared to on-the-job training, but this training may vary from a few days (manufacturing assemblers) to a few weeks (appliance repairs) to several months (welders and machine tool operators). It is typical that the higher paying jobs require more lengthy training periods.

Also, even though entrance into some occupations may not require a high school education, thorough entry examinations requiring the demonstration of basic educa-

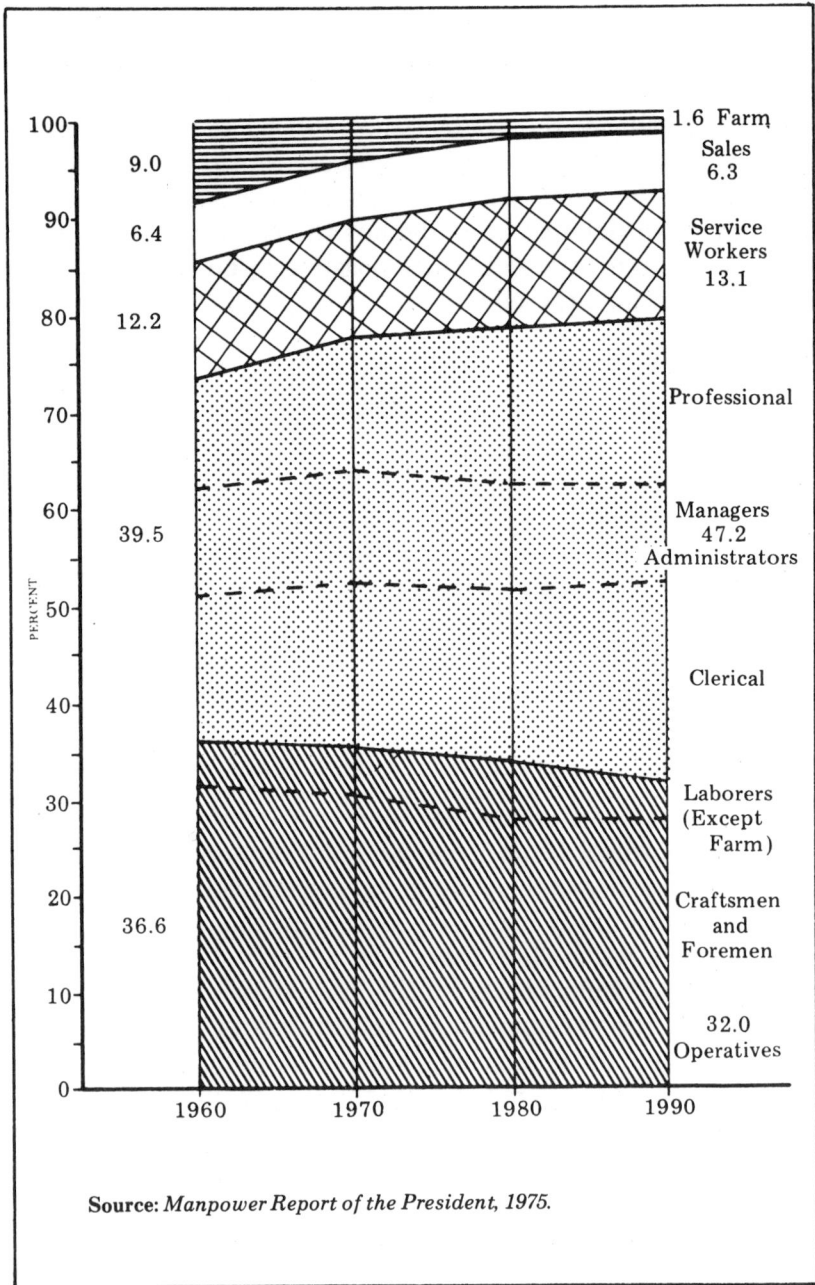

FIGURE 9. Certain types of jobs are increasing in numbers, while others show a trend toward decreasing numbers.

tional skills are often a prerequisite. This is a typical trait of most government service jobs. More rigid physical specifications must be met for construction occupations and for jobs that require driving.

Age requirements may be an obstacle for younger individuals without a high school education. For instance, such occupations as bartending, route driving, and security guards may require one to be 18 to 21 years old.

Personal experiences can prove to be a decisive factor in gaining employment. For example, motorcycle mechanics, a high growth occupation, are mostly self-taught or have received training in informal work situations. Experienced mechanics in this field earn wages ranging from three to ten dollars an hour.

In general, the categories with the most potential employment growth for this educational group are those of (1) mechanics and repairers and (2) health and social service occupations. Present evaluations and future projections indicate that the former classification receives much higher pay than the latter. The health and social service occupations available to those without high school educations are typified by the hospital orderly, an occupation from which one cannot be promoted without considerable additional education.

Those areas which promise the least occupational growth are in construction occupations and in occupations in transportation activities. The trend of increased introduction of labor-saving techniques in both occupational groups is projected to continue into the foreseeable future, thereby curbing the demand for unskilled labor despite the favorable growth rates expected of the respective industries.

The growth of leisure industries in the future may prove to be a high employment area for those with less formal education. With increased mobility and higher standards of living, the next few decades should witness an expansion of leisure industries which in turn should generate jobs more conformable to unskilled labor. The effects of the energy crisis on this segment of occupations is still unknown, but the chances are that leisure industries will continue to be a growth area.

Potential for "success" in the job market for individuals lacking a high school education will depend upon their ability to acquire a skill which is in relatively strong demand. As mentioned above, the occupations of mechanics and repairers provide the greatest opportunities for skill acquisition. To a lesser extent and with slightly smaller projected growth rate, opportunities will also be substantial in industrial production and related occupations—machine tool operators, assemblers, power truck operators, welders, and so forth. Finally, select occupations, such as skilled cooks and chefs, should provide opportunities for advancement in growing leisure industries. However, as long as employers can find workers with high school educations, they will generally prefer them, if only because of the demonstration of stability. Unless one has a special skill or direct contact with employers (perhaps relatives), to enter the occupational world without at least a high school diploma is to be at a serious disadvantage, for the competition there is enormous.

Occupations for People with a High School Education

Although there are many skilled occupations which can be obtained with or without a high school education, the options are much greater for the holder of a diploma, it being used as a screening device for many apprenticeships as well as for many jobs. For example, in industrial production and related occupations the graduate can qualify both for long-term training programs that do not come under the apprenticeship category and for the wider range of apprenticeship opportunites that do require a high school diploma.

With the introduction of more labor-saving techniques, the labor demands of the industrial production sector will shift more and more toward skilled labor for maintenance and repairs. Therefore, competition among non-graduates for the relatively few skilled jobs for which they can qualify can be expected to increase. High school graduates will hold a decided advantage in that there will be far fewer restrictions on their occupational choice in industrial production skills.

There will also be a wider variety of office occupations available to high school graduates. This is especially true if the graduate has had courses in typing, business arithmetic, and bookkeeping. Although on-the-job training is the usual mode of introducing individuals to many office occupations (statistical clerks, file clerks, and bookkeeping clerks), some occupations, such as secretaries and stenographers, require pre-entry formal training.

In general, growth in office occupations is expected to be faster than the average. Greatest opportunities are as skilled typists and stenographers. However, high demand in some occupations may be misleading in that the demand is due to high rates of turnover (bookkeepers). Also, expanding technology will make many office jobs obsolete (key punch operators). The continuing computer revolution is also expected to eliminate the need for some computer operating personnel because of increased incorporation of languages into the computer itself, making it easier and quicker to train personnel. This same growth in computer use is likely to make it essential that most office employeees have some knowledge of its use.

Service occupations, such as fire fighters, local police officers, and state police officers, are projected to have better than average employment opportunities, and in the case of state police officers growth is expected to be much faster than average. Though such occupations will be dependent upon government funding, the increasing concern for law enforcement and related civil services can be expected to provide impetus to growth. The expansion in law enforcement also comes from the increasing need for technical services to support officers in the field.

Although a high school education may be the first step in gaining employment in one of the occupations listed above, continuing education on the college level is often required. This is especially true for police officers in larger departments which require higher degrees of expertise.

Even though a high school education is usually the only formal education required in sales occupations, there are other difficulties for those seeking entry into this category. For example, experience is often a prerequisite, as well as being 21 years of age or older. However, sales occupations as a group are to have faster than average growth. Therefore, there is ample opportunity for individuals to get into the field and advance to higher paying and more prestigious jobs.

There are a few growth opportunities in the health services which offer very good opportunities for advancement without requiring formal education beyond the high school level. Specifically, dental lab technicians are trained on the job, and although they currently receive an average of about five thousand dollars per year with no experience, after approximately five years of experience the average salary rises to ten to fourteen thousand dollars. Medical assistants are also trained on the job for various duties but can expect slightly lower annual earnings than dental lab technicians. These two examples of health service occupations are both projected to have faster than average growth and to provide excellent employment opportunities for high school graduates.

Apprenticeship Programs

Apprenticeship programs may be a very attractive option for individuals who wish to acquire a skill which is projected to be in strong demand. This is even more true for high school graduates, who are in most cases preferred over non-graduates.

Growth in the demand for craft workers is projected to be about 20 percent by 1985, the average for all occupations. The least growth rate that applies to apprenticeship programs (and yet is still at the cross industry average) is expected in industrial production and related occupations. Even though substantial increased demand is projected for goods production, increased productivity and continued introduction of labor saving techniques will account for no more than average growth rate in employment. One exception to this situation is that the boilermaking occupation is expected to grow faster than average because of the increased construction of energy producing facilities.

Construction occupations have the widest variety of apprenticeship programs, ranging from bricklayers, carpen-

ters, and electricians to heavy equipment operators, painters, and plumbers. This category also appears to have the
most favorable overall growth rate.

One of the fastest growing occupations in the construction industry is that of asbestos and insulation workers. This
is largely due to the role of this occupation in energy
conservation moves. Heavy construction machinery operators are also expected to experience a much faster than
average growth rate. The only relatively large occupational
group in the construction classification which is expected to
have a slower than average growth rate is that of painters
and paper hangers.

Most apprenticeship programs in the construction
industry are designed with a preference for high school
graduates, and in some cases a high school diploma is
required. The wage rate of skilled workers in the construction industry ranges typically between eight and twelve
dollars per hour (union scale). Apprentices can expect to
start at about half of the skilled wage and receive periodic
increases. Length of apprenticeships vary from a low of two
to three years for cement masons to a high of five years for
plumbers and pipe fitters.

Mechanics and repairers form another large occupational grouping that has a variety of apprenticeship programs.
However, with the exception of maintenance electricians
most of these occupations (diesel mechanics, automobile
mechanics, and repairers) have very few available apprenticeship programs. Individuals acquire skills mostly through
on-the-job training and through informal instruction. This
occupational category is also projected to have a favorable
growth rate with special emphasis on industrial machinery
repairers, diesel mechanics, and maintenance electricians.

*Occupations for Junior College and Post-High School
Technical Training*

Those occupations requiring special training after high
school but at a less than four year level are expected to
experience faster than average rates of growth. In particular, health occupations, which belong to this group, are on

the rise because technological developments have allowed specialization in many areas with only one or two years of post high school training. Many of these fields are relatively new and as yet are very small; thus, they are likely to experience a long-term favorable growth rate, considering the general trend of increased health services.

Possibly misleading is the general rise in demand for the performing arts for individuals with post high school training. Even though practically all branches of the performing arts are expected to experience above average growth, the attractiveness of such occupations leads to overcrowding, which will continue to force keen competition and the likelihood that only those with the most outstanding talents and abilities will succeed.

Within this post high school training classification are also certain technical scientific occupations, such as drafting, engineering and science technicians, and surveyors. These occupations are to experience faster than average growth rates. On-the-job training is usually coupled with post high school formal technical training over periods varying from two to four years.

Finally, it will be fruitful to consider the increasing role of the paraprofessional. The high cost and relative scarcity of professionals in many fields leads to the use of lesser trained people to assume some of the less skilled of professional tasks. Paramedical personnel may be considered to have the lead in the development. The situation is not so clear for such occupational groups as paralegals, where they may be a threat to the professionals already practicing.

It appears that growth of paraprofessional occupations will vary widely across the country in the years ahead, partly because of differently defined labor markets. However, it seems that paraprofessional training programs have good growth potential, and although they are not structured in the same way as apprenticeship programs, their related opportunities can be simultaneously developed for on-the-job training and acquisition of certain areas of professional expertise through formal education. Such a development should relieve many professions of an overburdening work load, and it should result in savings to the consumer.

Occupations for College-Trained Manpower

Office occupations requiring a college degree consist of a wider variety of disciplines, but most are business-related degrees. In general, projected growth rates are quite favorable, most being average or above average. Exceptions to the rule are advertising workers, who can expect keen competition, particularly if lacking in advanced degree work or experience, and lawyers, who, because of conditions of oversupply, can also expect keen competition. On the other hand, market research workers, who may possess a variety of market-related degrees, can expect a much faster than average growth rate in their field.

Because of declining growth and increasing supply, individuals who seek to teach on any level can expect keen competition. Increasing standards will lead to the need for more advanced degrees in order to compete at all. However, opportunities should expand in specialties such as education for the handicapped and early childhood education, and in schools with disadvantaged populations.

Employment of health and regulatory inspectors will progress at a faster than average growth rate which will likely continue for some time into the future in light of increasing government regulation. Problems of pollution and ecological considerations should also stimulate this field. Also, as firms become more aware of the possibility of savings by hiring trained personnel in this area, even more opportunities should become available.

Demand should stay favorable in most branches of engineering. In many of the scientific and technical occupations, an advanced degree will be essential in order to compete in the job market effectively. Though faster than average growth is expected in practically all the related fields, increasing supply and increasing demand for greater qualifications beyond a bachelor's degree will bring about the need for more advanced degree work. This is equally true for mathematicians and physicists. An exception is in the field of chemistry in which good opportunites will be available to all levels of degree holders (from bachelor's degree to a doctorate).

None of the various occupations in health services is projected to have a below average growth, most being above average. This includes the various practices of physicians, dentists, and pharmacists. The same outlook holds for veterinarians, registered nurses, medical technologists, physical therapists, and speech pathologists and audiologists, the latter two of which are to have much faster than average growth rates. There are no longer the shortages in these fields which have prevailed so long; nevertheless, there is high demand in smaller geographical areas and the overall rate of growth will remain high.

Social science occupations are typical of professions in which advanced degrees are required to be able to compete in the labor market. Even at the Ph.D. level, competition will be keen for such professions as history, political science, and sociology, especially for teaching positions. However, economists and other social scientists whose training has application outside educational institutions should find good employment opportunities with private firms, particularly if such highly demanded skills as computer and statistical abilities have been acquired.

Social service occupations will have varied growth rates, which are perhaps reflective of changing social priorities and views. School counselors and home economists are to have slower than average growth rates, and competition for employment may be difficult without advanced degree work or work-related experience. Demand for more individuals in the clergy is on the decline for all Protestant denominations, but the demand is on the increase in the Catholic religion because of a persisting higher birth rate. Employment opportunities for rehabilitation workers are expected to increase faster than average and to be even more favorable for advanced degree holders. Opportunities for licensed architects and landscape architects are expected to expand much faster than average. Keen competition can be expected in the communications field for radio and television announcers. However, favorable opportunities will be available for technical writers and newspaper reporters.

Computer specialties should be given attention because they have offered such attractive opportunities over the past two decades. The rate of growth in the computer industry is expected to increase at a slower rate for 1970-85 than the rate experienced during the 1960s. The following jobs within the industry are all expected to increase: data processing, machine repairmen, systems analysts, programmers, computer and peripheral equipment operations. The projected demand for keypunch operators is expected to decrease for the coming decade.

Overall, the projected demand in the computer field is expected to increase 30 percent—from 765,200 to 997,600— for the 1970-80 period. Roughly 200,000 jobs are expected to be the result of growth and 300,000 from the replacement of incumbents, for total expected openings of roughly 500,000. The greatest portion of this anticipated growth is expected to be absorbed by the services industry and its effort to increase the quality of the computers.

The employment situation in library science is expected to grow at a slower rate for 1970-85 than was experienced during the 1960s. However, the projected demand is expected to exceed projected supply by roughly 2,000 positions per year on the average. The usual minimum requirement remains the bachelors degree in library science; however, some positions may be available for persons with less training. The overall labor market in the field of library science is expected to tighten in the next decade. As a result of this trend, one can expect the competition to increase the basic entry requirements of the field. In many cases applicants will find a masters degree most helpful, and the bachelors degree should become a requirement for most positions.

THE ECONOMIC WORTH OF AN EDUCATION

A college education for our children has become part of the American dream since the second world war. Indeed, for the first thirty years after that war, a college degree in most disciplines was almost a guarantee of career success. After a depression and an all-out war, the supply of educated persons was low, while the technological developments of that period and the increasing complexity of society had created a swollen and expanding demand. However, by 1970 that general shortage situation had ended. The pace of demand increase had slowed, and supply had caught up with demand in general. Now, many parents are asking, "Will a college education be a good investment for my child?" While they recognize that career preparation is not the only reason for college attendance, it is certainly one of the reasons, and career prospects affect the desirability of the college degree.

Evaluating the Decision to Attend College

In considering whether or not to attend college, it is wise to keep in mind three time frames: (1) the two-year associate or technically related degree, (2) the four-year B.A. or B.S., and (3) the various graduate programs that extend beyond four years. The longer the time frame, the greater will be the uncertainty as to the return on the educational investment.

Given the high rates of growth projected in occupations such as health services, scientific technicians, and potentially, paraprofessionals, it appears that the two-year degree will increasingly be a sound investment. However, four-year degrees require closer inspection because of the greater variety of disciplines and hence the greater variation in returns. The longer period of schooling plus the greater cost requires the choice of a career that is soundly projected to be in demand at least four years in the future.

Based on most projections, one would appear wise to avoid limiting oneself to a liberal arts degree without adding some specialized training beyond it. The job opportunities available with such a degree are likely to be little greater than those without any degree. This is also true of mathematics, physics, and various disciplines of social science. If one is bent upon entering such fields, the need for graduate work will be imperative; thus, a larger time frame and increased cost must be considered.

There is also a wide variation in returns to graduate education. As stated above, in many fields a graduate degree will be essential in order to be able to compete in the job market. However, even such fields as law are now becoming overcrowded, demonstrating that in some fields graduate education does not and will not in the foreseeable future command a premium as it once did.

Another major consideration should be the limited probability of entrance into particular graduate schools, especially in the medical field. In view of this, it is not wise to be single-goal oriented over such a long period of time. Associated with this problem is the quality of the college or university which one is able to attend. Some empirical work has been done demonstrating significant earnings differences of graduates from institutions of varying quality (Wales, 1973).

In terms of what might be a wise choice of occupation in the future, the strength of demand for engineers, accountants, and computer programmers are but a few examples. However, most fields such as these can experience a relative turn around over the period of a few years. Therefore, if an individual is to attend a four-year program, it appears that the best hedge for employment security is diversity. For example, computer skills can complement many different types of degrees, making one more employable and in many cases providing a choice of careers.

The pursuit of "dual career" preparation may take additional time, but in the long run it may be well worth the effort. This may be especially true for highly technical careers in which people are trained for a relatively narrow occupational category. It may be advisable for graduate degree seekers to pursue the same objective of preparation for more than one career.

The decision to attend college in the future will basically be affected by two things. The first is expected returns, which if they are to be realized will require considerable expertise in choice of career, choice of college, and long-range planning. The second factor is the cost, which no one expects to decline in the foreseeable future.

Naturally, these factors have to be weighed against alternative choices in other occupations. A major point of comparison is that in virtually all non-college choices there is not the acute sacrifice of income during the training period that there is while attending college. This expense cannot be counted totally as a cost, however, if one enjoys learning for its own sake and can afford the luxury of intellectual and social development separately from economic returns. One possible strategy would be to pursue a two-year degree which offers relative occupational security but which can be used as a stepping stone to a four-year or graduate degree without difficult transition problems.

Taken on the average, a college education was counted over many years to provide a financial return on the investment at the rate of around 12 percent. In a time of low interest rates, that was a better return than that offered to alternative uses of capital. Now the average return is calculated at about 8 percent, and many high grade bonds will bring a better return without risk. College for the sake of a diploma is probably no longer a good investment. Both parent and youth must ask supplementary questions: Are my motivations more intellectual and social than economic? Does the career that interests me require training at that level? Are my desires and commitments in that direction more important to me than financial return on the dollars invested?

Post-High School Options

If a parent is to be effective in helping a child choose a successful occupation, the process should probably begin before high school. A more correct statement may perhaps be that the parents should try to ensure that the child has acquired a skill which will be acceptably marketable upon graduation from high school. One method of approach is to develop interests in pre-high school years that can be further cultivated in high school and transformed into a marketable skill.

Greater potential exists in schools which have well developed vocational education curricula in conjunction with traditional curricula. The realization of skill potential in children may require a relaxing of traditional attitudes on the part of parents concerning the value of academic and vocational education. Also parents may be forced to change attitudes concerning the male and female work roles.

A productive decision as to what course of action to pursue after high school should be based on careful planning and consultation with knowledgeable guidance counselors. Essentially, the high school graduate can (1) attend college, (2) pursue a skilled trade through an apprenticeship or other on-the-job training program, (3) enter directly into employment, (4) join the military, or (5) become self-employed (a wide-open field for the versatile).

The last option may not be so unheard-of as it might first appear if the individual has acquired a highly demanded skill (motorcycle mechanics) while in high school and has also gained some experience. This may be more true for certain regions of the country than others. However, in general capital costs and the need for greater management expertise are projected to increase in the future and thus may become even more prohibitive to self-employment, although it should never be discouraged by parents.

The choice of entrance into the military should be made with a plan as to what technical training or skill can be acquired that can be brought back into the civilian labor market and put to use in case one decides after some experience that a full military career is not desired. Many skills in civilian life are taught in the military.

Going directly into the labor market produces its hazards as well as its rewards. Approximately one-third of the jobs in the U.S. economy can be held by anyone with reasonable basic education skills, manual dexterity, and the ability to drive an automobile. Another third requires on-the-job training, and the remainder requires formal pre-entry education and training. One needs to choose an occupation in which lack of higher formal education is not a barrier to reasonable advancement, or in which the needed education can be obtained in conjunction with continued employment. In this case experience will prove invaluable in later years.

Other factors that parents may be wise to advise children to investigate are (1) starting pay and benefits, (2) opportunities for advancement in terms of responsibility and pay, (3) length of training period, (4) necessity of relocation, and (5) the security of the chosen occupation. This last item will require considerable knowledge of future projections.

SOME SPECIALIZED AREAS

A few specialized prospects merit special mention. Among them are careers in the armed forces and the prospects posed by energy development.

Armed Forces

The military provides a realistic alternative for many persons who are seeking special kinds of job training. That is to say that many of the skills which can be attained in military training can be used after one leaves the military and enters civilian life. Early retirement possibilities to be followed by a second career add to the attractiveness of military service. However, increasing criticism of the pension costs may limit those and other perquisites in the future. The military offers an alternative for those persons who are not motivated to pursue college education, as well as for college graduates who enter its officer corps. The armed forces also offer a good chance to obtain practical experience in a variety of jobs. While the military offers training for many vocational positions, it also provides its officers with an opportunity to gain a college education through various extension programs with major universities.

A list of the major job categories in the military includes: administrative specialists and clerks, electrical and mechanical equipment repairers, crafts, service and supply handlers, infantry, gun crews and seamanship specialists, electronic equipment operators and repairers, communications and intelligence specialists, medical and dental specialists, and other technical specialists. If the private sector is broadly defined, many of these military job categories include specific occupations that have parallels in the private sector. Specific examples include: personnel administrators, automotive mechanics, lithographic specialists, food service, seamanship skills, teletype repairers, radar and air traffic controllers, medical aides, photographers, weather analysts, musicians, and so on.

In general, the military provides a wide choice for specialization in vocations which require both training and experience. For those occupations which do not require a license, but only experience, the military is a viable alternative. Also, it should be noted that even when the military cannot license an individual, it can provide the necessary training for licensing by other governmental and quasi-governmental agencies.

In addition to these job-specific skills, the military may provide some general skills that can be useful in the private sector. Perhaps the best example of this would be the leadership skills that are taught in the military. Also, the military discipline is useful for many jobs, and some employers prefer people who have these personal attributes. Other skills include written and oral communications as well as various organizational habits which are the result of operating in a highly structured situation. These personal characteristics are of immense value to private employers.

The Role of Energy

Occupational opportunities in the energy sector are expected to expand substantially. However, in terms of the whole economy the energy sector is not likely to have a major impact on employment.

There is a much higher concentration of skilled craftsmen and engineers in the energy sector compared with other sectors. Occupations for which there may be a serious shortage in the future are nuclear welders, various fields of engineering, and boilermakers. Because of the significant lead time required for training in these fields, there has been little indication of a more favorable supply in the future, especially concerning engineers.

Some problems which may arise concerning ample labor supply in the energy sector are connected with relocation. For example, with continued emphasis toward coal production, a large part of increased production is expected to come from western states (Rocky Mountain and Upper Great Plains regions), which have relatively little manpower trained in coal mining. Some of the problems exist for nuclear energy development, which in certain areas may experience shortages of plumbers and pipe fitters. Also, the petroleum industry may have problems in filling new openings for chemical engineers. However, as implied above these are local labor market phenomena. They are not projected to have a significant impact at the national level.

Although the energy sector itself is not to have a significant impact on employment opportunities considering the economy as a whole, the developments and growth in this sector are crucial to the whole economy. Practically all employment projections take as given an ample energy base in the formulation of those projections.

The development of alternative sources of energy over the next decade is bound up in the world price of oil; the lower the price the less impetus for development of other sources. Here, an essential role is to be played by the federal government. This is especially true considering the development of events beyond 1985, because a rationalized energy policy that is to be effective in that time period must be implemented years before.

Industries that are dependent upon high energy consumption will be most affected by energy price variation. Therefore employment growth in these industries will be more sensitive to those fluctuations.

Alternative energy strategies are not expected to have very different impacts upon the overall level of unemployment. However, allocation of unemployment among industries could have a significant impact upon various population groups and therefore upon the distribution of income.

SPECULATION BEYOND 1985

Most projections concerning employment, industrial growth, and general economic trends do not go beyond the 1985 outlook. Nevertheless, as related to future employment opportunities and growth, there are some trends that may be perceivable, and there are certain developments that will prove crucial to economic prosperity and ample employment opportunities. These trends and developments are perceived as going beyond 1985 or coming into existence after that date. In general, such perceptions also are based on assumptions such as those found in the *Occupational Outlook Handbook*.

One trend that is likely to continue through the end of the century is increasing labor mobility. This will in large part be due to changing life styles and diminishing strength of regional ties. Another major impetus to this increased mobility will be the better information flows to workers who will become more aware of employment opportunities in various parts of the country. However, part of this information flow should concern knowledge of particular locales where the opportunities arise, if it is a boom/bust employment cycle, and long- and short-run costs of relocating in another town.

Industry relocation itself should also become an integral part of the information flow. Corporations with vast amounts of planning expertise available may find it more feasible to relocate closer to sources of energy supply or closer to their markets. It is not likely that in the future it will be as advantageous to relocate because of cheaper labor supply. Increased unionization will reduce the attractiveness of such relocation, but in the longer run increased labor mobility itself, with its implied greater options to the worker, should make wages more homogeneous within occupational groups.

Unionization itself will encounter challenges to growth in the decades ahead. With its period of blue-collar growth largely past, continued expansion depends upon success in organizing white-collar occupations. The obvious example to this is the increased rate of unionization in the public sector. As white-collar work expands into massive, factory-like operations, these workers can be expected to demand a voice in making the rules of the work place. Lower level managers and supervisors, the military, and agricultural workers are other candidates for union organizations. The same forces which may restrict employment and union growth in some sectors may expand it in others. For instance, though highly skilled labor will continue to be in strong demand in larger construction projects and in industry, technological developments geared toward cutting costs, particularly for consumer housing, may reduce such a demand in related occupations for this sector but expand it in manufacturing the parts needed for such housing.

Technological development is a two-edged sword. Part of its usefulness is to reduce costs of goods and services, but its never-ending process increases the need for specialization of skills, which in turn become sensitive to future technological change. What this means in terms of employment is that the individual should become keenly aware of the applicability of a specialized skill within the employment spectrum as applied to different industries. Implied in this is the factor of difficulty in making the transition to another skill less sensitive to technological change.

The trend toward demanding an increasing quality of work life will affect employment opportunities in several ways. For example, better devised and applied safety and health regulations are necessary for a more equitable cost distribution among employers. Yet, more expertise will be needed in this area in order that employers can realize actual savings from properly applied regulations. This, in turn, will require greater worker participation in planning, organizing, and control.

The above example may not prove to be untypical of many methods devised to increase the quality of work life. With an increasingly educated and knowledgeable work force, there is reason to believe that worker-management cooperation in such areas should become stronger with signs of increased productivity and reduced costs. Opportunities for those involved in certain aspects of planning and control will be dependent upon training or acquiring of skills that are peripheral to their particular modes of employment.

It appears that the possibilities of self-employment will in general decline in the future. Prohibitive factors are the increased cost of capital investment and the wide variety of expertise which is becoming necessary to run a business. Individual choice should be based partly on the degree of job security, level of pay, benefits, and retirement plan that can be obtained as compared to the opportunities and rewards of self-employment.

Government's role in providing employment opportunities in the future will in part vary with the business cycle. However, a main long-term influence should be ensuring that crucial sectors of the economy (i.e. energy) are developed to the extent that they are not impediments to economic growth. The choice of employment in the government sector should be made with a comparison of similar occupations in the private sector and with some understanding of the possibilities of switching to the private sector (or vice versa) in the future.

The projection of future economic developments and how these developments will affect employment opportunities comes to rest on two essential and closely related government policies. The first is energy. As mentioned before, the long lead time necessary for planning and construction of energy facilities will make post 1985 projections directly dependent on what is done in the previous decade. Indecision and lack of a rational and deliberate energy policy delineating priorities of development seem to be the worst obstacles in the near future. This is also coupled with the ever-growing environmental concern.

Given a common understanding and agreement between environmentalists and developers, and given government policies designed to accelerate energy development, it is possible that energy independence can be achieved by 2000. Even with a slower trend it does not seem unlikely that the United States will become self-sufficient within the working lives of those being born now.

The second crucial—and what may be *the* crucial—factor in the future is international trade. Traditionally the U.S. has operated a high wage economy based on productivity rates far above those of our low wage competitors. Now our competitors have technology equal to our own or better, while retaining much of the low wage advantage. Thus, a dilemma: Such competition is a threat to U.S. jobs since many foreign products have prices lower than U.S. production costs; yet to keep the goods out to protect jobs is to burden U.S. consumers with higher prices.

Hence the future is full of uncertainties and challenge. But there is an essential assurance. With appropriate government policies, there will be ample opportunities for the well prepared.

ADDITIONAL READING

Carey, Max L. "Revised Occupational Projections to 1985," *Monthly Labor Review*, November, 1976.

Mangum, Garth L. *Employability, Employment, and Income.* Salt Lake City: Olympus Publishing Company, 1976.

U.S. Department of Labor, Bureau of Labor Statistics. *Occupational Outlook Handbook*, 1976-77 ed., BLS Bulletin 1875. Washington: Government Printing Office, 1976.

Wales, Terence. "The Effect of College Quality on Earnings: Results from the MBER-Thorndike Data," *Journal of Human Resources*, Vol. 8, 1973, pp. 306-315.

CHAPTER ELEVEN

Launching the Career

We have emphasized the fact that a person's career is a life-long process. Its development begins in infancy, and it is in a state of constant change and renewal until the time of death. It is not proper, then, to speak of "launching the career" as if it were an event clearly demarcated with regard to time and place. However, there is a point during the course of an individual's career at which he or she takes an important step into the world of work. We have spoken of that point as being the transition point from school to work, but even that is too specific, because entry into the work force often takes place before completion of school, and education almost inevitably continues in some form after entry into the work force. But there does come a time when the work activity assumes a new importance in the life of an individual, a time when work is no longer a convenience or a temporary activity, a time when a job suddenly becomes a conscious part of a career, when the long-range implications of work become apparent, and when today's job has direct meaning to the overall career plan.

Sometimes this important event occurs when the individual secures a part-time job—maybe even the first part-time job; sometimes it doesn't take place until all training has been completed and the individual enters the labor market full time; and sometimes it occurs when the individual seeks and finds a specific volunteer job. Often it is remembered by the individual as the "first job." It involves a number of things, from seeking out a specific type of job to making a personal commitment to a specific occupation or type of work.

In a book titled *Your Child's Career,* we would be remiss not to discuss that important event in the child's career. What are the steps involved? What can parents do to help? And what can the student and the parent expect as the child—now a young adult—moves into a new relationship with work and the world of work?

There is no better place to begin than at the beginning.

PARENTAL RESPONSIBILITIES

Early work experiences will accumulate to influence your child's career activity, as we have said before. As the child passes through the stages of career development, his or her career growth is occurring just as surely as physical growth. If you were to stand and stare at your child, you could not see any physical growth taking place, but you can certainly prove that it is happening by keeping track of the child's height periodically in a written record.

In many respects, keeping a written record of the child's career growth is much more vital than tracking physical growth, since the career can be even more dramatically and purposefully developed and formed than can physical growth. We go to great lengths to see that our children receive proper nutrition and exercise so their physical selves will be enhanced. No less crucial is seeing that their personal careers are given proper nutrition through appropriate training and schooling inputs. Their career exercise comes through significant work experiences. There would almost surely be serious deficiencies in diet with an adverse result of physical growth without careful parental planning and supervision. Likewise, crucial gaps in your child's career development will occur without proper parental involvement. We have talked about the nature of that involvement throughout this book.

To avoid a stunted or undernourished career for your child, there are a number of things which you can do. A simple written exercise may give some revealing insights into your child's career growth pattern. On a blank sheet of paper list some vital areas for proper career growth which you have experienced in your own life, leaving blank space after each heading. Some areas which you might include are: significant schooling, work experiences in the home, work experiences away from home, hobbies or special interests, civic or other volunteer involvements, church experiences, other organizational involvements, family involvements which influenced your career, and crucial career decisions or turning points. The areas you list should be ones that are pertinent to you. Now, under each item list some of the things which come to mind in just a few words. For example:

Work outside the home

 Lawn mowing business

 Paper route

 Farm work

 Stock clerk

 Janitor

 U.S. Army

 Car salesman

 Teaching assistant

 Sales worker in Wyler's Department Store

Family involvements which influenced my career

 Parental emphasis of education

 Expectation for part-time work

 Father's death

 Older children enrolling in college

 Going to work with dad

After accumulating such a list, reflect upon why each of these things has made an impact on your career. After you have pondered these items, consider other things that come to mind which have been influential in shaping your career. Jot them down. Now, jot down some things you feel would have made an important difference in your career *if* they had happened to you.

After reflecting upon your own career in this fashion, use a fresh sheet of paper to list what you feel would be significant areas for your child, drawing from your own experiences as well as experiences or opportunities you wish you had had. Now, list under the items for your child the experiences which have already occurred, and follow the exercise through to conclusion, as you did for yourself. Are there gaps and blank spots which need attention? What can you do to see that these happen at the appropriate time? Consultation with a school counselor or other appropriate professional, such as a career counselor, might be helpful as a follow-up to this exercise.

Parental Involvements

One role of parents is to assist the child to a careful, accurate discovery of himself or herself in relation to the world of work. This occurs through helping to make available appropriate experiences, and by aiding the child in making an accurate evaluation of self in relation to the experiences. A number of career development theorists agree that a career does not just happen at a given point in time but takes place developmentally throughout the life cycle. It would be well for parents to understand the career stages through which they might expect their children to pass. We have defined those stages in earlier chapters, but some thoughts from Donald Super's theory will serve well to illustrate the process. He suggests that from birth to age fourteen there is a growth stage during which career-related self-concepts develop through identification with key figures in family and school. There is a fantasy substage which occurs from ages four to ten, during which role playing in fantasy is important. From age eleven to age twelve interests or likes are major determiners of goals and activities. The age from thirteen to fourteen is another substage where children begin to recognize what their capacities or abilities are, and where job training requirements are considered.

Another major stage, exploration, covers approximately ages fifteen to twenty-four. (Super speaks of exploration in a much broader sense than we have used it here.) During this time, self-examination and occupational exploration in school activities and part-time work occurs. From age fifteen to eighteen, tentative choices are made after having considered needs, interests, capacities, values, and potential opportunities. These choices are tested in relation to school courses, work, and other experiences. From ages eighteen to twenty-one, reality factors are given more credence as the person has work, training, and other experiences. During the period from twenty-two to twenty-four years, the career choice which has been made is given trial in the form of an entry-level career job. (Keep in mind that the age levels given above are *not* definitive; they are offered only to provide a guide to the sequence of development. Every individual will develop at a different rate, and you should not be concerned if your child is ahead of or behind the schedule outlined above.)

Parents, then, will find it a useful experience to fantasize with their young elementary school children about careers. As the child enters into junior high school, parents can carefully view and selectively reinforce likes or interests as determiners of activities, course work, and goals. In the later stages of the junior high school years, parents should realistically review with the child his or her performances, achievements, and capabilities, and relate these to the interests which have become apparent. In turn the general training requirements for selected career fields could be considered, with reference to future career decisions which will occur later. During the high school years, further focusing and narrowing occurs and tentative career choices take place. Parental assistance—and the assistance of counselors—is especially important here, since these choices need to be made with consideration of previously identified or presently discernable interests, needs, capacities, values, and potential employment opportunities. Needed training and education, future income, demand for workers, and location of job opportunities will all need to be carefully weighed.

Discrepancies between self-concept and reality as related to these career choices should be tested in school courses, work, and other experiences. Appropriate evaluations, revisions of plans, and new starts are all part of the process. Upon completion of high school the child must make such decisive career choices as: Shall I continue with more schooling or go to work? If I elect more schooling, where will I get it? What type of schooling do I wish and for how long? If I decide to work, where will it be and what type of work?

The parents can be passive, or they can provide an active supportive role with such things as suggesting alternatives and discussing the consequences of choosing a given course of action. Discussing in advance potential parent support—both financial and otherwise—for advanced schooling is another important parental involvement.

Your Child Is Unique

You will do well to help your child to a self-discovery of personal uniqueness and to an acceptance of this as a very positive and desirable aspect of self. This includes discovery of the fact that he or she has certain strengths or plusses, as well as certain weaknesses or negative personal traits. Unfortunately, some children and parents are prone to see any weak traits as personal points of shame or of tragedy. The truth is that *everyone* has both positive and negative characteristics. The important thing is to develop an accurate self-concept and then take whatever one *is* as a starting point and make the best use one can with it.

It is unfortunate and unnecessary to let personal shortcomings become a source of debilitating frustration and discouragement. But it is also eventually going to prove a mistake to refuse to *accurately* assess strength areas. See them as they are—no more, no less—and then they can be used to advantage. Parents can be a valuable help to children in this area, both through their personal observations and through such evaluative resources as teachers.

Let's take a step beyond the recognition that every person has both plusses and minusses and scrutinize what some of these might be and how to deal with them. Physical limitations may be a problem for your child, since young people vary so radically in size and physical maturation. The youngster who is small may need to show ingenuity and persistence. For example, one sixteen-year old who looked about twelve tried repeatedly to get a job at a fast food restaurant. He was told he was too small, but he called back often during holiday rush periods, and finally his persistence paid off. He was hired to help out with the heavy customer traffic during one holiday, with a distinct understanding that he was temporary and would be terminated after the rush. He worked very hard but he also had prepared well for just this break. Earlier, he had often watched the workers prepare the hamburgers and other food items. He had practiced at home, and when the chance came his practice paid off. He knew he was good with his hands, and he had developed this quickness doing work at home. Soon it was obvious that he was faster than most of the other workers. Within a short time he demonstrated he excelled in this type of work. He was hired on a permanent basis. About a year later he represented his place of business in a statewide competition for speed in preparing hamburgers, and he won the contest.

The point is to recognize a limitation and then work around it so it does not become an unsurmountable obstacle.

Inexperience is another definite limitation. "Nobody will hire me because I have no experience; but how can I get any experience unless they will hire me?" Most of us have heard this common lament among youths seeking their first job. The usual response is something like: "Keep trying and don't get discouraged." While words of encouragement are appropriate, there is more that can be done by parents to aid children in getting work experiences which will assist them in their subsequent job quests.

Parental encouragement can be coupled with assistance in gaining meaningful experiences.

A medical doctor wondered how he might involve his family in a meaningful work experience and at the same time help them to better understand his profession. After careful thought, he proposed to his children that they take responsibility for the janitorial work at his office. When he told them the fee he had been paying for the service and told them it would be theirs if they maintained the quality of service he was receiving, they readily accepted.

It took some extra work on the part of the doctor and his wife to teach the children how to perform their new jobs and to aid them in organizing their work. The children had to arrange their schedules so as to be available for work early each morning before school. The children soon became well acquainted with their father's work area as well as the people who worked with him. An added indirect advantage was that the money expended for custodial work stayed in the family. As they grew and matured, the children were given the opportunity to change jobs and gain new experiences by doing filing, typing, and reception work as well as eventually performing minor medical assistance duties.

Just as it is important for your child to recognize, accept, and work around personal weaknesses or limitations, so is it vital to properly recognize, accept, and exploit personal strengths. This advantageous use of personal strengths is often much more difficult than overcoming weaknesses. Too often, strengths or assets are thought of in too narrow a fashion. Positive traits which are conclusive in success are sometimes not considered to be talents or abilities. For example, a child who develops the asset of punctuality has gained a vital force in the world of work. Although this seems on the surface to be a simplistic and easily acquired trait, it has far-reaching implications. A person who is truly punctual not only is on time to school, to appointments, to meetings, and to work, but also is on time with commitments, obligations, and assignments. The person who is punctual is sensitive to the value of time—both his or her own and others'. The punctual person must learn to schedule time effectively. The punctual person is meticulously honest in not stealing someone else's time.

Indeed, the child who develops the trait of punctuality has an invaluable trait for his or her career.

Reliability or dependability is another personal strength which will prove extremely useful in career worlds, as well as in every other phase of life. Many other traits fall into this same realm—cheerfulness, friendliness, honesty, determination, tenacity, flexibility, and the capacity to handle failures as well as successes graciously.

In quite another realm are strengths which fall in the area of abilities, aptitudes, or talents. These include such things as manual dexterity, eye-hand coordination, special perception, quickness in memorization, reading and writing skills, and mechanical, musical, or verbal aptitudes. To recognize these strengths, observation of a number of performance arenas is important. These may include activities with peers and siblings, school achievements, hobby involvements, and church activities. As important as recognition is the development of these abilities, which means helping to provide growth opportunities and experiences, and motivating through reinforcement and support.

Hobbies often furnish opportunities to build strengths and provide pertinent work experience. One girl and her father had aquariums with tropical fish as a hobby. The father noticed the girl had an unusually strong interest in the hobby and spent many hours caring for the fish, observing them, and reading background information. The girl also seemed to enjoy having people take interest in the aquariums, and when a neighbor seemed responsive the girl set up an aquarium for him in his home. The neighbor was so pleased with the girl's efforts that he not only paid for the cost of the fish and the equipment but also gave a bonus to the girl for her efforts. Noticing how elated the girl was over this experience, the father suggested he and his daughter form a partnership, with the father as the investment and consulting partner and the girl as the marketing and maintenance partner. The girl contacted professional people in the area and offered to rent them attractive aquariums for their offices or reception rooms which she would service. The proposition was generally well received, and she soon had rental units in a number of offices. Working with her father, she learned many valuable lessons in such things as purchasing of materials, profit margins, customer relations, and dependability.

Creative thought and effort will yield a variety of opportunities for childhood work experiences. Previous parental experiences may be drawn upon as a resource. For example, one father, a barber, had two teenage sons who needed some work experiences. They lived in an urban setting, and the family was rather baffled about how to find appropriate jobs for the boys. The father remembered working while he was a youth assisting a man who operated a furnace cleaning business. The family contacted a local furnace cleaner, and although the firm was not interested in hiring the sons, they did agree to give the father some part-time work, since he had some previous experience. The father accepted the offer to moonlight, and in the next few months he renewed and strengthened his skills in furnace cleaning. With the extra money he earned, he bought his own furnace cleaning equipment and started his own furnace cleaning business, employing his two teen-aged boys as his assistants. The business eventually became so lucrative that the father quit his work as a barber and worked at his furnace cleaning full time. The man is now preparing for retirement, and his two sons, who have grown into adulthood, are working in the business full time, and are gradually taking over for their father.

A Custom-made Career for Your Child

Now that we have scrutinized some of the considerations for a career, let's focus in on your child's specific career.

Too often, people simply let a career happen by just "evolving" into whatever seems by chance or circumstance to come along. Don't let this be the process for your child's career. Cause the career to develop which will bring the kind of life desired. Working closely with your child, you will want to help him or her choose a career field which optimizes the things which are important to the child.

As the choice is made, help the child consider not only what is gained but what is given up by making this particular choice. Your child should see clearly what the occupation is by asking questions about the training and education needed, about where he or she will live, about the people with whom he or she will associate, about monetary rewards to be gained, and about the kind of prestige to be enjoyed. The child should think carefully about what activities this work will entail, what hours will be worked, and what physical and emotional demands will be required.

Although choice of the occupation is a long-term process, try as soon as feasible to name the occupation, title it, and pin it down so that you and your child both know what it is you are aiming for.

Remember to be flexible and allow for modification if the decision made proves unfeasible. In the interim, start finding out as much as possible about the occupation by talking to people who work in this field, and by reading information about it from the local high school, college, or state Job Service career information library.

Now that you are focusing on the chosen occupation, make room in your child's life so it can really happen. The child must begin to get the necessary training to enhance success in the field, including classes, activities, and work experiences. Reality test the choice by taking a career I.Q. test, meaning a test of interests and qualifications. In this case, take a sheet of paper and write a description of the proposed career in as much detail as possible, drawing from whatever resources you wish. Take a second sheet of paper and draw a line down the middle. On one side write the word "interests," and on the other side write "qualifications." List as many of your child's interests and qualifications as you can. Then check each of these against the career description on the first sheet. If there is a positive correlation of an interest or qualification item with the career description, mark a plus; if a mismatch or negative match up, mark it minus. If you get a preponderance of negatives, you may need to reconsider. If there is an abundance of plusses—especially on key items—you may consider it a reaffirmation of the chosen field.

Major Launching Stages in the Career

The preparations and preliminaries for launching the main career, such as early training and experiences, are all important and will have a direct bearing on the eventual career. But there are a few easily identifiable points or launching stages when most young people actually make major career decisions or commitments that are pivotal in the whole future life style of the persons involved.

One major career launching decision occurs when the young person elects to leave school. For the majority of youth, this will not become a difficult choice until high school has been completed, but any parent may be faced with the circumstance of a child who decides to drop out of school prior to completing high school. For many parents this may appear to be instant tragedy and a source of major parent-child conflict. The best solution is probably not a head-to-head confrontation, with parents seeking to force the child back to school. A happier and more effective solution would probably be to take the opportunity to seriously discuss the implications of such an act in terms of career possibilities, present and future life style, and alternatives to the dropout route.

A time when nearly all parents and children must make major career launching decisions is upon completion of high school. Of course, this is preceded by the course selections and preparations made throughout the twelve years of schooling, but the pivotal point is the decision made and followed upon completion of high school. The parents play a vital supporting role in helping to supply needed information about the available alternatives. Scrutiny of the various options should be sure to include not only college, but also trade or technical schools, apprenticeship programs, and on-the-job training and learning opportunities. The typical American parents' dream of sending their children to college is only one of many good alternatives, as evidenced by the statistics which show that less than 20 percent of the jobs in the United States are held by college graduates.

So that proper consideration can be given to the various viable alternatives, you should help your children to get both good information and a chance to interact with individuals who can provide stimulating insights about each alternative. Such individuals can also help to evaluate your child's potential in relation to each alternative. School admissions offices, counselors, and company personnel workers can assist in this function.

Parents and children should carry out a reality check so that a realistic evaluation can be made of each alternative's potential. For example if your child is considering going to a business college in another city, a thorough investigation should be made to ascertain living costs and accommodations, tuition and fees, entrance requirements, graduation requirements, and lengths of time needed to complete the program. Further study should show what the possibilities are for employment following graduation.

After a careful analysis is made of the various alternatives, then a realistic determination must be made as to whether it is an actual possibility in terms of finances, personal motivation, and immediate as well as long-term outcomes. Your child will need to see how it can actually occur.

GETTING THE JOB

The most crucial aspect of the career launching process comes when the first career entry job is sought. Unfortunately, many people spend twelve or more years getting schooling and making other preparations for getting into the right career, and then when the time comes to actually begin work, they are quite haphazard or even casual about how they enter the job market. They simply accept one of the apparently available jobs. Don't settle for what *seems* to be available; instead, conduct a probing, thorough search. Once the career objective has been decided upon, seek jobs with the rifle approach rather than the shotgun approach. In other words, seek the job which will enhance the career.

Getting a job is a job in and of itself. In many cases and in some respects it is the hardest work a person does. It is difficult to maintain an eight-hour-a-day job hunting schedule, so the job seeker must pace himself or herself. Learning to use available resources skillfully will be a great asset in the job placement process, both for potential employer leads as well as for job information. Some good reliable resources are:

    Job Service (State Employment Service)

    School Counselor

    School Placement Office

    Former Employers

    Library

    Chamber of Commerce

    Yellow Pages

    Professional Organizations

    Newspaper Want Ads

    Unions

    Commercial Employment Agencies (Check in advance on their reputations, whether the fee is to be paid by employer or employee, and how much.)

    School Teachers

    People in the Community You Know

    Better Business Bureau

    Your Friends and Relatives

The old adage, "It's who you know that counts," is most certainly applicable here. People are prone to hire those they know. Pass the word along to friends, relatives, neighbors, and employers with whom you are acquainted. Advertising is an extremely important part of marketing products, and you are trying to help your child market himself, the most important product in the world, so spread the word. Don't keep it a secret that you are in the market and you are sold on the product.

Job-Hunting Strategies

On one occasion a young man zoomed into a service station on a motorcycle. He stopped alongside the surprised station operator who was lubricating a car. The barefooted youth was wearing only a pair of grubby, cut-off jeans. He was chomping vigorously on a wad of gum and still sat astride his motorcycle, racing the noisy engine. Casually pushing his wind towsled hair from his eyes with one hand, he said, "Hey, ya got any jobs?" The attendant looked at him for a moment, then replied, "No." The boy shrugged his shoulders and zoomed off. The attendant turned to a customer and said: "Actually, I am looking for a boy, but I sure wouldn't hire him."

The reasons the cyclist didn't get the job may seem rather obvious, but there may be more than meets the eye in this little incident. It is very possible that this boy was in many ways qualified for doing the job. But his grooming, his manners, and his approach told this prospective employer all he wanted to know in one brief moment. He could not envision this boy waiting on his customers and providing the kind of courteous, efficient service he desired to give. He did not see this boy showing him respect as an employer, and he was not impressed that he would be an employee who would be reliable and show good judgment. In short, this young man did not present himself in a way that would enable this employer to see him in the role which needed to be filled.

If you are going to be successful in helping your child to sell himself or herself, remember it includes a total sales program which involves proper packaging of the product (dress and grooming), clever and effective advertising (résumé, letter of application, and interview), proper timing, and appropriate presentation of the product (getting an appointment, interviewing effectively, follow-up to the interview, and so on).

The manner in which a job applicant presents himself or herself, no matter how good a prospect, becomes crucial to being regarded in a positive light. Presenting oneself to a prospective employer without preparation can be disastrous. The scout motto to "Be Prepared" is crucial in job seeking.

One must be dressed for the occasion—neat, clean, and sharp. But being overdressed for the interview or for the work situation can be as bad as being too casual. If the job requires dirty work and the people who are interviewing are dressed for doing dirty work, to report in a formal suit and tie or a long, delicate dress would place the applicant out of character. A good practice would be to go in advance of the interview and observe how employees in similar jobs in this place of work dress. Another possibility is to ask the person who sets up the appointment.

As your child prepares to meet prospective employers, it will be helpful to consider such practical items as good posture and courtesy. A firm, friendly handshake, a smile, eye-to-eye contact, and a pleasant conversational tone of voice are amazingly helpful in convincing an employer in one's favor. Enthusiasm is the spark which often lights the employment fire.

A good procedure for employer contacts is to fit into the accepted standards of good business contacts. A letter of introduction with an enclosed resumé is usually appreciated. A day or two after the letter, it is good to call in for an appointment for an interview. The applicant should not just drop in, expecting to be worked into a busy schedule. A drop-in appointment is often a source of irritation, whereas a scheduled appointment is usually planned for, and ample time is available. (Preparation for the interview will be discussed in detail later.)

Following the interview, an effective procedure is to write a short thank-you letter expressing gratitude for the interview, reaffirming interest in the job, and perhaps stating briefly why the applicant feels especially qualified for the job. This procedure allows the interviewer to "meet" the applicant several times—with the introductory letter and resumé, with the telephone appointment, with the interview, and again with the thank-you letter. All of these contacts are in good business taste. Chances are that few of the other candidates have been this thorough in their approach, and the prospective employer may think: "Say, this candidate is the kind of conscientious person who goes the extra mile, the kind of person we need in our organization."

The Job Interview

The job interview has been referred to as the twenty-minute lifetime, because a person's future may be so profoundly affected by those few moments. Years of preparation in school, in work settings, and in the home can go literally for naught if there is not effective communication in the one-on-one interview for the sought-after job. Although there are many factors to consider in seeking a job, all other factors pale by comparison to the interview, where the vast majority of jobs are won or lost. Since it is of such great importance, the interview should be shown proper respect through adequate preparation.

Any new behavior is awkward, and the job interview is no exception. It is only natural that a novice will be nervous and probably ineffectual. Here, the parent can be of great help to the child by practicing job interviews. After a number of practice efforts, rather than being nervous and clumsy in the interview your child will tend to feel as though he or she knows what to expect and how to handle the situation. The practice interviews should vary in format, from formal to informal. Some typical questions which might be asked would be:

(1) Why do you think you might like to work for our company?

(2) What jobs have you held? How were they obtained and why did you leave?

(3) In what type of position are you most interested?

(4) Why do you think you would like this particular type of job?

(5) What do you know about our company?

(6) What qualifications do you have that make you feel that you will be successful in this job?

(7) How long do you expect to work for us?

(8) How do you feel about your previous employers?

(9) How much do you expect to be paid?

(10) Are you flexible about your work hours?

(11) Are you willing to do whatever work you are asked?

(12) What are your future vocational plans?

(13) In what school activities have you participated? Why? Which did you enjoy the most?

(14) What courses did you like best? Least? Why?

(15) How do you spend your spare time? What are your hobbies?

A good general rule in interviewing is to try to be as positive as possible. Criticism or negativism about school, former jobs, former employers, friends, parents, or teachers is usually not well received by the interviewer. The potential employer is usually looking for someone who will be loyal, enthusiastic, and positive.

Most people, including interviewers, take certain pride in their place of employment. It is pleasing and impressive to them when an interviewee knows something about the organization. The more the interviewee knows, the more impressive it is. Therefore, it's worth spending a little effort to find out such information as the kinds of products produced or services rendered, the size and type of organization, the progress they have shown, new directions taken, and the company's achievements. It is important to know in advance the proper name of the employing organization and, whenever possible, the name of the interviewer. Almost always the interviewer will introduce herself or himself at the beginning of the interview. The interviewee should listen carefully for the name and then make it a point to call her or him by name during the interview.

The best approach is to smile and look the interviewer in the eye as the discussion begins. One should let the interviewer take the lead in setting the format for the interview, but it's a good idea to have some intelligent questions in mind in case the interviewer asks, "Well, what can I do for you today?" It's also a good idea to know what it is one wants to accomplish with the interview so that one can shape the conversation to include the points one wants covered.

For example, the interviewee should have clearly in mind his or her strengths in order to be able to insert comments about them at key points. He or she should also be aware of personal weaknesses, so that if they are brought up the interviewee won't be flustered and spend valuable time talking about flaws. The goal is to be frank and honest but to avoid unnecessary emphasis on the negative. An example of how to use the interview to advantage might be:

Interviewer: How are your grades in school?

Interviewee: Well, I have a C-plus average, which isn't particularly strong, but I did better than B work in my major, and this year I averaged B-plus overall. You might also be interested in knowing that I was a member of the school debate team which won the regional tournament. I also have worked part time throughout my last two school years and paid for all my own expenses.

At this point, the interviewee should stop and let the interviewer respond in whatever way she or he wishes. The interviewer may pursue the subject of grades further, but she or he has been given two other strength areas (debate team and work experience) for possible discussion. In other words, the interviewer hit a weak spot, but because the interviewee was prepared to deal with it, the response included one negative element presented in a poised, frank manner and four positive elements which would seem to more than offset the weak point.

It is important for the interviewee to be positive, pleasant, and enthusiastic, to be alert, to use good posture, and to be responsive. The interviewee should listen carefully to the questions and respond in a complete way but not ramble or give overly lengthy responses. He or she should maintain a comfortable, conversational demeanor, but show respect for the interviewer.

The interviewee will want to keep in mind this basic question: "What does the interviewer see as she or he looks at me?" What the applicant wants the interviewer to see is a new employee, and so the idea is to get that message across in as many ways as possible, both verablly and non-verbally. This includes telling about any skills, experience, training, and education which may help qualify the applicant for the job. One should not be apologetic about his or her qualifications.

There are other rules of job interviewing which seem almost to go without saying, and yet they are often violated. An applicant should always go alone for the job interview. The applicant should not smoke, eat, or chew gum during the interview unless invited to do so by the interviewer. One should be a little early for the appointment in case the interviewer is ready ahead of time, but not too early. The interviewee should be prepared for the interview to end on time in order not to encroach on someone else's time. If the *interviewer* chooses to prolong the interview, then it is appropriate, and the applicant should not appear anxious about it. As the interview ends, it is appropriate to thank the interviewer and be complimentary. One might say: "Thank you very much for the interview. I am very impressed by what you have told me about the job and your company. I surely hope I will be considered further for it."

After the interview is over, parent and child might find it profitable to discuss it and to carefully evaluate what has taken place. If a different approach is needed or if modifications are in order, they can be incorporated into the next interview. In that way, even interviews which do not result in employment become positive learning experiences.

The Personal Résumé

A carefully prepared résumé of one's qualifications, training, and experience says to a prospective employer: "I cared, and so I prepared." On the other hand, a hastily constructed, poorly prepared résumé may create quite the opposite impression and may very well be worse than none at all.

The résumé should contain only information about the job candidate that will help to convince the employer that this is the person for the job. (Obviously, a person would be foolish to take a job for which he or she was unqualified, since the result would be bad for both the employer and the employee.) The résumé should be a frank and honest—but positive—personal summary of education, work experience, personal achievements, interests, personal data, and references. The sample résumé in Figure 10 gives a basic format which will serve as a starting point to assist you and your child in writing a résumé.

The résumé should be neatly typed and carefully checked for spelling or typographical errors. Never give an employer a carbon copy of a résumé, because that seems to say, "You are not important enough to warrant receiving the original." The best résumé is a typed original with perhaps a heading at the top which says: A résumé of . . . (applicant's name) prepared for . . . (employer's name).

Once the basic format is established, typing extra copies goes quickly. If it is not possible to individually type each one, then printed reproductions can be used.

SUCCEEDING IN THE JOB

Once your child succeeds in obtaining the job, the truly substantial opportunity for career growth and development begins. All the preparations and training now are brought to the test of usefulness in the central arena of the career world. In a sense, the chance now comes for your child to see in perspective previous experiences and preparations and to draw effectively upon these as the need presents itself in situation after situation.

The first day will prove a special challenge. Any new behavior is a challenge, and the first few days on the job will be no exception. Remembering the first day in a new school may be a useful reminder that a new job can be expected to pose its problems. But the new job jitters will pass, just as the feelings of awkwardness, fear, and uncertainty disappeared at the new school after becoming acquainted not only with the people but also with the procedures and expectations. Just being on the job for an eight-hour stretch while under a nervous, emotional, and physical strain will be

```
                              RESUME
                           JAMES STALEY
                    Prepared for ACME Glass Company

PERSONAL DATA

        Address:    214 Elm Street, Stanton, Ohio    43221
        Phone:      (216) 428-9665
        Age:        16
        Marital
          Status:   Single
        Health:     Excellent
        Height:     5'10"
        Weight      155 lbs.

WORK EXPERIENCE

        Newspaper carrier (daily home route)
           May 1974 - Present
        Lawn mowing -- five regular customers for three summers
        Church renovating project -- painting, assisting carpenter
        Murray Fruit Farm -- pruning trees, picking and packaging
           fruit

VOLUNTEER AND CIVIC ACTIVITIES

        Chairman, scout troop neighborhood clean-up drive
           Summer 1974

RECOGNITIONS AND AWARDS

        Eagle Scout, Representative to school student council

EDUCATION

        Spencer Senior High -- general academic course
           'B' average (currently in eleventh grade)
        Rexfield Junior High -- general academic course
           'B' average
        Special courses -- typing, 40 wpm; mechanics, small electrical
           and gasoline motors

OTHER ACTIVITIES

        Intermural basketball, pony league baseball, two-year member
           of school forensics club (debate)

INTERESTS

        Hiking, camping, hunting and fishing, music (I play the guitar),
           and drama

REFERENCES

        Martin B. Jensen              Thomas Edwards
        (School Counselor)            (Newspaper Carrier Supervisor)
        Spencer Senior High           Stanton Sentinel
        1485 Ridge Drive              3775 South River Road
        Stanton, Ohio    43221        Stanton, Ohio    43221
```

FIGURE 10. This sample résumé shows a basic format and some of the information which should be included.

exhausting at first, but with time this should subside, and even though the work may be taxing, the worker usually becomes conditioned in whatever ways are needed to cope.

One of the most important areas of concern will be getting along with others. The American Management Association says that over 80 percent of the people who are terminated from the job fail because of the inability to get along interpersonally with fellow employees. This includes both supervisors and co-workers.

It would be a great service to your child if you could help him or her learn that a boss is not an enemy but a friend. If the right relationship is established, the supervisor can become an advocate, a confidante, a facilitator, a loyal supporter, and an emissary. Of course, the common approach is for a new employee to become privy to gossip and complaints made about the boss by the workers. This constitutes a delicate circumstance—trying to be loyal to the supervisor while attempting not to alienate the peers. This can be done if handled adroitly.

One young lady who was an outstanding secretary went to work for a new company. Her skills were so outstanding that just a short while after her hire she was given an advancement to work as the boss' secretary rather than being a member of the secretarial pool. This caused some jealousy on the part of the secretaries who had been on the job longer. Having a heavy work load and feeling pressure to produce well in the new position, the young lady began to skip her rest breaks, even though the other secretaries invited her to go with them. She also began to decline their invitations to spend the lunch hour with them, and she usually ate a sandwich at her desk while she continued to work. Hostile feelings quickly developed toward her from the other secretaries, and the negative feelings became so intense as to make the girl both uncomfortable and upset. She reasoned that she was only trying to do a good job. While her boss was initially pleased with her work, he began to receive negative feedback about her inability to get along with other staff members.

The young lady was wise enough to seek the help of a counselor, and it was pointd out to her that the extra ten minutes of work she accomplished during each of the break periods was hardly worth the hard feelings caused by appearing to snub her fellow workers. In a sense, she was also making them feel guilty for taking their rightful breaks, because her actions said: "You go ahead on a break if you have to, but I don't need a break." The counselor also pointed out that she missed an opportunity for personal interaction during the lunch hour. The young lady began going with the others on breaks and going to lunch with them. She also started sincerely asking their advice on certain matters and went out of her way to express admiration for their performances. When her work load was too heavy, she talked it over with her boss so adjustments could be made. Occasionally, she worked a few extra hours in the evening or on a Saturday when no one else was around. She also reorganized her work so she could be more efficient. The results were pleasing to the boss, to her co-workers, and to herself.

Being thoughtful of others, showing proper respect, being complimentary, being willing to admit one's mistakes, and being willing to apologize when in error are all vital worker traits which parents can help children develop. Being punctual, being willing to do more than asked, being a good listener, learning to follow instructions, not being critical or gossipy about others, being patient, and being understanding and tolerant of others, are also crucial traits. Other important traits include showing initiative without being pushy, being cheerful and friendly, being able to accept criticism gracefully, and being a team worker.

Your child must learn that there will be some failures along the way. Learning to take failures as well as successes in stride is a great accomplishment. Someone has said that success is picking yourself up one time more than you fall down. Succeeding on the job is a gradual process which takes a long time. Instant success is usually a story book myth. Each day of work is another step on a long career journey. While a given job—especially at the entry level—is not always going to prove totally challenging and satisfying, it will be a valuable source of experience if used properly for that purpose. The objective should be to excell on the job, whatever it may be. Many young people tend to be impatient and become quickly disenchanted with a job when they find routine kinds of duties attached to it. *Any* job has routine or undesirable elements. A mistake many young workers make is to job hop so often that they tend to always be placed in entry level work, which almost always lacks the challenge and excitement that more advanced jobs hold. If they would learn to stick with a job long enough to move to a higher level job, they would find more challenge in their present work, as well as a greater opportunity to move laterally or upward to a more advanced level of opportunity rather than moving to yet another entry-level job.

Before considering a change to another job, a person should always ponder the change in relation to long-range as well as immediate objectives. Will this change provide progress in the direction of the kinds of opportunities one eventually wants? When contemplating a change, a good general rule to follow is that the switch should be finalized and the final commitment to the new employer made only after talking to the present employer. If the worker has been effective in the job, often the current employer is willing to make favorable adjustments in salary, responsibilities, and duties in order to retain the good worker. The experiences the worker has had should be carefully weighed by the worker before accepting a new job. He or she should carefully examine his or her values at this stage in the career and realize that his or her worth is not remaining static but is ever changing.

SUMMARY

Your child's career is not only launched but well under way as she or he leaves infancy and enters childhood. The home is the first place of employment and serves as one of the most vital and long-lasting purposes in the lifelong career process. The role of parents in the career process is a key one, and they will be more effective if they are willing to be consciously and actively involved.

Early work experiences are a part of and form foundations for the later career experiences. Parents should actively reinforce work as a pleasurable and rewarding experience and help their children to get jobs, to have successful work experiences, and to understand the value of those experiences. For example, a newspaper route provides a childhood source of income and a work experience, but it also gives training which applies to many later circumstances. A child with a paper route:

(1) Learns the discipline of daily responsibility to others

(2) Gains the self-discipline of getting up early each morning

(3) Earns income dependent on her or his own careful follow through

(4) Learns lessons in interpersonal and customer relations

(5) Learns the added rewards which come from excellence of performance

(6) Can learn to streamline and make efficiency lighten work loads through such procedures as using a mail collection system

The parent can help a child to relate school volunteer work, hobbies, and other experiences to career objectives. The parents can assist the child in gaining the opportunities for experiences which will relate at the various age levels with career development stages.

The parents can coach their children in such job-finding skills as using job-finding resources, writing letters of application and résumés, practicing effective job interviewing, and conducting the job search.

Parents are in a good position to teach their children personal traits and work habits which are vital to succeeding on the job. They also can teach skills in interpersonal relationships, which after all will be the greatest determiner of success on the job. They can also help their children to keep an eye on the future and their long-range goals as well as on their present desires. By so doing, they can aid an orderly progression through a lifelong career.

Through precept and example, parents can help their children to see the need for proper balances between work and leisure, between family life and professional life. Without question, parents are the single greatest influence on an individual's career.

ADDITIONAL READING

Bolles, Richard Nelson. *What Color Is Your Parachute?* Berkeley, California: Ten Speed Press, 1973.

Crystal, John C., and Bolles, Richard N. *Where Do I Go from Here with My Life?* New York: Seabury Press, 1974.

Haldane, Bernard. *Career Satisfaction and Success.* New York: American Management Association, 1974.

Holland, John L. *Making Vocational Choices: A Theory of Careers.* New York: Prentice-Hall, 1973.

Irish, Richard K. *Go Hire Yourself an Employer.* Garden City, New York: Anchor Books, 1973.

Super, Donald E. "A Theory of Vocational Development," *American Psychologist*, Vol. 8, No. 4, pp. 189-190.

CHAPTER TWELVE

A Career Success Partnership: You and Your Child

So there you have it. If you didn't already know, it should have been driven home adequately in these pages . . . *you* are the key to the success of your children. You are largely the source of their initial life and work values. Yours is the first example they have to follow and the one which will be most lasting. Your attitudes toward work will be the ones they will absorb. If you seem to enjoy work around the house and yard or speak favorably about work experiences, and if you praise your children for their productive efforts, they are likely to enjoy work activities now and in the future.

Their initial exposure to the world of work will progress from home to neighborhood to community, and their occupational horizons at first will co-exist with your own. You will be the first to have the opportunity to teach them the roles which work plays in society, how we serve each other through work and find satisfaction in work well done. That can become a game during travel, as the nature of work and workers is pointed out. If they are to learn much about occupations beyond those immediately around and about them, it will be because you and the school make an effort to guarantee that broader exposure. It will be largely up to you to show them the relationships between their own interests, personalities, values, and preferred life styles and the occupations they will ultimately pursue. Those are difficult concepts, and it cannot be laid on too heavily at first, but little by little over the years subtle messages multiply and become a part of the individual's conscious and unconscious reactions.

Only you can teach them about work through home chores, and you can make that a negative experience of drudgery or a positive one of achievement and pride. You and they together will determine whether they seek and accept part-time and summer jobs during their growing up years and what they learn from them. At a minimum, they can learn the satisfactions of independence. They can also learn what it is like to be a small business operator or self-employed professional through newspaper routes or baby sitting. With a little extra effort on your part as they grow up, they can be exposed to actual work experiences in a number of settings. They won't have the opportunity for exposure to any appreciable proportion of the 30,000 occupational titles, but they can sample retail sales, construction, manufacturing, a lab, and an office, for instance, giving them a feeling for employment in some of the major types of work environments.

You have been proven by research to be the major influence in their decisions to leave or remain in school. Make that a conscious and deliberate decision for both you and your children, based on the alternatives of work now versus further training and a different occupation later. For most youth, the primary determinant of their choice to continue or leave school is whether they enjoy it and are successful at it. You can add pros and cons related to careers and to other considerations.

Who is in a better position to teach a child decision-making skills than the parent who determines whether the child is encouraged and allowed to choose among alternatives or simply given an order? Like swimming or tennis or work, decision making is learned only by actually making decisions and experiencing consequences.

Most youth get their early jobs through their parents, relatives, and family friends. In fact, all of their lives, just as in your life, these informal contacts will be the major source of job placements. Don't be reluctant to use your influence. You will not be doing any employer a disservice if you also take the time to teach your child diligence, dependability, and good conduct. And there is no reason to stop being helpful at any point. After all, you haven't stopped needing such help occasionally yourself. What *is* important to stop gradually is the influencing of decisions and the imposing of your judgments. Children will need your counsel at first, but it will not long be welcome unless it is actively sought.

How important is education in your child's working career? That, of course, depends upon occupational interest. Education has value beyond its career applications, of course, and you will not want to deny your child its cultural and intellectual joys if the child values and wants them. But as an investment in future income, the payoff for education largely depends upon the nature of the occupation being prepared for and the abilities, talents, and interests of the one pursuing the education. For career purposes alone, there is no reason to prolong education if the interest is in an occupation best learned on the job. Since you will probably pay for most of that education, you must be involved in the decision, one in which you must weigh the welfare of other members of the family as well as the one whose education is under consideration.

If this book has served its purpose, you will now have a clearer vision of your role and how to do it. It should have caused you to re-examine your own career development as well as anticipate that of your child. You probably remember your experiences as a mixed bag of joys and frustrations, achievements and disappointments. You undoubtedly conclude that work is not all there is to life—that family, recreation, and personal development are much of what makes life worthwhile. But you probably also agree that, unless you inherit wealth, earnings are a prerequisite to those enjoyments. As you look back over the years, you probably also reminisce that most of your joys came through achievements and most of those achievements involved work, whether for pay or not.

What is more important to you than your child's future happiness? Like yours, it is not all dependent upon career success. But a successful working career is a sufficiently crucial part of that happiness to justify a commitment from you that your child's career will be high among your parental priorities.

Index